Copyright and Other Fairy Tales

Copyright and Other Fairy Tales

Hans Christian Andersen and the
Commodification of Creativity

Edited by

Helle Porsdam

Professor of American Studies, University of Southern Denmark

Edward Elgar

Cheltenham, UK • Northampton, MA, USA

Published by
Edward Elgar Publishing Limited
Glensanda House
Montpellier Parade
Cheltenham
Glos GL50 1UA
UK

Edward Elgar Publishing, Inc.
William Pratt House
9 Dewey Court
Northampton
Massachusetts 01060
USA

Reprinted 2007

A catalogue record for this book
is available from the British Library

Library of Congress Cataloguing in Publication Data
Copyright and other fairy tales : Christian Andersen and the commodification of
    creativity / edited by Helle Porsdam.
        p. cm.
    1. Andersen, H. C. (Hans Christian), 1805–1875–Criticism and interpretation. 2.
    Copyright–History. I. Porsdam, Helle, 1956–

PT8120.C66 2006
839.8'136–dc22   2005050164

ISBN 978 1 84542 601 9

Typeset by Cambrian Typesetters, Camberley, Surrey
Printed and bound in Great Britain by Biddles Ltd, King's Lynn, Norfolk

Contents

Contributors

Michael Blakeney
Lee Davis
Lawrence Lessig
Fiona Macmillan
Helle Porsdam
Marieke van Schijndel
Joost Smiers
Uma Suthersanen
Stina Teilmann
Leslie Kim Treiger-Bar-Am

Introduction: Hans Christian Andersen, best of story tellers

Helle Porsdam

On 1 April 2005 at the University of Southern Denmark in Odense, Professor Harold Bloom came close to adding one more name to his list of the greatest and most original authors of the Western literary tradition – that of the Danish writer Hans Christian Andersen (1805–75). The famous Yale professor and author of numerous books on literary criticism had been invited to Odense, Denmark to deliver the Hans Christian Andersen Academy Lecture 2005 and to receive the Hans Christian Andersen Award 2005. The award of 50 000 euros was given to Harold Bloom in Andersen's native town of Odense with much pomp and circumstance on 2 April, the day that all of Denmark celebrated the 200th anniversary of the most famous Danish writer of all times.

There is perhaps a certain irony in the fact that it was Harold Bloom who became the recipient of this award. Hans Christian Andersen is not among the handful of writers who make up the Bloomian literary canon. The writers that constitute *The Western Canon: The Books and School of Ages*, as Bloom called one of his most controversial books from 1994, are 'strong poets' – those who have been strong enough to transcend that 'anxiety of influence' which all writers feel toward their literary precursors. The strongest of them all is Shakespeare, who is Bloom's hero. Shakespeare not only defined for the Western world the standards by which we judge all literature; he also defined for us what it means to be human. Modern literature has not added very much to what people could have already learned from reading Shakespeare, and Shakespeare has therefore become the precursor with whom all subsequent writers have had to contend.

Originality in literature for Bloom thus pretty much means the strength to kill off one's precursors – to not just become copies of these precursors. To what extent did Hans Christian Andersen possess such originality? This was clearly one of the more important questions that had presented themselves to Bloom when he agreed to deliver his talk in Odense. Having never done much work on Andersen before, he considered it a challenge to think the Danish writer into – or at least relate him to – his canon. He opened his lecture in this way:

> Andersen's prime precursors included Shakespeare and Sir Walter Scott, and his best work can be thought of as an amalgam of *A Midsummer Night's Dream* and the almost as magnificent 'Wandering Willie's Tale' from Scott's *Redgauntlet*, with a certain admixture of Goethe and of the 'Universal Romanticism' of Novalis and E.T.A. Hoffman. Goethean 'renunciation' was central to Andersen's art, which truly worships only one god, who can be called Fate. Though Andersen was a grand original in his fairy tales, he eagerly accepted from folklore its stoic acceptance of fate.[1]

Later in his talk Bloom emphasized, though, that it was only Andersen's fairy tales – and not his novels, dramas, poetry and travel writings – that 'are, for the most part, unique works that transcend their sources . . . Only in May 1835 did he find his own genre, the visionary stories that have been as widely translated and circulated as the Bible, Shakespeare, and *Don Quixote*'. Now, to the list of writers and works already mentioned as Andersen's 'prime precursors', Bloom added folk tales and *The Arabian Nights*.

Having thus established Andersen as an original writer – that is, not just a copyist of the writing of those that came before him – Bloom then attempted to pinpoint the characteristics of this originality. 'Defin[ing] precisely the qualities of Andersen's stories that go on making them imperishable' turned out not to be quite so easy though. Andersen's project in life, Bloom claimed, was 'how to remain a child in an ostensibly adult world'. 'Childlike in Denmark, Andersen was childish abroad'; yet, if he was a visionary story teller, 'his fairy-realm was malign'. Andersen may have invented what in the last two centuries has been called 'children's literature', but it is a literature that is full of atrocious and cruel creatures. Andersen's is not a benign and beautiful universe – 'after some early stories he is no more available just to children than are Kafka and Gogol. Rather, Andersen wrote for extraordinarily intelligent children of all ages, from nine to ninety'. Ultimately, this children's writer who did not really write for children, but for adults, defies interpretation – 'I believe', said Bloom, 'that we still have not learned how to read him . . . if there is an aesthetic wholly equipped to analyze Andersen's peculiar power, I have not encountered it'.

TRUST THE ORIGINAL, NOT THE TRANSLATION?

Bloom's amazement at discovering the grown-up side of Hans Christian Andersen's fairy tales, and the role that this amazement may have played in his concluding that Andersen defies interpretation, is interesting. Anybody with enough knowledge of the Danish language to be able to read Andersen in the original is aware that Andersen wrote stories that might be read aloud to children, but that were designed in such a way as also to be of interest to the grown-up(s) reading them aloud. The difference between the way in which

Andersen is perceived by his countrymen and by readers who cannot read him in his own language may well have something to do with his translators. 'The bad translations of H.C. Andersen's fairy tales have given the English-speaking world a distorted and one-sided view of H.C. Andersen', complained one of the first Danish scholars to write about Andersen's reception in the English-speaking world, Elias Bredsdorff.[2] And he continued:

> People know that he has fantasy and originality, but that he was an inspired artist only very few Englishmen realize. The English understand that [Andersen's] countrymen use him commercially in the tourist industry, but they are surprised that he has been assigned a big and significant place in literature. Andersen's fairy tales are still appreciated by English children, but they outgrow him and are not tempted to rediscover him when they grow up – understandably enough perhaps, considering the boring way in which [the tales] are often presented. (Bredsdorff 1954, 520)

Bredsdorff may not have been quite fair in his assessment of the work done by Andersen's translators, however. Instead of claiming that miserable translations are to blame for Andersen being read only by children, argues Viggo Hjørnager Pedersen, 'one might just as well claim that the translations have to a large extent been shaped by their being regarded as children's literature' (Hjørnager Pedersen 2004, 15–16). Besides, Andersen's influence on English literature is much greater than Bredsdorff's condemnation makes us think. Andersen is 'to all intents and purposes an English writer, read by millions of people who do not understand a word of Danish, and exerting more influence on English children's writing than any native Briton until Lewis Carroll' (ibid. 16). Danes may well regret this, but they would do well to remember that to millions of people around the world – Andersen having, as Bloom noted, been translated almost as widely and into as many different languages as the Bible itself – Andersen is known only in translation, that is, as a copy.

'Whose Ducklings Are They Anyway?', Hjørnager Pedersen therefore asks, and the story he tells of the English translations of Andersen's tales and stories is a very interesting one. The first of Andersen's works to appear in English was *The Improvisatore*. It was published in England in 1845 and had been translated by Mary Howitt – from the German. Andersen's novel had become a big hit in Germany, and Howitt, who was living in Germany between 1840 and 1843, seems to have known some Swedish, but no Danish. In this, Howitt was no different from the majority of English translators who 'worked either directly from the German, or used German translations as cribs' (ibid. 18). *The Improvisatore* got very favourable reviews in the English press. 'As a book of pleasing travels and admirable reflections we know of none better; and we can sincerely recommend it to our readers,' wrote a reviewer in the *London Journal*, for example (quoted in Bredsdorff 1954, 434).

The real turning-point in Andersen's career in the English-speaking world came only a couple of years later, and what made Andersen a household name in England were not the two novels that followed *The Improvisatore* so much as the tales and stories that were translated into English. During 1846–47 – only a few years later than they appeared in Danish – nine different selections of Andersen's stories and tales by six different translators appeared in English. The 44 stories and tales for which Andersen received instant fame are more or less the same stories and tales for which he is known to this day in the English-speaking world (and through the English-speaking world to the rest of the world, too) – 'The Princess on the Pea', 'The Little Mermaid', 'The Tinderbox', 'The Emperor's New Clothes', 'The Wild Swans', 'The Swineherd', 'The Ugly Duckling' and 'The Nightingale', to mention just a few. Many of his later stories and tales were not exactly children's stuff – they are the ones that contain the cruelty on which Harold Bloom commented and which he did not really know what to do with. These later tales appeared in one or two editions, but at the same time the far more popular 'children's stories' from his earlier years 'were republished, pirated, and adapted in a great and ever growing number of versions. The result was that the Andersen people knew toward the end of the century, and the Andersen they know today, came to be perceived as the author of somewhere between 5 and 50 tales, not of the 156 that he actually wrote' (Hjørnager Pedersen 2004, 73–4).

Early translators like Mary Howitt were partly to blame for relegating Andersen to the nursery, but they were operating under certain moral and practical constraints. Victorian prudery as to what was proper for grown-ups to read aloud to children was one such constraint. Books written for young children should neither be too frightening nor too violent, and sexual overtones or references definitely had to be toned down. Andersen's work, of course, was full of violence and did contain many more or less overt sexual references. Furthermore Andersen's often class-related humour was felt to be too blunt or critical of the political status quo. Hjørnager Pedersen mentions as an example of this a particular translation of 'The Tinderbox'. Whereas Andersen's queen is very human and down-to-earth – she 'could do more than just ride in a coach' (directly translated from the Danish) – the queen in the translation 'does not just ride in a coach, but "looks grand and condescending", which rather undermines the idea of her being a common-sense, practical woman' (ibid. 105). To this was added more practical considerations concerning the tastes of the publishers and buyers of Christmas books for children. This was a genre that became very popular during the nineteenth century, and publishers considered it the ideal venue for Andersen's work. Being a translator was hard work and did not pay all that well, after all, and for all of these reasons translators found themselves forced into adjusting Andersen's stories to prevailing tastes.

What then of later translations? According to Hjørnager Pedersen, later translations – even those that appeared well into the twentieth century and those that are published today – seem to rely heavily on the earlier translations (which in turn relied, as we saw, on German translations). One might even speak of a 'family of translations', an interdependence 'between the majority of the English translations, which seem to make up a large family of texts. Some translators obviously paraphrased their predecessors – and in some cases, this was already known – but, in addition, many more or less independent translators have borrowed from the tradition, so that it is difficult to find a modern edition that is not in some way or other indebted to older ones' (ibid. 353). If we add to this the fact mentioned above that to most of the world, Andersen is known in 'an *imitation*, a translation that is [sometimes] so free that it begins to look like a new work' (ibid. 17), the line between that which is the original and that which is the copy in relation to Hans Christian Andersen starts to become very blurred indeed.

HANS CHRISTIAN ANDERSEN AND COPYRIGHT

Andersen's first work started appearing in Denmark in the 1830s. Throughout his lifetime his stories and tales were translated as they appeared. In fact some of them were published in English even before they appeared in Danish. Bredsdorff lists 18 stories, two novels, one travel book and the definitive edition of Andersen's autobiography as having appeared in English before they appeared in Danish (Bredsdorff 1954, 621–2; Hjørnager Pedersen 2004, 73).

Inevitably, some translations were better than others. Of this however Andersen could not himself be the judge. While he was quite good at German and French, he did not speak English very well, and even though he attempted on more than one occasion to learn the language, he never succeeded. How difficult it could be to engage in conversation with Andersen in English, the American writer J. Ross Brown described in his book *The Land of Thor*, from 1867. When he visited Denmark in 1866, he called on Andersen, who tried to tell him about his latest fairy tale, 'The Beetle':

> 'Have you seen my last – the – what do you call it in English? – a little animal –'
> 'Mouse,' I suggested.
> 'No, not a mouse; a little animal with wings.'
> 'Oh, a bat!'
> 'Nay, nay, a little animal with wings and many legs. Dear me! I forget the name in English, but you certainly know it in America – a very small animal!'
> In vain I tried to make a selection from all the little animals of my acquaintance with wings and many legs. The case was getting both embarrassing and vexatious. At length a light broke upon me.

'A mosquito!' I exclaimed, triumphantly.

'Nay, nay!' cried the bothered poet; 'a little animal with a hard skin on its back. Dear me, I can't remember its name!'

'Oh, I have it now,' said I, really desirous of relieving his mind – 'a flea!'

At this the great improvisator scratched his head, looked at the ceiling and then at the floor, after which he took several strides up and down the room, and struck himself repeatedly on the forehead. Suddenly grasping up a pen, he exclaimed, somewhat energetically, 'Here! I'll draw it for you;' and forthwith he drew on a scrap of paper a diagram, of which the accompanying engraving is a fac-simile.

'A tumble-bug!' I shouted, astonished at my former stupidity.

The poet looked puzzled and distressed. Evidently I had not yet succeeded. What could it be?

'A beetle! A beetle!' I next ventured to suggest, rather disappointed at the result of my previous guess.

'A beetle! A beetle! – that's it; now I remember – a beetle!' and the delighted author of 'The Beetle' patted me approvingly on the back, and chuckled gleefully at his own adroit method of explanation.'

(quoted in Bredsdorff 1954, 273–4)

At the time of this encounter, Andersen was 61. He was world famous and received fan calls and letters from all corners of the world. One fan was another American by the name of Horace E. Scudder. Scudder was an editor with the *Riverside Magazine for Young People*, which was published out of Boston, and he first wrote to Andersen in 1862: 'I assure you it is with no small pleasure that I write thus to one who has doubtless many honourable insignia, but who is to me and to all my fellow children in America, young and old, simply Hans Christian Andersen, best of story tellers' (Hersholt 1948, 18). Scudder received no answer to this gracious letter. In fact, he had to write three more letters to Andersen before the latter finally wrote back. What prompted the Danish writer to answer Scudder's fourth letter, dated 13 March 1868, was Scudder's proposition of 'an arrangement', according to which Andersen would receive $500 for 12 new stories to be published in the *Riverside Magazine*. 'It is understood', Scudder wrote, 'that these stories shall not have been published in English beforehand' (ibid. 23).

To Andersen, Scudder's offer of remuneration for his work was highly welcome. He did have slight misgivings at first about the *Riverside Magazine* being the right venue for his stories: 'On a cursory perusal of the *Riverside Magazine* I must confess that it is my impression that the greater part of it is written for very young people, and though I know that my tales are read by young and old, and that the former enjoy what I would call the exterior, the latter the inner part, I think that my stories are not entirely on their right place in the said *Magazine*' (ibid. 25). In the end however the thought of finally getting paid for his translated work won him over, and he granted Scudder a near monopoly of the translation rights for new stories: 'I oblige myself to take care that any new stories or tales, which I may send to the *Riverside Magazine* are not published, neither in Danish nor in any other language until three months after they have been sent to you' (ibid. 31).

Between 1868 and 1875, Andersen received about $2200 in royalties through Scudder from his American publishers (ibid. 11). Before 1868, he had received nothing at all from the United States. His royalties from England amounted to £368 – a ridiculously small amount, which can only be accounted for by the fact that there was no international copyright protection during Andersen's lifetime (Bredsdorff 1954, 623). English and American publishers could – and indeed did – print whatever part of Andersen's oeuvre they wanted without paying him anything. It was only with the Berne Convention for the Protection of Literary and Artistic Works in 1886 that an author's right to be paid for translations of his or her work was established. When Andersen wrote to a friend in 1836 that, 'unfortunately I belong to such a small nation that even though my work is among the most well-read of works, it will hardly be able to feed me' (ibid. 622), he hardly knew how prophetic his words would be.

Paradoxically, furthermore, as Andersen's fame grew in England and later also the United States, it became harder to interest respectable publishers in publishing the later stories in an English translation. The more popular Andersen became, the more likely it was that cheap pirate editions would be published, and the lack of protection for the author, the translator as well as the publisher of work done by non-English (or non-American) writers created problems for the more serious publishing companies who wanted to treat 'their' authors fairly. One interesting case in point is Richard Bentley, the first English publisher to publish Andersen's work. In 1846 Bentley offered Andersen £50 for each work of more than 320 pages that the writer might yet produce – provided that Andersen himself paid for the translation of such a work, and that it had been published in neither Denmark nor Germany.

A few years later though, in 1850, Bentley had to renege on his offer:

> I regret to tell you that the last book I published of yours did not succeed – in fact it left me with a loss. This I attribute, beyond public caprice, to the present state of the Copyright Act, which does not protect a publisher in what I have always considered his just rights – that is, the Law at present here will not allow the right of a foreigner to have copyright here, nor to assign it. The effect of this is, that Publishers hesitate to give money when their work may be pirated, but it also operates injuriously inasmuch as the booksellers will not purchase on speculation a book at a fair price, when a cheaper edition may appear in the market next day. In this state of things – for this is a recent decision – I do not know what to do – it clearly will not be in my power to purchase copyright.[3]

Bentley pretty much lost interest in dealing with foreign writers when he lost a lot of money in 1855, because the House of Lords rejected his claim to the right to publish a number of American writers with whom he had signed a contract. The subject, he wrote to Andersen, 'sickens me':

In consequence of the decision of the House of Lords, declaring that no foreigner had copyright in English, I lost 1000£ a year. All the property which I had acquired in *this class* of works was declared *valueless*! property for which I paid upwards of £23 000! – Had the House been content with making the law prospective it would not have been unjust, but to sacrifice an individual who has acquired this property by regular purchase *under the sanction of repeated* Decisions of all our Courts (that a foreigner first publishing here did possess copyright) – *was* and *is* a monstrous wrong, and calls for redress. But what can an individual do against such fearful odds – and so I am sacrificed for the public good! Such a monstrous wrong would not be done, I believe, even in Russia, but for England, which professes to encourage literature, and seeks to draw all learned men and all men eminent for art or science to her, thus to refuse their claim to the fruit of their labours, it is a high crime against the principles she vaunts her desire to carry out. The subject sickens me, so I will quit it. (ibid. 191–2)

When a collection of Andersen's tales and stories was published in Denmark in 1872, Andersen sent a copy of the book to Edmund Gosse, who subsequently asked the Danish writer's permission to translate it and find a publisher for it in England. He received Andersen's permission, but wrote to Andersen the following year that his efforts on the latter's behalf had been in vain:

No one here in London will risk the publication of a translation of your last stories. Perhaps this will surprise you as much as it did me, but the reason of it lies in the extreme popularity of your works amongst us. Unless a very cheap and common edition were brought out, – and this would not be worth your while or mine, – the publishers fear that the translation would at once be pirated by other publishing-houses, and they themselves would lose their profits. Added to this is the difficulty of an already-existing translation in America. You know there is no copyright-treaty between England and Denmark, or between England and America, so your works are open to double danger. (ibid. 299–300)

Andersen died two years later, in 1875, and thus never saw the work done by Victor Hugo and other authors and publishers, organized in the International Literary Association, towards an international conference on copyright. Convinced that something had to be done about a copyright situation that protected the copyrights of a state's own citizens, but allowed the violation of copyrights held by citizens of other countries, members of the International Literary Association persuaded the president of the Swiss Federal Council to host a diplomatic conference in Berne in September 1884. This was the first time that representatives from different governments worked together on a draft agreement. Two more years were needed for negotiations before the Berne Convention could be signed on 9 September 1886 by ten countries. Great Britain, Germany and France were among the signatories – but not the United States, which only joined the Berne Union in 1989 (Marlin-Bennett 2004, 53–4).

After the Berne Convention, which itself has seen several revisions, other conventions and treaties have followed, all of which have strengthened the copyrights of authors and publishers. In 1970 the World Intellectual Property Organization (WIPO) was founded as an independent international organization. It became a specialized agency of the United Nations in 1976 and has been instrumental in institutionalizing rules representing the interests of the dominating parties in an increasingly global trading system. Twenty years later, the WIPO Copyright Treaty was signed. It builds on the provisions of the Berne Convention and revisits the protection of copyright in light of the challenges posed by the Internet and related digital advances (ibid. 56). Throughout, the trend has been toward an ever greater commodification and privatization of copyrights, the 'winners' being the global media companies, and the 'losers' being the general public and lesser-known authors who neither wish nor know how to write the sort of best-selling novels on display in bookstores in every major international airport.

What would Hans Christian Andersen have thought of this trend? While probably happy finally to be able to make some real money, my guess is that he would have agreed with many scholars – and this includes several of the scholars contributing to this book – that copyright is not and should not be considered as 'property'. It is, rather, 'a specific state-granted monopoly issued for particular policy reasons' (Vaidhyanathan 2001, 253). Andersen could not have anticipated the tensions coming to the fore a hundred years after his death between market interests and privacy, and between commodification and the commons. Nor could he have foreseen the questions that, as Renée Marlin-Bennett puts it, 'remain central to what should be an ongoing global debate' in the Information or Digital Age:

> Who is making the rules about property rights? How are the rules being made? Are protections for rights holders strong enough? Do we need more rights and better-enforced rights? How is the public interest protected? Are we preserving a global knowledge commons? Are we allowing people to control the flow of information in ways consistent with their own needs and those of the public? (Marlin-Bennett 2004, 249)

It is these and related questions that the contributors to this book take up and discuss possible answers to. The idea to look at the issue of copyright against the background of Hans Christian Andersen and his work was fostered in the autumn of 2004 as the bicentennial of his birth was coming up. Professor Lawrence Lessig preceded Harold Bloom; on 4 November he delivered the Hans Christian Andersen Academy Lecture 2004 at the University of Southern Denmark in Odense on '(Re)creativity: How Creativity Lives'. Present on that occasion were the other contributors to this book who met again the following day to discuss 'Hans Christian Andersen and Copyright'.

As it turned out, Andersen presented an ideal focus and/or point of departure for such copyright discussions.

THE EIGHT CHAPTERS

The first chapter is an adaptation of the lecture Lawrence Lessig gave in November 2004 at the University of Southern Denmark in Odense. As the title indicates, Lessig is concerned about how creativity lives – how culture gets created and then gets spread. Strictly speaking, he argues, all culture is remix – creative work being produced by some author, say Hans Christian Andersen, 'mixing bits of culture and his own creativity together'. Most of us are aware of the way in which writers remix and reuse the work of their precursors; what we may be less aware of is that readers also remix. Lessig reminds us that 'every act of consuming culture is an act of constructing culture. Through both, cultures get made.'

With the emergence of digital technology within the past 15 years, the reader now has immediate access to cultural sources of all kinds. While the new technology has empowered the individual reader and has created a more democratic form of speech from which society as a whole benefits, the use of the Internet has also turned every act into a copy. Actions that were previously free have now become regulated, even illegal. Remixing by using digital technology 'is rendered illegal, because in a world where all uses produce a copy, and in a world where all copies are copies of presumptively copyrighted material, one needs permission first, and this permission is not coming'.

The way to go, says Lessig, is not to reject copyright law altogether, but rather to find ways to fit copyright law to the digital technology. His own attempt to do so involves the non-profit corporation Creative Commons that has been internationalized through the iCommons Project. The idea is to provide each individual creator with a choice of licence. Depending on the licence chosen, the creator can limit certain commercial uses of the creative work in question, for example, just as he or she can permit or not permit modifications of the work. This sort of arrangement, argues Lessig, encourages cultural remix without destroying the underlying regime of intellectual property.

The other eight contributors to this book share Lawrence Lessig's concern about the present state of copyright law and the way in which it threatens the remix of culture and creativity. Whether or not to remain within the underlying regime of intellectual property law, and what sort of reforms are needed if we do decide to remain within this regime – these fundamental questions form the subtext for these eight contributors, just as they do for Lessig. The second and third chapters by Stina Teilmann and Uma Suthersanen, respectively, give us a very useful historical survey of copyright law. In 'On real nightingales and mechanical reproductions', Stina Teilmann takes as her point of departure three of Hans Christian Andersen's stories – 'The Princess on the Pea' (1835), 'The Swineherd' (1842) and 'The Nightingale' (1844) – for an analysis of the way in which 'authenticity' became an important marker of value during the nineteenth century. For Andersen – as for other nineteenth-century writers – the important thing was to be 'authentic' or 'real', and the emphasis on 'authenticity' had important consequences for copyright law. Whereas copyright originally, in the early 1700s, was an author's right in a material copy (the original) to make more material copies, the object of copyright (the work) came during the nineteenth century to be defined as 'immaterial'. 'This served to separate literary and artistic property entirely from the physical property of manuscripts and artworks, as well as from the physical objects of the copies of a "work" ' – a separation that 'is crucial for modern copyright law'.

Uma Suthersanen looks at the genesis of international copyright law in 'Bleak House or Great Expectations? The literary author as a stakeholder in nineteenth-century international copyright politics'. As writers were becoming stakeholders with economic and societal interests that had to be protected domestically as well as internationally, they began lobbying for the establishment of reciprocal copyright protection between different states. Charles Dickens is a famous case in point. Dickens visited the United States in 1842, and during this visit he repeatedly advocated for the protection of British works and the protection of international copyright law. The jury is still out as to whether Dickens's motives were of a pecuniary kind or whether they were of a more lofty and idealistic kind. Suthersanen uses Dickens and his fight for copyright protection to trace both the interplay between nineteenth-century literary authors and copyright awareness, and the history of the entry of the United States into the world of international copyright law. 'The nineteenth century is', as she points out, 'an archive of many such issues.'

'Adaptations abound. Versions of Hans Christian Andersen's tales are countless', writes Leslie Kim Treiger-Bar-Am in 'Adaptations with integrity'. She looks at an author's right to control such adaptations and other modifications of literary, visual and musical artworks. More interested in an author's moral right of integrity than in the economic interest in copyright that may also give copyright owners control over derivative uses, Treiger-Bar-Am centres her analysis on UK law and its enactment of section 80 of the Copyright, Designs and Patents Act 1988. Her premise is that the moral right of integrity is a right of expression, arising directly from the principles and the case law of freedom of expression, and her argument is that 'modifications to all artforms, and of all types, ought potentially be actionable pursuant to the integrity right'. Like Lawrence Lessig, Treiger-Bar-Am also points to the reader or viewer as a potential modifier of an original work. Such a modifier is also an author and must be protected accordingly: 'Freedom of expression is both the justification for the author's integrity right and for defences to claims pursuant to the right.' The integrity rights spectrum thus ultimately requires 'a balancing of autonomies of expression of author, modifier and reader'.

In 'What might Hans Christian Andersen say about copyright today?', Fiona Macmillan points to copyright's failure to further creativity and culture as primarily due to the fact that 'we have allowed the process of commodification to take over copyright without really asking what the costs and consequences of this commodification are'. The original rationale for copyright – that it encourages the production of the cultural works that enable culture and democracy to develop – has been sadly misused to allow a build-up of private power over cultural output. One consequence of this copyright-facilitated aggregation of private power is that big 'media and entertainment corporations are able to act as a cultural filter, controlling what we can hear'. This ability to control and manipulate markets severely limits the range of cultural products on offer, thus effectively homogenizing world culture. Another major consequence is a loss of the commons or public domain. Corporate control of the commons not only limits the public's access to cultural works; it also limits the opportunity for resistance and critique of the political status quo. Even though attempting to surmise Andersen's attitude toward this picture of cultural homogenization and domination is 'a risky business', Macmillan concludes, 'Some disruption of the current copyright consensus might very well be a fitting tribute to Hans Christian Andersen'.

One area that illustrates the inappropriateness of the property paradigm within copyright law is traditional cultural expression. In 'Hans Christian Andersen and the protection of traditional cultural expressions', Michael Blakeney examines the agitation for the protection of traditional cultural expression as an artefact of the international intellectual property regime. He shows how this agitation originated with calls for the protection of folkloric works within the context of the Berne Convention and then under UNESCO, and how it has been adopted as a cause of action by groups of indigenous peoples. This is not unproblematic however. Using Andersen's first four tales – 'The Tinder Box', 'The Princess on the Pea', 'Little Claus and Big Claus' and 'Little Ida's Flowers', all published in 1835 – as an illustration of the way in which cultural creativity has always included folkloric borrowings, Blakeney cautions that 'An intellectual property regime which provides for the protection of traditional cultural creativity should also permit the natural development of culture through permissible borrowings'. He goes on to examine justifications for the protection of traditional cultural expression and concludes with a testing of these justifications by an examination of the situation in Australia, where this branch of the law is the most elaborated.

Lee Davis's focus in 'Should the logic of "open source" be applied to digital cultural goods? An exploratory essay' is the economic role of copyrights for digital cultural goods. Digitization has made possible the expression of almost all cultural works in virtual form on the Internet; they are easily accessible to anyone, anywhere in the world. Davis is especially interested in 'the implications of one of the most compelling developments in recent years: that the copyright has inspired its own antithesis, with the growth of the "open source software" (OSS) movement'. With the new digital technology, readers and users can play around with and manipulate works of art of previous centuries, for example the works of Hans Christian Andersen. 'The results', she writes, 'might be highly creative. But they might just as easily be "mush". Whatever the case, the stories created would be far from Andersen's original work.' The question is therefore whether OSS, in its facilitation of continuous free public access to software innovations, jeopardizes the preservation of older works of art. Ultimately, 'solutions . . . need to be found', Davis concludes, 'that both enable artists to maintain the integrity of their work, and enable other interested parties to experiment with these works in new ways'.

The solution to the problems outlined by Davis, as indeed to many other copyright-related problems, Marieke van Schijndel and Joost Smiers would argue, is simply to give up on copyright law altogether. In the last chapter of the book, 'Imagining a world without copyright: the market and temporary protection, a better alternative for artists and the public domain', van Schijndel and Smiers suggest a thought-experiment: that we join them in a journey into a world without copyright. It is, they acknowledge, not an easy thought-experiment to conduct; most of us find it very difficult to imagine a world without copyright. It may be worth our trouble though. Having discussed (in order then to dismiss) various models that have been presented as alternatives to the current copyright regime – one of which being Lessig's Creative Commons model – van Schijndel and Smiers propose a model of their own: the usufruct model. This is a civil law alternative to the Anglo-American notion of copyright as property – 'characteristic for usufruct is that one does not have the ownership of an item; however, one is entitled to the usage of the fruits of the item'. There are a number of practical matters that still need to be resolved with respect to the usufruct model, van Schijndel and Smiers admit, but the matter may well take care of itself in the end: 'With digitization in mind, our guess is that we will not have to wait much longer before the copyright system will crumble.'

NOTES

1. Harold Bloom, 'Trust the Tale, not the Teller'. Lecture given at the University of Southern

Denmark on 1 April 2005 on the occasion of the 200th anniversary of Hans Christian Andersen. Not yet published. Manuscript in author's possession. The author wishes to thank Professor Bloom for having graciously given her a copy of his talk.
2. Bredsdorff (1954), p. 520 (my translation from the Danish – all subsequent translations from this book are my own).
3. Bredsdorff (1954), p. 624 – the story of Andersen and copyright in England and the United States is based on Bredsdorff, (1954), pp. 622–5.

BIBLIOGRAPHY

Bredsdorff, Elias (1954), *H.C. Andersen og England* [*H.C. Andersen and England*], Copenhagen: Rosenkilde & Bagger.

Hersholt, Jean (1948), *H.C. Andersen og Horace E. Scudder: En brevveksling* [*H.C. Andersen and Horace E. Scudder: An Exchange of Letters*], Copenhagen: Gyldendal.

Hjørnager Pedersen, Viggo (2004), *Ugly Ducklings? Studies in the English Translations of Hans Christian Andersen's Tales and Stories*, Odense: University of Southern Denmark Press.

Marlin-Bennett, Renée (2004), *Knowledge Power: Intellectual Property, Information, and Privacy (Ipolitics)*, Boulder, CO: Lynne Rienner Publishers.

Vaidhyanathan, Siva (2001), *Copyrights and Copywrongs: The Rise of Intellectual Property and How It Threatens Creativity*, New York: New York University Press.

1. (Re)creativity: how creativity lives

Lawrence Lessig

I come from California, the land of the technology-obsessed. It's also the land of Hollywood, where the people are Hollywood-obsessed. But in this chapter, I would like to ask you to forget about technology and to forget about Hollywood, and to focus instead upon culture. In particular, upon how culture gets created and how culture gets spread, and about the relationship between authors and readers. My aim is to remind us about the importance of both at a time when the importance of one has been forgotten.

In 1865, Lewis Carroll published the extraordinary work, *Alice's Adventures in Wonderland*. Sometime in the twentieth century (it depends upon where you are), the Carroll's copyright expired, and the work passed into the public domain. In 2001, as a demonstration of its new E-Book Reader technology, Adobe created an e-book version of this public domain text. The e-book was produced from a text created by the Gutenberg Project, a project designed to make works in the public domain available for free on the Internet.

But when *Alice's Adventures* got translated into its Adobe E-Book version, the freedoms of the public domain had mysteriously disappeared. There was a button on the very first page that listed the 'permissions' that ran with the book. If you clicked on that button, you were given a list of 'permissions' that were in fact restrictions on the uses you could make of *Alice's Adventures in Wonderland*. So, for example, the permission reported that 'no text selections can be copied from this book to the clipboard'. It reported that 'no printing is permitted on this book'. It reported, 'This book cannot be lent or given to someone else.' It reported, 'This book cannot be given to someone else.' And finally, the permissions reported, 'This book cannot be read aloud.'

This final 'permission' was too much for the community that gathers around the Internet. A firestorm broke out, as Adobe was asked to explain how it could be distributing a public domain children's book but restrict the right to read the book aloud. Adobe responded, 'Don't be silly. Obviously, we don't intend to restrict the ability of people to read a book aloud. We instead simply intend to indicate that the technology of the E-Book Reader is not permitted to be used to read the book aloud.'

The distinction was lost on most, but the 'silliness' was important not so much because of the substance of Adobe's restriction, but because of growing anxiety about the way technology might affect culture – anxiety about both how technology might affect the writing of culture and, more importantly, how it might affect its reading. Or put differently, how technology might affect the creativity of culture, and how technology might affect how that creativity gets remixed.

Think a bit about this concept of 'remix'. Think a bit about 'remix' in particular before technology got into the mix. Think about it before Hollywood got into the mix.

By 'remix', I mean a very familiar idea. We begin with some creative work – work which some author produced by mixing bits of culture and his own creativity together. That work is then remixed by others, through the addition of other creative work, or even through simple criticism of that work. This is remix. And in this sense, life is remix. In this sense, culture is remix. Knowledge is remix. Politics is remix. Remix is how we create. Remix is how we recreate. Remix is how we are human, and how we as humans make culture.

Now most of us are familiar with the ways writers remix. For example, the Brothers Grimm took folk tales from their tradition, and they ported those stories to a more popular style for their time. They were successful remixers. Indeed so successful were they at remixing that they thought everyone was just a remixer. Thus when the Grimm Brothers grabbed some of H.C. Andersen's stories, believing they were simple remixes of Danish stories, Andersen had to inform them that his stories were his alone, though no doubt informed by a tradition that was not his alone. And perhaps most famously in the United States, Walt Disney was a successful remixer. He too took creativity from many, including the Brothers Grimm and H.C. Anderson. He too remixed them to fit the work of each within the culture for which he was producing. Thus with the Grimms, Disney remixed their bloody, moralistic stories into something much nicer. With H.C. Andersen's 'The Little Mermaid', which is not that bloody, and not sufficiently moralistic for many of Andersen's critics, he made a happy story from an unhappy tale. And most profitably, Disney took the creativity of a creator called Buster Keaton, in a work called *Steamboat Bill, Jr.* – a work that had no blood and was absolutely amoral – and turned that work into something called *Steamboat Willie*. In each case Disney was a remixer, taking the creativity of others and producing it, updating it, translating it into creativity that his culture, a culture of his age, could accept.

That's the remix of the writer. Less familiar however is the remix of the reader. You watch a movie – for example Michael Moore's *Fahrenheit 9/11* – and then you whine to your friends about either how it's the best movie you've ever seen or the worst movie ever made. By that act, you're remixing Michael Moore's creativity into your life, and sharing that remix with others. And both acts help construct, or reconstruct, a culture. Or you choose to watch Walt

Disney rather than reading H.C. Andersen. That too is a choice about how a culture will get remixed, and thus remade. Every act of consuming culture is an act of constructing culture. Through both, cultures get made. Every act of reading and choosing and criticizing and praising past culture is an act through which present culture gets made.

Now in our tradition, this practice of remix is 'free'. Free as in unregulated. It is completely free for the reader; it is essentially free for the writer.

As a reader, you don't need permission to criticize Michael Moore. You don't need authorization from Disney to recommend his *Little Mermaid* over H.C. Andersen's. The acts of reader-remix are unregulated by the law. Indeed because the law of copyright regulates (in its essence) 'copies', and because the ordinary use of copyrighted works by readers does not produce a copy, the remix of the reader is by design free of legal constraint. No doubt books and movies cost money to buy. So the reader is constrained in that narrow economic sense. But even here the constraint is mitigated by institutions like libraries or free TV. And in any case, the regulation of an economic constraint is different from the regulation of a legal constraint.

The writer faces more constraints. He too is within our tradition free to remix, but not as free as the reader. For the writer, some types of remix are unfree because they are expensive. And some types of remix are unfree because they are constrained by law.

For example Alfred Hitchcock's 1954 movie, *Rear Window*, was based upon an earlier short story by Woolrich, titled 'Had to Be Murder'. Hitchcock was thus constrained in his ability to remix Woolrich's story in two different ways. First, because the technology of filmmaking was expensive, his remixing was expensive. And second, because Woolrich's story was still under copyright, Hitchcock's remix needed the permission of the copyright holder. He was thus not free to remix it without the permission of the copyright holder. In both senses then, Hitchcock was constrained. And in this sense he was less free to remix than his reader. But in my view these constraints on the writer have historically been both limited and reasonable. To the extent that the constraints were economic constraints, they reflected real scarcity within a market. To the extent that they were legal constraints, for most of our history they were relatively limited.

These constraints depend upon technology. Indeed we could say that the difference between the reader and writer depends upon technology. Hitchcock was constrained by the costs of making a film. But that constraint for him was manageable; for a reader, or even another filmmaker, that cost would have been disabling.

In the past 15 years we've seen a radical change in technology. The emergence of digital technology has meant a radical change in the way culture gets made and spread and remixed. That change in turn is changing the opportunity for remixing culture. It is expanding that opportunity, by closing the gap between reader and writer.

So for example the Beatles produced an album called the *White Album* that inspired the musician Jay-Z to produce an album called the *Black Album*. And that album inspired a musician called DJ Danger Mouse to produce the *Gray Album*, which was literally a synthesis of the tracks of the *White Album* and the *Black Album*. Without the changes of digital technology, this form of creativity would not have been possible.

Or consider the changes in the context of film. In 2004, the film *Tarnation* was debuted at Cannes. It was said by many to 'wow' Cannes. This film cost $218 to make. The director had been given an iMac by his friends, and using film that he had shot through his whole life, he produced a film that was of such a quality to win awards at many international festivals, as well as rave attention at Cannes.

Or perhaps most important have been the examples of remix using digital technologies in the area of politics. It is of course impossible to describe the power of these creations in written form. That is in fact the point. But there has been an explosion of creative political commentary, using images and sounds from the culture around us, remixed using digital technologies to either artistic or political end. None is more powerful than a remix of Lionel Richie's 'Endless Love', as a duet with President Bush and Prime Minister Blair (available at http://atmo.se).

In all of these examples, the point to recognize is the potential that this change in technology creates. Anyone with a $1500 computer has the opportunity to take sounds and images from the culture around us and remix them in a way that produces culture differently – that changes, that is, the way that culture gets remixed by changing the creative potential and, most importantly, the democratic potential of this culture. These new technologies change the freedom to speak by changing the power to speak, making that power different; no longer just a broadcast democracy but increasingly a bottom-up democracy; no longer just *New York Times* democracy, but increasingly a blog democracy; no longer just the few speaking to the many, but increasingly peer to peer.

The reader becomes the writer in this world, and the writer in this world becomes a reader. For as cultures get spread without a distributor standing in the middle, the way cultures get made and remade changes.

In this sense, technology has exploded the potential for remix. But that potential is now threatened by two other effects technology has produced. One effect is the most obvious: the explosion in the 'piracy' of copyrighted material. And the second effect will follow from the first: the reaction to this 'piracy'.

The first effect is the explosion in content 'shared' without the permission of the copyright holder. This piracy has inspired a 'war', a war which Jack Valenti has referred to as his 'own terrorist war' (apparently the terrorists are our children). This war has induced the creation of new weapons, of both law and technology, designed to protect intellectual property by effectively disabling the Internet's original design. Rather than facilitating the efficient spread of content, these weapons disable the efficient spread of content. We thus break the way the Internet was designed to protect Hollywood from the threat that this technology presents.

But while the Internet in practice has weakened the reach of copyright law, in principle the network radically expands the reach of copyright law. To see the point, think for example about a book. If you imagine all the uses of a book in the world before digital technologies, many of these uses were essentially unregulated. If you read a book, that's an unregulated use, because to read a book is not to produce a copy. If you give someone a book, that's an unregulated use, because to give someone a book is not to produce a copy. If you sell someone a book, that's an unregulated use, because to sell somebody a book is not to produce a copy. If you sleep on a book, that's an unregulated use, because to sleep on a book does not produce a copy. These ordinary uses of these bits of culture are, before the Internet, free. Then at the core of these uses is a set of uses which are properly regulated by the law. For example if you publish, it requires the permission of the copyright owner, because to publish a book is to invade a proper exclusive right protected by copyright.

Enter the Internet, where every act is a copy. Now, magically, without the resolution of any legislative body, actions that before were presumptively free are now by default regulated. Ordinary uses of culture become controlled, and new uses of culture using these digital technologies become essentially illegal. Thus remix in this culture is rendered illegal, because in a world where all uses produce a copy, and in a world where all copies are copies of presumptively copyrighted material, one needs permission first, and this permission is not coming.

So for example DJ Dangermouse knew the Beatles never give permission to remix their work. Jonathan Caouette, the director of *Tarnation*, discovered that while his film cost $218 to make, it would cost $400 000 to clear the rights to the images and sounds used in the background of the film. In these cases and many others, the consequence of the way the law regulates today is that permission is required and yet permission is not coming, rendering much of this creativity illegal.

Illegality doesn't stop this form of creativity. But it does stop our schools from teaching this kind of literacy, and it does slow the spread of technologies for facilitating it – as manufacturers fear liability from the misuse of their technologies.

But over time however this illegality will be converted into impossibility.

For today, the rule renders these forms of creativity illegal. Tomorrow, as the technology of digital rights management (DRM) becomes increasingly embedded in the infrastructure of our culture, the capacity to engage in these forms of creative re-expression will be removed. DRM, designed to protect against 'piracy', will have the (perhaps unintended) effect of blocking this form of digital remix.

This consequence for DRM is not well understood. When DRM technology was first proposed as a response to 'piracy', there was a battle about whether 'fair use' would be preserved. But the 'fair use' at issue in those debates was the right to make multiple copies of a particular work. It was not the right to engage in remix. That earlier battle has produced a modern settlement. The settlement will produce a world where we will have strong digital rights management technologies, but a liberal 'fair use' policy where by 'fair use' the law means the right to make a limited number of copies within your own home. So for example you have the right to buy creative work and with that right we'll include the right to make X free copies within the home.

This compromise of course solves the architecture of revenue problem for creative industries from the nineteenth and twentieth centuries – industries that depended upon controlling copies. But it destroys the potential for digital remix. For the same tools used to lock down culture to prevent 'piracy' are tools that will make it effectively impossible to remix culture – at least without the permission of the culture owner, and again, that permission is not coming.

The problem here is not the technology. Nor is it something called 'copyright'. The problem is a regime of copyright not fit to the technology. The current regime of copyright is cumbersome, bloated, expensive and too lawyer-centric. It's a world where the costs of doing right are too high, and the scope of control is simply too great. It's a world where the limited exception to free use that copyright law used to impose is now the rule. It's a world where what before was a small amount of regulation in the creation and the spread of culture now covers all creativity and a great deal of the spread of culture. It is a radical change in the scope of regulation. Thus just when the technology could mean that anybody could engage the kind of creativity that Walt Disney did, the law intervenes to say that no one can do to Walt Disney what Walt Disney did to the Brothers Grimm. Or, we could say, no one could do to the Disney Corporation what Walt Disney did to H.C. Andersen. Technology enables; the law and technology disables.

Our response to this change should not be to reject the law. It should instead be to fit the law to the new technology. It should be to find ways to respect rights while making it easier to do what is right.

One idea to facilitate just this sort of change is the non-profit corporation that I run called Creative Commons. Creative Commons has as its objective a simple way to mark content with the freedoms the creators intend the content to carry. If you go to our website, http://creativecommons.org, you are given a choice to publish creative work subject to a license you select. That license permits you to limit commercial uses of your work; it allows you to permit or not permit modifications of your work; and it allows you to say that if modifications of your work are allowed, then others should release their modifications under similarly free terms.

These choices produce a license. This license comes in three layers. One layer is a human-readable commons deed, which expresses, in terms understandable to any, the freedoms associated with the content. The second layer is a lawyer-readable license, designed to guarantee the freedoms that are expressed associated with the content. And the third layer is a machine-readable expression of the freedoms associated with the content, so that machines can begin to gather content on the basis of the freedoms.

These three layers are essential together. We have to make the freedoms associated with content on the net understandable, unchallengeable and usable. And by so marking content, we can encourage a wide range of creativity consistent with the underlying copyright law. Or put differently, we can encourage a kind of creativity that encourages others to build on the creative work of others, consistent with the underlying regime of intellectual property.

This project has been internationalized through the iCommons Project. In more than 60 countries around the world right now, iCommons is porting the legal code of this three-layer license, so that in those jurisdictions, you will be able to select a license appropriate to that jurisdiction, while guaranteeing a common framework understandable and portable to creators around the world.

This is of course just one project. But its aim suggests the more general point. We need to adapt the law to fit the opportunities of digital technology. Those opportunities are most important the chance these technologies give to a much wider range of creators. Some of these creators depend upon exclusive rights to sustain their creativity. Some do not. Our system of intellectual property protection should not make either kind of creativity impossible.

The existing regime of law and technology, encouraging the range of 'piracy' that it does, makes it hard for the first kind of creator to succeed. The succeeding regime of law and technology – regulating all uses and enforcing that regulation through DRM – will make it very hard for the second kind of creator to exist. We need not choose between these two forms of creator. We could have a regime that supported both.

In 1874, Hans Christian Andersen received a letter from a child in the United States. The letter thanked Andersen for his creativity, and it included a small amount of money. It was the first of many letters that Andersen would receive – all from children, all sending money, and all to his great embarrassment.

Andersen had been the target of a campaign in the United States to raise awareness about the 'pirate nation' that the United States was. Until 1891, the US did not protect foreign copyrights at all. This children campaign was a brilliant effort to create political demand for the United States to respect foreign creative work. It was an effort to bring the United States into the modern era, respecting the rights of creators.

When the US finally recognized the rights of foreign copyright owners, it was said to have matured as a nation. But the regime of copyright that secured that maturity was still essentially limited. The law throughout the nineteenth, and most of the twentieth centuries left ordinary uses of culture free. It didn't purport to regulate readers. And it only incidentally regulated writers. It no doubt created property for the authors, but that property did not enable the control of the readers.

Digital technologies have changed this balance. While on the one hand, they have exploded the opportunity for the reader to be the writer, on the other hand, they have inspired a movement to change that technology, so as to reassert control over the reader, and the writer, in a way that we have never known before.

The maturation of American copyright law in 1891 was a long overdue change. But this change in copyright law around the world, induced by the threat that 'piracy' presents, should be resisted. We have the chance to continue a tradition that writers have enjoyed through the creative work of more than just writers. The technology has democratized creativity. It has enabled a generation of Andersen creators – not privileged but talented; not just writers but readers.

Before we lose this opportunity, we should understand its potential. The democracy in a broad range of remix creativity is more valuable than the control these new technologies will enable. We need to resist this control, and experience this democracy.

2. On real nightingales and mechanical reproductions

Stina Teilmann

Hans Christian Andersen (1805–75) lived in a century during which 'authenticity' came to be an important marker of value. The Romantic Movement in art and literature celebrated 'authentic expression'. Philosophy and political thinking began to emphasize the significance of 'authentic being'.[1] As a result 'authenticity' was given a new sense in the nineteenth century. No longer a mere synonym for 'authoritative' and 'authorized' ('legally valid'), 'authentic' became important in the sense of 'being real and actual' as opposed to 'counterfeit' or 'copied'.[2]

Andersen shared his contemporaries' fascination with authenticity. Indeed some of his most famous fairy tales reveal an intense concern with the significance of being authentic or 'real'. Thus the opening lines of 'The Princess on the Pea' (1835):

> Once upon a time there was a prince who wanted to marry a princess. But she had to be a real princess. He travelled all over the world to find her, yet everywhere he went, something was the matter. There were certainly enough princesses, but he couldn't be sure that they were real princesses – there was always something that wasn't right. He came home and was very sad because he so wanted to marry a real princess.[3]

A princess comes and knocks on the door, and she claims to be a real princess. The old queen, the prince's mother, gives her 20 mattresses and 20 eiderdowns on which to sleep, and puts a dried pea underneath. The next morning, when the princess complains how badly she has slept, the royal family knows that she has told them the truth:

> *Now* they could tell that she was a real princess, because she had felt the pea through twenty mattresses and twenty eiderdowns. Only a real princess could be that sensitive. (Andersen, 2003, p. 62)

The prince marries the real princess and the pea is placed in the Royal Museum where you can still see it – unless it has been stolen – and thus be assured of the authenticity of the tale. And the story ends triumphantly, after filling barely one page of print: 'See, that was a real story'.

In 'The Swineherd' (1842)[4] we find a similar preoccupation with things real. Again, a prince is looking for a suitable bride; he has set his mind on the emperor's daughter. To impress the princess he sends her a gift of the most authentic things that his kingdom has to offer: a rose 'that smelled so sweet that you forgot all your worries', and a nightingale 'which sang as if it kept every lovely melody in its throat'. The princess and her ladies-in-waiting open the present in great excitement. First they see the rose and agree:

'Oh, it is so nicely made,' all the ladies-in-waiting said.

But a nasty surprise awaits them:

The princess touched it and looked as if she were about to cry. 'Ugh, Daddy,' she complained. 'It's real.'

The emperor implores his daughter to open the other box before she gets too upset. This one contains the nightingale, which sings so beautifully that no one is able to think of a bad word to say about it. However, an elderly courtier praises it by means of an odd comparison:

'How that bird reminds me of the dear departed empress's music box' . . .

and the princess exclaims:

'I refuse to believe that it's real.'

However the messenger who has delivered the gift assures her that it is real:

'Then let it fly away,' the princess said. There was no way she'd allow the prince to call on her. (Andersen, 2003, p. 132)

In the end, the princess gets what she deserves. She is thrown out of her father's palace for kissing the prince dressed up as a swineherd, and as she had failed to appreciate 'the real thing' – the nightingale – the prince will have nothing more to do with her.

'The Nightingale' (1844) tells us of a bird presented to the Emperor of China. This nightingale sings so beautifully 'that the Emperor got tears in his eyes'. And when the nightingale sings even more beautifully, 'its song went straight to his heart' (Andersen, 2003, p. 143). One day the Emperor receives a package with the word 'Nightingale' written on it. The Emperor opens the box:

Inside the box lay an artificial nightingale; it was supposed to look like the real one, but it was covered with diamonds, rubies, and sapphires. As soon as you wound it up, it sang one of the melodies that the real one sang, and its tail went up and down, gleaming of silver and gold.

It is intended that the two nightingales should sing together in a duet of unprecedented quality:

> but it didn't quite work because the real bird had its own style, and the artificial bird had only its mechanical parts. 'You can't blame it for that,' the imperial music master said. 'It keeps perfect time, just the way I like it.' Then the artificial bird had to sing by itself. It was just as popular as the real one, but of course it was also much prettier to look at: It glittered like brooches and bracelets. (Andersen, 2003, p. 144)

The mechanical bird sings the same tune 33 times and still does not grow tired. Meanwhile the real nightingale flies away to the green forest. It is thought to be a most ungrateful creature. But the Emperor still has the best bird:

> The imperial music master lavished praise on the bird – assured everyone that it was better than the real nightingale, not only because of its apparel with all those beautiful diamonds but also because of its inner qualities. (Andersen, 2003, p. 145)

With the real nightingale one can never know what comes next; the artificial bird can be opened and displayed, its 'human ingenuity' can be admired. However when the Emperor falls ill, the mechanical bird is of no use, it has no restorative powers. Only when the real nightingale returns and sings to the Emperor is Death chased away.

One of the foremost commentators on the nineteenth century's fascination with authenticity and 'being real' is Walter Benjamin. In his essay 'The Work of Art in the Age of Mechanical Reproduction' (1936), Benjamin discusses authenticity in the light of its correlate, the 'reproduction'. As the value of authenticity became a norm in the arts, so there developed a focus on the definition of its opposites: in particular 'reproduction' and 'copy'. Benjamin is renowned for the argument that new techniques of reproduction in the nineteenth century changed the perception of art. However what is not always acknowledged is the fact that in this process the word 'reproduction' gained a distinct new meaning.

As becomes clear from Benjamin's argument, 'reproduction', in its new sense acquired in the nineteenth century, is to be defined in contrast to the 'original'. Benjamin delineates the polarity by observing how mechanical reproductions can never take the place of originals:

> Even the most perfect reproduction of a work of art is lacking in one element: its presence in time and space, its unique existence at the place where it happens to be. This unique existence of the work of art determined the history to which it was

subject throughout the time of its existence. This includes the changes which it may have suffered in physical condition over the years as well as the various changes in ownership. The traces of the first can be revealed only by chemical or physical analyses which it is impossible to perform on a reproduction; changes of ownership are subject to a tradition which must be traced from the situation of the original.[5]

In 'the age of mechanical reproduction', in Benjamin's celebrated formulation, a polar opposition developed between an original artwork and its reproduction. Originals were distinguished for their authenticity or, as Benjamin terms it, their 'aura'. Reproductions are functions of originals – an original work originates in the personality of the author (through a creative and organic process) while a reproduction originates in an original work (by a technological and mechanical process) – and it is characterized by its unconcealed lack of authenticity. Benjamin draws attention to the fact that new techniques of reproduction have made it possible to manipulate the representation of the original work. Since the invention of mechanical image making, reproductions of artworks have signalled in all sorts of ways that they are reproductions and not originals. As Benjamin notes:

> process reproduction is more independent of the original than manual reproduction. For example, in photography, process reproduction can bring out those aspects of the original that are unattainable to the naked eye yet accessible to the lens, which is adjustable and chooses its angle at will ... technical reproduction can put the original into situations which would be out of reach for the original itself. (Benjamin, 1936, p. 222)

In our day a pictorial reproduction may contain potentials and properties which are essentially different from its original. Posters and postcards can represent well-known artworks the way we prefer to see them; representations are not expected always to remain faithful to an experience of the original.[6]

It is important to realize that the sharp opposition between original and copy, which we take for granted, stems from a reconceptualization of the 'work' and the 'reproduction' that took place in the nineteenth century in the context of copyright law. The debate concerned the definition of the object of copyright: the 'work'. In the course of the nineteenth century 'the work' became a central term in copyright law, and most European laws of copyright defined the work as immaterial.[7] As a logical consequence of this debate, the definition of what constitutes a 'copy' (whether authorized or unauthorized) had to be negotiated. The question of infringement would depend on this definition.

The debate was taking place throughout Europe; we shall concentrate on the impact it had on British and French copyright law. In following the debate in two legal traditions of copyright (common law and Continental law), we can note that there is an overlap in terminology due to the shared Latin element of the English and the French languages. (This of course has also created some dangerous *faux amies*.)

According to *Copinger and Skone James on Copyright* (Garnett et al., 1999), the 'most fundamental' as well as 'historically the oldest' way of infringing copyright is to make copies without the copyright holder's consent: to make unauthorized copies.[8] Infringement, in this case, is assessed on the basis of an alleged illicit 'copy': the infringing object. Yet astonishingly, the earliest copyright laws, the Statute of Anne 1710 and La loi du 19 juillet 1793, do not contain any definition of what constitutes such an infringing object. The text of the Statute of Anne states that copyright is granted for a maximum of 21 years to 'the Author of Any Book or Books already Composed and not Printed and Published, or that shall hereafter be Composed, and his Assignee, or Assigns';[9] and that it is an infringement to 'print, reprint, or import, or cause to be printed, reprinted, or imported such Book or Books without the Consent of the Proprietor'.[10] At the time, copyright was a 'right in copies'. In printing, since its introduction in England by William Caxton in the late fifteenth century, a 'copie' referred to both the manuscript or other 'matter prepared for printing'[11] as well as to the various 'written or printed specimen of the same book'.[12] In the latter sense, a 'copie' (of a book) was synonymous with an 'example' (of a book);[13] none of these carry the implication of being derived from an 'original'. The former sense, denoting a material document, is what would now be termed the 'original'. Copyright, in 1710, was thus an author's or his assignee's right in a material copie – the original – to make more material 'copies'.

The French revolutionary law of 19 July 1793[14] bestowed an exclusive life-long right on authors to 'sell and distribute their works within the French Republic, and to transfer the exploitation right to their works in part or in whole'.[15] This right, which united the right of reproduction and the right of distribution, came to be named the *droit d'édition*.[16] *Contrefaire* was the term for infringement by what we would call copying.[17] An infringer, a *contrefacteur* of the *droit d'édition*, would be someone who, without the consent of the author, made and sold an *édition contrefaite*:[18] a 'counterfeited' publication of his work. According to article 3 of the 1793 law, such 'infringing examples, printed or engraved without the written permission of the author, were to be officially seized at the request of the author'.[19] As in Britain, the author, who was the copyright holder, had the right to make *exemplaires*: 'examples' of a book. In French, as in English, *exemplaire* and *copie* were synonyms in early printing. Both referred to the various specimen of a book. In addition, both terms signified that from which the printed book is copied.[20]

An infringing 'copy' or 'example' required no definition in early British and French copyright law. This is because of what Benjamin Kaplan has labelled the 'printing–reprinting formula' of early copyright law.[21] The principles of this 'formula' derived from the systems of royal privileges (which had worked until 1695 in Britain and until 1777 in France),[22] supplying early copyright law with its most fundamental dichotomy: that between authorized and unauthorized copies (in the sense of 'examples') of books. 'Copies' or 'examples' (of books) were not conceived of in relation to a 'work'. Significantly, as printing terms, there was no ontological difference – in neither English nor French – between the 'copie' (as a specimen of a book) and the 'copie' (as the 'original' wherefrom more samples are made). Making samples – copies or examples – of a book meant to proliferate the master's 'copie'. And there were authorized samples and 'counterfeited' ones. Unauthorized ones 'counterfeited' authorized samples rather than a 'work'.[23]

This fundamental dichotomy accounts for the limited scope of copyright law until the first half of the nineteenth century. Copyright law simply prohibited the printing and disposing of books without permission from the copyright holder. In Britain there was copyright infringement only insofar as a person had (re)printed a copyright volume without authorization.[24] Likewise in France, copyright infringement occurred only to the extent that books were printed and pictures were engraved without written consent. Further explanation was unnecessary because what was forbidden by copyright law was to repeat the act of copying (printing or engraving) which had already been performed by the copyright holder, or by someone authorized by the copyright holder. One was not allowed to print a book, or (in France) to engrave a picture, if one were not authorized so to do. Infringement was conceived of in verbs: to 'print, reprint or import' and to 'sell and distribute'. What we nowadays think of as 'copying' in copyright law was never so named but was understood in terms of specific technologies creating 'examples': printing and engraving for the purpose of multiplication and distribution.

Early copyright law worked to authorize some acts of 'copying' while outlawing others. This approach continued into the nineteenth century. The French Revolutionary Copyright Act of 1793 remained in force until 1957. In other words, no legislative effort was made in France for more than 150 years to replace the definition of copyright infringement. In Britain the 1842 Copyright Act repeated much of the language of the Statute of Anne. Copyright continued to be held in books. The primary offence of copyright was defined as 'the printing or causing to be printed, either for sale, or exportation, any book in which there is a subsisting copyright, without having the written consent of its proprietor'.[25] Similar principles were subsequently adopted in British copyright in relation to art. The famous case, *Hanfstaengl v. Empire Palace* (1894),[26] illustrates this extension from literature to the plastic arts. The case concerned a *tableau vivant* modelled on a painting – its figures, the way they were dressed, their positions and the background – wherein the claimant, Hanfstaengl, held the copyright according to the 1862

Fine Arts Act.[27] This Act was the first to afford copyright protection to paintings, drawings and photographs. The court, in *Hanfstaengl*, found that there had been no infringement. Lord Justice Lindley observed that the Legislature of the 1862 Fine Arts Act had had in mind to 'restrain people from producing something which would compete in the market with the originals or with authorized copies of them'.[28] As is implied, copyright law does not prohibit (unauthorized) prolification or representing in itself. Rather, it prohibits copying – multiplying and distributing – with the aim of profiting.[29]

By the turn of the twentieth century a major change in copyright law had taken place. A definitive end had been put to the printing–reprinting principle. In the 1908 edition of Eugène Pouillet's *Traité théorique et pratique de la propriété littéraire et artistique et du droit de représentation*, (the authoritative work on French copyright law until it was replaced by Henri Desbois's *Le droit d'auteur en France* in 1950),[30] it is spelled out that if French copyright law speaks only of printing – *l'impression* – this should be understood in its historical context.[31] Printing, we are told, was the only mode of *reproduction* known in 1793.[32] Pouillet et al. (1908) makes it clear that what is banned is any unauthorized reproduction, regardless of the technological means.[33] The method of reproduction is treated as irrelevant. It is argued, for example, that it is an infringement to transcribe a manuscript by hand without permission.[34] The approach of Pouillet et al. (1908) is the culmination of a process which began at the time of Eugène Pouillet's predecessor, Augustin-Charles Renouard, in the 1830s.[35] Renouard employs the term *copier* to define what constitutes *contrefaçon*: infringement.[36] However, *Le Robert* dates the first instance of *reproduction* in the sense of 'multiplication', as in copyright law, to 1839.[37] The fact that *reproduction* had acquired this new denotation is reflected in the 1879 edition of 'Pouillet'. There we learn that *reproduction* without the permission of the author constitutes *contrefaçon*.[38] In 1908, as noted, the term *reproduction* had become so dominant in French copyright law that the authors of 'Pouillet' feel compelled to explain why the 1793 Act referred only to printing and engraving. Today, according to the French Intellectual Property Code (which derives from the law of 11 March 1957), the *droit de reproduction* has replaced the *droit d'édition* and is one element in the author's *droit d'exploitation*.[39] Infringement of the author's exploitation right is defined thus: 'Any representation or reproduction in its entirety or partially without the consent of the author or his beneficiaries is illegal.'[40] Reproduction is defined thus: 'The material fixation of a work rendering possible an indirect communication of the work to the public. Means of effectuating such a fixation are, in particular, printing, design, engraving, photography, casts, all the graphic and plastic arts, as well as mechanical, cinematographic or magnetic recording.'[41]

In Britain a similar change has taken place. The 1911 Copyright Act was the first British Act to draw together – for purposes of protection – many different classes of works: books, paintings, sculptures, engravings and so forth. This Act defined copyright as 'the sole right to produce or reproduce the work or any substantial part thereof in any material form whatever'.[42] Any unauthorized 'production' or 'reproduction' of a copyright work 'in any material form whatever' now constitutes a violation of copyright. *Bradbury, Agnew, and Company v. Day* (1916) is emblematic of the change in copyright law. It was held that a *tableau vivant* that imitated a cartoon was an infringement. Thus the judgment in *Hanfstaengl v. Empire Palace* was overruled.[43] Profit is no longer the issue. Nor is it a matter of 'commodities' competing in the marketplace. The emphasis is on simulation: resemblance or similarity in themselves are deemed to infringe. Emphatically, the term 'reproduction' entered into the core of copyright in 1911. The word had figured neither in the 1842 Copyright Act nor in the Fine Arts Act of 1862.[44] It had however appeared in the 1870 edition of Copinger's commentary on the Law of Copyright in Works of Literature: 'Copyright may be infringed . . . by reproduction under an abridged form.'[45] A further related change in the 1911 Act was that the term 'work' had replaced 'books' to denote the object of copyright protection.

'Reproduction' continues to be the central term defining infringement by 'copying' both in the 1956 Copyright Act and in the current Copyright Designs and Patents Act 1988; here a number of acts are 'restricted' by copyright. The first restricted act in the 1956 Act was 'reproducing the work in any material form' (s. 2 (5)). Infringement consisted and continues to consist in performing this and certain other defined acts without authorization. In the 1988 Act 'infringement by copying' is the first category of infringement and 'copying' is defined as: 'to reproduce in any material form' (s. 17 (1)).

The adoption of the term 'reproduction' in British copyright law has received little comment over the years. However, an objection is raised in the ninth edition of *Copinger and Skone James on Copyright*:

> the word 'reproducing' in section 2 (5) of the Act of 1956 may be more ambiguous . . . than the words 'printing or otherwise multiplying copies' in the Act of 1842 . . . it is submitted that the word 'copyright' itself indicates that the right given is confined to copying in some form the work to which copyright protection is afforded and does not extend to an independent production of the original.[46]

And the passage concludes that there is no infringement if the matter is merely that 'the later work "reproduces" the earlier' (143). Clearly, to 'copy' and to 'reproduce' are seen by the authors of *Copinger and Skone James on the Law of Copyright* (1958) as not quite synonymous. Accordingly they argue:

> The question therefore appears to turn solely upon the interpretation of the expres-

sion 'reproduction' and the definition of that word in section 48 (1) of the Act of 1956 does not assist, as this definition merely includes certain special forms of reproduction. It is apprehended, however, that the word 'reproduction' in the Act of 1956 has the same sense as the word 'copy' has acquired in copyright law. Various definitions of 'copy' have been suggested, but it is submitted that the true view of the matter is that, where the court is satisfied that a defendant has, in producing the alleged infringement, made a substantial use of those features of the plaintiff's work in which copyright subsists, an infringement will be held to have been committed. (147f)

Thus 'reproduction' is to be interpreted as 'copy' in the sense the latter has acquired in copyright law over the years. And this sense is 'to make a "substantial use" of a copyright work'. The adoption of 'substantial use' as the norm for infringement in copyright law has often been explained as a change from a quantitative to a qualitative criterion. Under the 'quantitative' measure of early copyright law, generally speaking, only unauthorized printing of copyright books *in toto* was illegal. There was no prohibition of partial copying. According to a quantitative criterion for infringement the decisive factor is 'how much' has been taken.[47] For a qualitative criterion of infringement the question becomes rather one of the nature of the similarity.

In early copyright law, infringement involved both multiplication and distribution of a book in copyright. Under current copyright law, 'reproduction' does not imply that a copyright work has been reproduced in large numbers and disseminated. Copyright has changed from being a tool to control the printing or 'counterfeiting' of books into a widely inclusive law that prohibits 'reproduction' in 'any material form' or 'fixation'.[48] To be sure, new technologies and the appearance of a vastly greater quantity of potential subject matter (photographs and industrial products for example) had put pressure on copyright systems throughout the nineteenth century. In order to meet the demands for protection not only of art and literature, but also of such nebulous entities as 'designs' and 'products', copyright law had had to become more flexible. How were such changes possible without disrupting the theoretical framework of copyright law?

Something had occurred at a conceptual level to render this possible. First of all, the definitions of copyright infringement and *contrefaçon* had been freed from their historical ties to a particular technology: printing (and, in France, engraving). The broader terms of 'copy' and *copier* were generally adopted in the early nineteenth century to designate the acts restricted by copyright. At a later stage, 'copy' and 'reproduction' became synonyms: to 'copy' and to 'reproduce' (*copier* and *reproduire*) have now become synonymous in copyright law. This is rather more extraordinary than it may seem from our perspective. As legal terms, 'copy' and 'reproduction' have specific semantic values. However the choice of terms in copyright law (as in all law) relies on the denotations that words have outside the law.[49] And the etymologies of the two terms are quite distinct. To 'copy' in both French and English has a long history as a verb that applies to writing. Since the fourteenth century, according to *Le Robert*, *copier* had meant to duplicate or accurately to transcribe a text.[50] By the same token, the *Oxford English Dictionary* records the primary and earliest meaning of to 'copy' (1387) as 'to make a copy of (a writing); to transcribe (*from* an original)'. In both French and English 'to copy' implies a relation of strict causality.[51] A copy repeats its source with accuracy.[52] As such, copying can result in both duplication and multiplication. But it works according to a serial principle: every new copy can potentially function as a substitution of its source, could take its place as the 'original'. This is exactly what Benjamin says a 'reproduction' cannot do. It is important to realize that although 'copy' in both French and English is quite a 'copious' word, with many connotations, the term 'copy' entered copyright law with the specific sense it had acquired in printing. The construction of early copyright law must be understood in the context of the book trade.[53]

'Reproduction' – which is not a Latin word – can be traced back no earlier than the seventeenth century. In French – as in English – it designated then, as now, the process by which 'something renews itself',[54] or 'the action or process of forming, creating or bringing into existence again',[55] such as the reproduction of the living species.[56] In the seventeenth century, 'reproduction' was most significant in a biological context. However in the eighteenth century it became linked to pictorial representation. One could by then 'reproduce' an image.[57] In the early nineteenth century a further denotation was added to 'reproduction', namely that a reproduction could be 'a copy or a counterpart, especially a copy of a picture or other work of art by means of engraving or some other process'.[58] The new meaning of 'reproduction' was related to new technologies, including photography, stencils, duplicators and [printers'] clichés.[59] Reproduction as multiplication became a possibility in a 'parallel relation': an infinite number of reproductions, including reproductions of reproductions, is possible, but all reproductions point back to their first origin, always displaying a degree of similarity between themselves; and none of the reproductions could take the place of or be a substitute for 'the original'.

And so we must ask how, during the nineteenth century, copy and reproduction – to 'copy' and to 'reproduce', *copier* and *reproduire* – became synonyms. The words started to be explained in terms of each other. And both were employed in copyright law to refer to the creation of 'equals': copies and reproductions, made according to a 'model'. 'Copy' and 'reproduction' however are peculiar synonyms. As we have seen, they have dissimilar connotations: one is associated with texts and exact repetition, the other with images and regeneration; the one is crafted and may be taken (or mistaken) for the original, the other is organic, always approximate and evidently so. Since they became synonyms the meanings of both words have broadened considerably. By 1870 a key could be 'copied' or 'reproduced'.[60] In 1916 a *tableau vivant* could be a 'copy' or a 'reproduction' of a cartoon.[61] About five decades later, in 1964, you could furnish your home in 'reproduction' or 'copy'-style furniture.[62] Today we live in a 'culture of the copy'[63] where magnetic, photographic, digital technologies of copying and reproduction have obscured the distinct etymologies and histories of the two words.

It was, I suggest, precisely the synthesis of the two terms and their combined connotations that made copyright law flexible. It was only when 'copy' ceased to be an 'example', that is exclusively a printing term (as Pouillet argued in 1908), and when 'reproduction' became a form of copying (as Copinger and Skone James stated in 1958), that copyright law was enabled to extend the reach of its protection, and the range of its prohibitions.

In the nineteenth century the opposition 'authorized copy'–'unauthorized copy' was replaced by the dichotomy – entirely familiar to us – of the 'original work' and the 'copy'. A 'copy' no longer designates that which printings are made from. 'Copy' has ceased to be 'example' according to copyright law. Copies are now copies of an 'original work', that only printers still refer to as 'copy'.

It has not been fully appreciated how this shift has determined the way copyright law has developed in the twentieth and twenty-first centuries. The new dichotomy between the original work and the copy or reproduction continues to be absolutely fundamental in copyright law, as in our general understanding. Modern copyright law could not exist without it. In the course of the nineteenth century most European laws of copyright came to recognize that the object of copyright protection was a literary, artistic, musical or other 'original work'; and that a 'work' is immaterial.[64] This served to separate literary and artistic property entirely from the physical property of manuscripts and artworks, as well as from the physical objects of the copies of a 'work'. This separation is crucial for modern copyright law.[65] Even so it must be acknowledged that the extraction of the immaterial work from all of its material instantiations is not a simple task.[66] Arguably the exercise would not have been possible outside of the cultural context of the debate over authenticity in art, literature and philosophy. The new polarity between authenticity and inauthenticity provided a conceptual framework within which copyright law could establish a distinction between an 'authentic' original work and an 'inauthentic' copy. The original work was the authentic expression or *pensée* (which is of course immaterial) emanating from a creative person and manifesting its 'aura'. This is the real nightingale who sings with his own voice. The copy is the inauthentic, material – or even mechanical – version. Like the late Empress's music box and the artificial bird, the copy is the product of a technological process. In these terms the work–copy dichotomy has been introduced into copyright law. And it is thanks to this dichotomy that 'substantial use' has become a copyright infringement. Inasmuch as the 'original work' is immaterial, it may be manifested in a variety of material forms. Similarity (which comes in degrees) has thus surreptitiously installed itself as a factor in determining whether or not something is a copy (or a reproduction). In Benjamin's terms, it is only when we recognize the 'similar' that we are able to realize the 'difference', and to identify the differences, the lack of authenticity, of the 'aura'.

Copyright infringement is no longer restricted to acts of unauthorized copying. The consolidation of the new regime of copyright law took place when (unauthorized) 'reproduction' became the main term for infringement. In 'the age of mechanical reproduction', as Benjamin has named it, the reproduction (and the copy) have become the sign of inauthenticity, devalued and mass-produced.

Today the Internet has made Benjamin's argument only more pertinent. Benjamin proclaimed that the 'aura' of art has been rendered problematic by the invention of mechanical reproduction. 'Authenticity' however is a concept that emerges in opposition to the copies. In fact the principal mechanical technology that Benjamin has in mind, namely photography, has been given its own criteria for authenticity. No one would dispute that Edward Weston or Henri Cartier-Bresson's negatives are laden with authenticity. And in our mundane age of the xerox machine we admit the superiority of the 'master-copy' as compared with other copies. On the Internet however there are nothing but instantaneous samples with no original: all has equal claim to be original. An original has the same ontological status as a copy. None of them is distinct in terms of aura, authenticity or simulacrum. There are only exact likenesses, incessantly recurring and entirely without material instantiation. Thus the Internet gives new validity to Benjamin's argument. Once we realize this, light can be shed on some of the current problems with copyright in digital works. Technically speaking, there is no such thing as a digital 'reproduction' of a digital work. There is only the creation of identical samples; every use of a digital work requires the generation of such a sample. The problem is that – as Laurence Lessig and others have pointed out – in legal terms, a sample is a copy.[67] In that way an act, which is technologically determined, may acquire the status of an intentional, infringing act. Copyright law cannot cope with the order of sameness on the Internet, for it has been shaped to protect 'original works' from 'reproduction' in a world of pre-digital technology.

Hans Christian Andersen may be seen as an allegory of this tale of the development of copyright. He tells the story of a real princess, but it is 'really' only a version of the story. A few decades earlier the Brothers Grimm had been telling 'authentic' fairy tales gathered from the *Volk*. Andersen, self-consciously and playfully, alludes to the artifice of his own story: 'See, that was a real story.' As such he is simulating the tradition of Grimm, offering us a likeness of a fairy tale. From Grimm to Andersen we witness an epistemic shift in *mentalité*. Hans Christian Andersen created the inauthentic fairy tale, and exploited the endlessly fascinating possibilities of likeness. That fascination continues to this day, not least in the resistance of those charming tales to the aura that real fairy tales ought to have – but would never claim for themselves.

NOTES

1. On this topic see for instance Abrams (1953) and Trilling (1972).
2. See the *Oxford English Dictionary*: 'authentic' and 'authenticity'.
3. Hans Christian Andersen (2003), p. 61.
4. For further perspectives on the tales of 'The Swineherd' and 'The Nightingale' (which is discussed later) in relation to copyright law, see Fiona Macmillan's contribution to this volume.
5. Benjamin (1936), pp. 219–53, 222.
6. Andy Warhol's representation of Leonardo Da Vinci's *Last Supper* takes this regime of representation to a new limit. See also Leslie Kim Treiger-Bar-Am's discussion in this volume of the way copies or reproductions of an artwork are less 'original', that is, more distant from their origin, than the unique original.
7. See for example Kohler (1892); Pouillet (1879); Renouard (1838); and Law (1770).
8. 'The exclusive right to prevent copying or reproduction of a work is the most fundamental, and historically the oldest, right of a copyright owner', Garnett et al. (1999), p. 392, § 7-08. Today in the UK the copyright holder has the exclusive right to copy the work (the reproduction right), to make performances, broadcasts, adaptations, and to issue copies to the public.
9. 8 Anne c. 19. (1710) (I).
10. 8 Anne c. 19. (1710) (I).
11. *OED*: 'copy' as that from which something is copied (Caxton 1485).
12. *OED*: 'copy' without reference to an original (Caxton 1477).
13. *OED*: 'example' (1530).
14. *La loi du 19–24 juillet 1793. Décret relatif aux droits de propriété des auteurs d'écrits en tout genre, compositeurs de musique, peintres et dessinateurs.*
15. 'Vendre, faire vendre, distribuer leurs ouvrages dans le territoire de la République, et d'en céder la propriété en tout ou en partie', La loi du 19 juillet 1793, art. 1.
16. The *droit d'édition* stood in opposition to the *droit de representation* (the right of public performance) which had been protected by an Act of 1791. This dichotomy continues to exist in French copyright. For more on this see Spoor et al. (1980).
17. The term derived from *Ancien Régime* laws protecting royal privileges in books. Thus *contrefacteurs* had been made subject to corporal punishment by a Royal Decree of 27 February 1683. The Royal Decree of 30 August 1777 banned *contrefaçons*: unauthorized copies of books wherein a printer or an author held a privilege. For more on this see Dock (1963).
18. La loi du 19 juillet 1793, arts. 4–5.
19. 'Les exemplaires des editions imprimées ou gravées sans la permission formelle et par écrit des auteur', art. 3.
20. *Le Petit Robert CD-ROM*. Version électronique du nouveau Petit Robert (1997), Paris: Dictionnaire Le Robert. From the sixteenth century *exemplaire* referred to both an '*exemple, modèle à suivre*' and '*chacun des objets reproduisant un type commun*'. Likewise, *copie* as

a printing term referrred to both the manuscript (or matter prepared for printing): '*écrit à partir duquel on compose*' and to the '*reproduction (d'un écrit)*'.

21. Kaplan (1967), p. 20.
22. See Armstrong (1990) and Loewenstein (2002).
23. The traditional French term for infringement, *contrefaire*, is emblematic of this dichotomy in its implication that counterfeited *exemplaires* of a book imitate authorized ones.
24. The most important infringement cases in eighteenth century British copyright, *Millar v. Taylor* (1769) and *Donaldson v. Beckett* (1774), concerning the nature of literary property (whether copyright was a natural right or a privilege), show how the nature of the 'copy' was not yet an issue.
25. 5 & 6 Vict. C. 45 (1842 Copyright Act). See furthermore (1842), *The Law of Copyright, regarding Authors, Dramatic Writers, and Musical Composers; as altered by the Recent Statute of the 5 & 6 Victoria, analysed and simplified with an Explanatory Introduction, and an Appendix, containing, at full, the New Copyright and the Dramatic Property Acts. By a Barrister*, London: James Gilbert, p. 17.
26. *Hanfstaengl v. Empire Palace* (1894) [1894] 2 Ch 1 (CA).
27. 25 & 26 Vict. C. 68 (29 July 1862). An Act for amending the Law relating to Copyright in Works of the Fine Arts, and for repressing the Commission of Fraud in the Production and Sale of such Works.
28. *Hanfstaengl v. Empire Palace*, p. 6.
29. In *Hanfstaengl v. H.R. Baines & Co Ltd* (1895) the House of Lords confirmed this view. See *Hanfstaengl v. H.R. Baines & Co Ltd* (1895) [1895] AC 20.
30. Desbois (1950).
31. Pouillet et al. (1908), p. 422.
32. The 1793 Act speaks of 'printing' and 'engraving'; engraving, presumably, is also to be understood in terms of the history of technology.
33. 'La contrefaçon est indépendante du moyen employé pour la fabrication', p. 458. Interestingly, it is necessary to state that copying an infringing copy, 'copier une contre-façon' (p. 463), is itself an infringement.
34. 'La copie est faite à la main; l'œuvre n'en est pas moins reproduite; elle circule, elle est portée à la connaissance du public, et cela sans autorisation du public', p. 423.
35. Renouard (1838).
36. Reproduction did not yet have the meaning it has gained in modern copyright law, as is evident in this passage: 'La pensée dont il a déposé l'expression sur son œuvre originale lui confère un droit sur les objets où l'expression de la même pensée serait reproduite, en vertu et par application des mêmes principes que ceux qui confèrent le droit de copie à l'écrivain qui a confié sa pensée au papier', p. 77. 'Reproduce' here refers to an element of the creative process, while 'copying' implies a technological process.
37. *Le Robert*. The definition of reproduction which goes back to 1839 is: 'Le fait de reproduire (un original), d'en multiplier les exemplaires par un procédé technique approprié.'
38. Pouillet (1879), p. 375ff.
39. Which consists furthermore of the *droit de representation*.
40. Art. L.122–4. 'Toute representation ou reproduction intégrale ou partielle faite sans le consentement de l'auteur ou de ses ayants cause est illicite.'
41. Art. 122–3. 'La reproduction consiste dans la fixation matérielle de l'oeuvre par tous procédés qui permettent de la communiquer au public d'une manière indirecte. Elle peut s'effectuer notamment par imprimerie, dessin, gravure, photographie, moulage, et tout les art graphiques et plastiques, enregistrement mécanique, cinématographique ou magné-tiques.'
42. Copyright Act 1911, s. 1 (2).
43. *Bradbury, Agnew, and Company v. Day* (1916) 32 TLR 349.
44. The Fine Arts Act made it illegal for anyone without the consent of the copyright holder to 'repeat, copy, colourably imitate, or otherwise multiply for Sale, Hire, Exhibition, or Distribution . . . a [copyrighted] work or the Design thereof', 25 & 26 Vict., c. 68, s. 6.
45. Copinger, *Law of Copyright in Works of Literature*, vi, 101. Cited from *OED*. The *OED* cites a further example from Kay & Johnson's *Reports of Cases in Chancery II*, (1856), 285:

'Having regard to the international treaties, the Plaintiff reserves his right of reproduction, which is a sufficiently apt word in this case.'

46. *Copinger and Skone James on the Law of Copyright* (1958), p. 143f.
47. An early application of the qualitative criterion can be found in *Bramwell v. Halcomb* (1836) K.B. (3 My. & Cr. 737, 40 Eng. Rep. 889). For a more recent application of the 'substantial use' test see *Ravenscroft v. Herbert* (1980) R.P.C. 193.
48. On the early development of copyright law see Becourt (1990), pp. 143, 231–87; Deazley (2004); Feather (1994); Matthyssens (1954), pp. 15–57; Sherman and Bentley (1999).
49. Even if we imagine the relationship between ordinary language and legal terminology as a matter of contingency, it would be hard to maintain that legal terms do not borrow connotations from the same words in extra-legal contexts.
50. 'Copier fidèlement un texte, un passage important', *Le Robert*: 'copier'.
51. The *OED* records how in the eighteenth century one could also talk about 'copies' of pictures. A 'copy' of a picture seems to have been used mainly in a derogatory sense; a copy of a picture would be understood to be a slavish copy. Likewise in French, a *copie* of a picture amounts to a *plagiat*.
52. As such to 'copy' is distinct from, say, to 'imitate', as in a quotation from 1667 given by the *OED*: 'An Ode of Horace, not exactly copy'd, but rudely imitated', Cowley, *Greatest Works*, 125.
53. On the connection between booksellers' guilds and copyright, see for example Armstrong (1990); Blagden (1977); Eisenstein (1979); Johns (1998); and Laligant (1991).
54. 'Action par laquelle une chose renaît', *Le Robert*.
55. The *OED* records an example of this use from 1659.
56. The verbs *reproduire* and to 'reproduce' are traced back to the sixteenth century. In *Le Robert* as 'produire de nouveau' (1539). The *OED* records a use of 'reproduce' from 1611 in the biological sense: 'to bring again into material existence; to create or form anew': to form a lost limb afresh or to generate new individuals.
57. For instance the 'reproduction' of nature by art and the idea of 'reproduction' as truthful representation. *Le Robert* dates *reproduire* in the sense of 'répéter, rendre fidèlement, donner l'équivalent de (qqch.)' to the eighteenth century.
58. The *OED* dates this use back to 1807.
59. *Le Robert* records an 1839 use of *reproduction* in the sense of 'le fait de reproduire (un original), d'en multiplier les exemplaires par un procédé technique approprié'.
60. See *Le Robert*.
61. *Bradbury, Agnew, and Company v. Day* (1916). Supra note 43.
62. See the *OED*.
63. On 'the similar' see Baudrillard (1995) and Schwartz (1998).
64. On the immateriality of the work in copyright law see Teilmann (2005), pp. 19–24.
65. In broad terms the division means that purchasing a copy of a book is not accompanied by a right to reproduce its contents. Conversely, the owner of the copyright of a literary work has no control over the material copies; they can freely be sold and, perhaps, resold.
66. It was indeed a difficult operation and many legal scholars of the nineteenth century struggled with the distinction. Pouillet (1879), for instance, found it necesssary to specify that unauthorized reproduction of a reproduction is unlawful. See note 7 supra.
67. See for instance Lessig (2004).

REFERENCES

Abrams, M.H. (1953), *The Mirror and the Lamp. Romantic Theory and the Critical Tradition*, Oxford: Oxford University Press.

Andersen, Hans Christian (2003), *The Stories of Hans Christian Andersen*, selected and translated by Diana Crone Frank and Jeffrey Frank, Boston, MA: Houghton Mifflin.

Armstrong, Elizabeth (1990), *Before Copyright. The French Book-Privilege System 1498–1526*, Cambridge: Cambridge University Press.

Baudrillard, Jean (1995), *Simulacra and Simulation*, trans. Sheila Faria Glaser, Ann Arbor, MI: University of Michigan Press.

Becourt, Daniel (1990), 'La Révolution française et le droit d'auteur pour un nouvel universalisme', *Revue internationale du droit d'auteur*, **143**, 231–87.

Benjamin, Walter (1936), 'The Work of Art in the Age of Mechanical Reproduction', reprinted in Hannah Arendt (ed.) (1968), *Illuminations*, London: Collins/Fontana Books.

Blagden, Cyprian (1977), *The Stationers' Company. A History, 1403–1959*, Stanford, CA: Stanford University Press.

Copinger, W.A., F.E. Skone James and E.P. Skone James (1958), *Copinger and Skone James on the Law of Copyright*, 9th edn, London: Sweet & Maxwell.

Deazley, Ronan (2004), *On the Origin of the Right to Copy: Charting the Movement of Copyright Law in Eighteenth-Century Britain (1695–1775)*, Oxford: Hart Publishing.

Desbois, Henri (1950), *Le droit d'auteur en France*, Paris: Dalloz.

Dock, Marie-Claude (1963), *Étude sur le droit d'auteur*, Paris: Librarie Générale de Droit et de Jurisprudence. R. Pichon et R. Durand-Auzias.

Eisenstein, Elizabeth L. (1979), *The Printing Press as an Agent of Change. Communications and Cultural Transformations in Early-modern Europe*, Cambridge: Cambridge University Press.

Feather, John (1994), *Publishing, Piracy and Politics. A Historical Study of Copyright in Britain*, London and New York: Mansell Publishing.

Garnett, Kevin, Gillian Davies and Jonathan Rayner James (1999), *Copinger and Skone James on Copy*right, 14th edn, London: Sweet & Maxwell.

Johns, Adrian (1998), *The Nature of the Book. Print and Knowledge in the Making*, Chicago, IL: University of Chicago Press.

Kaplan, Benjamin (1967), *An Unhurried View of Copyright*, New York: Columbia University Press.

Kohler, J. (1892), *Das literarische und artistische Kunstwerk und sein Autorschutz*, Mannheim: Drud und Verlag von J. Bensheimer.

Laligant, Olivier (1991), 'La revolution française et le droit d'auteur ou perennité de l'objet de la projection', *Revue Internationale du Droit d'Auteur*, **147** (janvier), 3–123.

Law, Edmund (1770), *Observations Occasioned by the Contest about Literary Property*, Cambridge: J. Archdeacon.

Lessig, Laurence (2004), *Free Culture: How Big Media Uses Technology and the Law to Lock down Culture and Control Creativity*, New York: Penguin Press.

Loewenstein, Joseph (2002), *The Author's Due: Printing and the Prehistory of Copyright*, Chicago, IL: University of Chicago Press.

Matthyssens, Jean (1954) 'Les projets de loi sur le droit d'auteur en France au cours du siècle dernier', *RIDA*, **4** (juillet), 15–57.

Pouillet, Eugène (1879), *Traité théorique et pratique de la propriété littéraire et artistique et du droit de représentation*, Paris: Marchal et Billard.

Pouillet, Eugène, Georges Maillard and Charles Claro (1908), *Traité théorique et pratique de la propriété littéraire et artistique et du droit de représentation*, 3rd edn, Paris: Marchal et Billard.

Renouard, Augustin-Charles (1838), *Traité des droits d'auteurs dans la littérature, les sciences et les beaux-arts*, Vol. 1, Paris: Jules Renouard.

Schwartz, Hillel (1998), *The Culture of the Copy. Striking Likenesses, Unreasonable Facsimiles*, New York: Zone Books.

Sherman, Brad and Lionel Bentley (1999), *The Making of Modern Intellectual Property Law. The British Experience, 1760–1911*, Cambridge: Cambridge University Press.

Spoor, J.H, W.R. Cornish and P.F. Nolan (1980), *Copies in Copyright*, Alphen aan den Rijn: Sijthoff & Noordhoff.

Teilmann, Stina (2005), 'Framing the law: the right of integrity in Britain', *European Intellectual Property Review*, **27** (1), 19–24.

Trilling, Lionel (1972), *Sincerity and Authenticity*, Cambridge MA: Harvard University Press.

3. *Bleak House* or *Great Expectations*? The literary author as a stakeholder in nineteenth-century international copyright politics

Uma Suthersanen

It was the best of times, it was the worst of times. It was a far, far better copyright treaty than any the world had ever attempted before. It began with Great Expectations; by the end, the participants felt, if not quite like Les Misérables, at least as if they had emerged from a Bleak House. What the dickens was it? It was the Diplomatic Conference on Certain Copyright and Neighboring Rights Questions, convened at Geneva, Switzerland, from December 2 through 20, 1996.[1]

It is a well-accepted tenet in the twentieth century that authors deserve protection against all forms of misappropriation of their works, and that stand-alone international copyright treaties are one of the best means of achieving worldwide protection.[2] This argument began in the nineteenth century, a century which saw, perhaps not uncoincidentally, the genesis of international copyright law. The virtual disappearance of the author in twenty-first-century copyright discourse contrasts sharply with the rise of the author in the early nineteenth century as exemplified by the two most recent international copyright treaties adopted at the conference mentioned in the above quote.

Whilst the eighteenth century can be viewed as the era which saw the end of patronage, especially in Britain, and the rise of the middle classes and the 'common man', the nineteenth century saw authors and writers finally becoming local economic and societal stakeholders. The nineteenth century also saw such stakeholders realizing that their interests had to be protected both in the domestic and in the transnational markets. By the mid-nineteenth century, most European publishers and authors had perceived the need to establish reciprocal copyright protection between different nation states. Belgium for instance was forced to conclude a bilateral treaty with France to protect the latter's authors, whilst the United Kingdom's *bête noir* was the United States.

It is another well-accepted tenet in the twentieth century that the US had become the major intellectual property producer and exporter in the world. Not only does the United States today take active participation in setting international norms for intellectual property rights, it also seeks to encourage other countries to sign and ratify these norms, such as the Internet treaties, through bilateral trade agreements.[3] The US has, within the last hundred years, been transformed from Long John Silver to Judge Dredd. The US adopted a very different stance in the nineteenth century in respect of authorial interests and international copyright law. Until 1891, American copyright law denied copyright to foreign citizens and the United States was 'notorious in the international sphere as a significant contributor to the "piracy" of foreign literary products'. Moreover the tendency to reprint foreign works freely was encouraged by the existence of tariffs on imported books that ranged as high as 25 per cent.[4]

The European campaign to bring the United States into the nascent global copyright system is well documented. However there are some interesting points that can be derived from looking at the debate by applying an author–stakeholder analysis. In particular this chapter looks at the interplay between authors such as Charles Dickens and copyright awareness. Charles Dickens, like so many authors of his day, was convinced of his ability to turn the tide of opinion towards a copyright regime which protected foreign authors. As one commentator notes:

> unlikely coalitions formed during the nineteenth century, whose common objective was to change the international copyright laws. Among them were Americans with international reputations such as Henry Clay, John Jay, Henry Wadsworth Longfellow, Louisa May Alcott and Samuel Morse; educational institutions, including Longfellow's alma mater Bowdoin College, the University of Virginia and the University of California; miscellaneous groups such as the American Medical Association and the citizens of Portland, Maine; and Europeans Charles Dickens, Edmund Burke, Harriet Martineau, and Gilbert and Sullivan.[5]

Dickens's attempt to influence the course of international copyright law is also inextricably linked to the rise of the author as a cult figure in society and as a key stakeholder in the economy. This chapter traces, in part, the history of United States's entry into the world of international copyright law in the nineteenth century. We trace this history vis-à-vis Charles Dickens's attempt, in 1841, to persuade the Americans to pursue an international copyright agreement, and also the backdrop of nineteenth-century literary authorship. The nineteenth century is an archive of many such issues.

AUTHORS AS STAKEHOLDERS

Rise of Literature and the 'Author'

The nineteenth century was an extraordinarily successful one for literature, with thriving publishing and the emergence of many writers. The century produced not only novels, but also large numbers of histories, geographies, biographies, religious works and political treatises. In respect of novels alone, between 1837 and 1901 approximately 50 000 novels were published in Britain, thus replacing poetry as the most important form of literature produced by British writers. This means that the some 3500 novelists of the Victorian period were averaging 17 novels apiece.[6]

Although it has been suggested that the reason for this astounding success in literature is the relative lack of authorial interest in copyright,[7] this cannot be true as the nineteenth century is also noted for the deployment by authors of appropriate rhetoric to emphasize their noble art and profession of writing. The romantic 'authorship' rhetoric is still prevalent today. A fundamental reason, it is suggested, for the adoption of authorship rhetoric is the need to present arguments for the extension of copyright in both economic and humanistic terms. Authorship rhetoric was also required to solve the paradox of the writing profession – the master–servant/apprentice relationship had accepted imitation as being part of the creative act; these acts were suddenly viewed as misattribution of authorship and plagiarism. Nineteenth-century authors had to convince the public not only of their worthiness but also of their right to remuneration from their writings. One should note that by the end of the eighteenth century, copyright had yet to impact upon authors' lives in terms of remuneration – most authors were paid a lump sum for their work as opposed to sales-based royalties, and moreover authors were required to assign their copyrights to their publishers – much like today's academic journal authors.[8]

Wordsworth, and other authors, successfully brought intellectual property issues to national attention, and several copyright statutes, furnishing increasing protections, were promulgated in England in the mid-nineteenth century. The most important of these was the Copyright Amendment Act of 1842 (the Talfourd Act), which was the first major piece of legislation put forth by and for authors.[9] The Act was revolutionary in establishing the term of copyright as the author's lifetime plus seven years or 42 years from publication – whichever was longer. It therefore specifically aligned copyright with the lives of authors. A lot of this struggle was due entirely to authors battling out the notion of 'professional authorship' in the nineteenth century. The notion of 'authorship' was debated intensely – from an intrinsic and an extrinsic perspective.

Intrinsic Perspectives: Personhood and the Right of Integrity

Authors had begun to conceive of themselves as private personae, whereby works emanated from them rather than from the Divine Being. The Romantics stressed the individuality of literary works – Immanuel Kant, and Johann Gottlieb Fichte, in particular, insisted that authors did not imitate nature, but rather 'spoke' original works derived from their inner personalities.[10] Writers such as Charles Dickens and Thomas Carlyle, although very much dependent on the proceeds of their writing for economic survival, still insisted on a romantic view of the artist as aesthete, and the dignity of literature.[11] England's Romantic Poets such as Wordsworth, Coleridge and Shelley similarly waxed lyrical about the notion of the author as a solitary and unique genius.[12] The discussion on authorial originality and invention often resulted in criticism of the then accepted classical practice of imitating the past or nature.[13] Wordsworth in particular was emphatic on this point and embarked on a crusade by persuading the lawyer-litterateur, Thomas Noon Talfourd, to propose a copyright bill so that he could pass on property rights in his works as an inheritance. Wordsworth was clearly driven by economic motives; however he also viewed his works as a personal emanation, which was intimately linked to his conception of self. For him, literary property 'embodied an aspect of essential character; a function of individual identity, it was inalienable'.[14] He sought protection for his literary creations not only for financial reasons, but also because they were inextricably linked to his identity. Similarly Talfourd compared literary property to a person's character:

[W]hy do you protect moral character as a man's most precious possession, and compensate the party who suffers in that character unjustly by damages? Has this possession any existence itself half so palpable as the author's right in the printed creation of his brain?[15]

International copyright law was also often proffered as a means of protecting not only the pecuniary interests of foreign authors but also the local stakeholders such as indigenous writers, publishers and printers – the latter set of people represented the cultural heritage of the country. This was further boosted by the sudden clamour for moral rights as the new form of technologies and mass markets caused authors new concerns for their reputations on such markets. The 1837 Clay Report in the United States, for instance, included a petition by several British authors whose complaint was that British authors were 'exposed to injury in their reputation and property' and that their works were

liable to be mutilated and altered, at the pleasure of [American] booksellers, or of any other persons who may have an interest in reducing the price of the works, or in conciliating the supposed principles or prejudice of purchasers in [the United States].

Indeed the petition emphasized the point of integrity right by noting that the lack of effective protection for foreign authors may confuse the American public 'as to whether the books presented to them as the works of British authors ... are the actual and complete productions of the writers whose names they bear'.[16]

Extrinsic Perspectives – Market and Trade

Although the nineteenth century is often hailed as the first century that witnessed the popular novel and the large reading public, this is not strictly true, as popular seventeenth- and eighteenth-century writers such as Defoe, Fielding and Richardson had a large public eagerly awaiting yet another *Robinson Crusoe* or *Tom Jones* or *Pamela*. The book historian Marjorie Plant also notes that despite the low level of education in the mid-eighteenth century, novels were a widely consumed commodity especially with the rising popularity of the circulating libraries and the inculcation of the reading habit amongst women.[17] Realistically however, the 'reading classes' during the eighteenth century were still relatively limited to the upper and 'commercial middle classes'. Moreover the booksellers (that is, the book trade) practised in a cartel and thus remained very much in power.[18] Authorship was still a struggling profession by the end of the eighteenth century.

The system of patronage had reduced considerably by the nineteenth century, being viewed by many authors as being demeaning and compromising of their independence.[19] Authors now started to have new sources of income – journalism and periodical literature. Dickens, for instance, found initial fame in the success of *The Pickwick Papers* which was published in monthly parts, whilst *The Old Curiosity Shop* was originally published in a magazine.[20] The relative rise and success of literature in the nineteenth century was also a result of the availability of a large and devoted market for the works that new writers and new technologies produced.[21] The promise of higher income was a result of the technological improvements in the nineteenth century which led to many conflicting situations for authors. Technological advances meant improved printing and dissemination of books across the globe, which in turn led simultaneously to increased print runs and improved sales of books. However simpler printing technology meant higher rates of piracy, whilst authors were being led to expect higher income returns.

The success of Dickens's *Pickwick Papers* relied on his publishers, Chapman & Hall, exploiting newly available technologies and distribution mechanisms, whilst the 'novel in parts', a format to which Dickens was so partial, had an easy captive market with the circulating libraries.[22] Although such libraries had existed since the Restoration period, the nineteenth-century circulating library was removed from being under the aegis of provincial booksellers to a national business.[23] A further impetus was that the anti-competitive Booksellers' Association was taken to task not only by public pressure but by leading authors of the day such as Dickens and Tennyson who, perversely, also advocated a free trade in books.[24]

With the expansion of the market for popular books in the nineteenth century, the book trade grew proportionately, enabling publishers to pay more for manuscripts. Consequently the author's status changed and the profession of authorship slowly emerged. This inevitably led to copyright being viewed as an important economic tool for the protection of both authors and the industry that disseminated the written work. Not only was the domestic market considered important – a persistent element in the nineteenth century was the attempt of authors to obtain international copyright protection. All these attempts indicate the absence of completely altruistic motives of the authors.[25] While the language of 'natural rights' is abundant, an underlying rationale is 'financial rights'. Thus Seville notes that the early debates prior to the 1842 Copyright Act were fought on factors such as fairness, equality, sales and profits.[26]

The battle was also fought on behalf of the public interest, and arguments ranged from societal needs such as cheap books to educate the public, to economic policies. The anti-copyright rhetoric employed the arguments of free trade, education, monopolies and utilitarianism, to counter the pro-copyright rhetoric of natural rights of authors and their valuable contribution of literary works to society.[27] Indeed it is popularly believed that Macaulay's famous 'tax on readers' speech relied heavily on competitive market rhetoric and turned the tide of opinion against a more generous copyright regime for authors.[28] 'Copyright is monopoly, and produces all the effects which the general voice of mankind attributes to monopoly', Macaulay declared. Whilst he supported the fact that authors should be remunerated, and that the least exceptionable way of doing so was by copyright law (albeit a monopoly), nevertheless for the sake of the public good he argued strenuously that the 'evil ought not to last a day longer than is necessary for the purpose of securing the good'. Moreover Macaulay's speech was prescient in terms of copyright ownership eventually being divorced from the authorial rhetoric of remuneration and personality:

> My honourable and learned friend dwells on the claims of the posterity of great writers. Undoubtedly, Sir, it would be very pleasing to see a descendant of Shakespeare living in opulence on the fruits of his great ancestor's genius ... But, unhappily, it is scarcely possible that, under any system, such a thing can come to pass. My honourable and learned friend does not propose that copyright shall descend to the eldest son, or shall be bound up by irrecoverable entail. It is to be merely personal property. It is therefore highly improbable that it will descend during sixty years or half that term from parent to child. The chance is that more people than one will have an interest in it. They will in all probability sell it and divide the proceeds. The price which a bookseller will give for it will bear no proportion to the sum which he will afterwards draw from the public, if his speculation proves successful.

But perhaps the incursion of 'market' and 'trade' language into the debates on copyright is not surprising given the huge growth in the reading public, which in turn resulted in the writing profession being imbued with a consumer-driven market culture, as opposed to the previously more leisurely patronage culture. Sometimes the anti-copyright arguments cleverly drew upon the same natural rights rhetoric of the authors, but from the societal perspective. Thus the rights to education, knowledge and access to information were transformed to point out the potential of copyright to hinder diffusion of knowledge, to place a barrier to cheap editions of works and to act as a censorship tool.[29]

Dickens and the Copyright Debate

Despite all these changes, authors had yet to come together in the UK, prior to the 1842 Act, and form a guild or trade association.[30] Hence the importance of individual authors such as Dickens and Wordsworth due to the lack of organizational structures unlike the publishing and print trades. In the United States, Dickens encountered many of the same problems of lack of author societies or organizations. Although Dickens's role in national British copyright law was small compared to that of William Wordsworth, his involvement in the history of copyright law is still notable due to his somewhat disastrous campaign for international copyright in the US.[31] Charles Dickens's involvement with copyright had begun early, with his admiration of Talfourd, especially after the latter was appointed as an arbitrator to a dispute between Dickens and his publisher over the copyright of two of his novels.[32] This friendship even entailed the dedication of *The Pickwick Papers* to Talfourd.

Domestic protection was to no avail without international protection. Book piracy had affected the British book trade since the eighteenth century when Irish printers had pirated copious amounts of English books. This activity ceased when Ireland ceased to be a colony and became part of the Union in 1800. However Irish piracy was soon replaced by French, Belgian and American piracy. Parisian printers, in particular, were notorious for supplying British tourists with cheap reprints of the latest publications such as Walter Scott's books – although mass importation of foreign reprints was prohibited, the London publishers could do nothing to bar individual tourists from importing single copies of pirated books as part of their personal baggage. These foreign editions soon infiltrated bookshops and circulating libraries.[33]

New rights were needed and were effected by bilateral and international treaties with pirating nations.

AMERICA THE PIRATE

Early Copyright Privileges and Laws

The United States, during the eighteenth and nineteenth centuries, was an especially big problem as unlike France and Belgium, there was no indication that she was willing to be part of international copyright law. In the late eighteenth century most of the books sold in the US were imported.[34] By the nineteenth century, it was a net debtor in flows of cultural innovation. In marked contrast to its stance on international patent negotiations and conventions, where it was a strong advocate and leader, copyright law was virtually nonexistent in the US. In the beginning, printers and publishers protected their markets by securing agreements among themselves.[35] At some point in American history, the need for greater and more secure protection arose as the first real stakeholder in US copyright history arose and faced the very same difficulties faced by London and Paris booksellers vis-à-vis regional booksellers. The American publishing industry – led by its main lobbyist Noah Webster, the author of the first American dictionary – was keen to protect its works across state borders.

The first state copyright law entitled An Act for the Encouragement of Literature and Genius was passed in Connecticut in 1783;[36] this was soon followed by Massachusetts, Maryland, Georgia and New York, New Hampshire and Rhode Island. The Continental Congress (prior to the Federal government) actually passed a resolution recommending states to secure to US authors or publishers copyright for a minimum term of 14 years.[37] By the time the Constitutional Convention was held in 1787, all but Delaware had passed copyright legislation.

The Articles of Confederation did not offer any protection to literary and artistic property – however the United States Constitution included a copyright clause[38] (Article 1, cl.8), and pursuant to this clause, Congress enacted the first copyright statute, the Copyright Act of 1790, which secured to authors, publishers or their legal representatives two 14-year terms of copyright protection in books, pamphlets, maps and charts. The Act however limited copyright protection to 'a citizen or citizens of these United States, or resident therein'. Section 5 of the Act stated explicitly:

> [N]othing in this act shall be construed to extend to prohibit the importation or vending, reprinting or publishing within the United States, of any map, chart, book or books, written, printed, or published *by any person not a citizen of the United States, in foreign parts or places without the jurisdiction of the United States.* (emphasis added)

As noted by some commentators, this provision constituted a piracy provision, which was the result of a developing country protecting its fledgling culture and industry whilst exploiting the works of developed countries such as France or the UK.[39] Moreover the lack of copyright protection to foreign authors was commonplace in the late eighteenth and early nineteenth centuries due to the absence of an international copyright agreement.[40] This lack of copyright protection to foreign authors in the 1790 Act was particularly irksome to English authors – between 1800 and 1860, almost half of the best-sellers in the United States were pirated, mostly from English novels. Compared to a legitimate English edition, an American pirated edition was approximately one-tenth of the total cost.[41]

Dickens in the United States

One means by which authors gained control over their works during the mid-Victorian era was through customary usages within the profession. Both British and American publishers developed a system of 'courtesy of the trade' whereby publishers would respect the first publishing house to announce the publication of an edition of a foreign work.[42] In the UK the customary privileges had been used to the advantage of the London booksellers, allowing them to publish their titles without competition from the provincial booksellers.[43] In the US, this system protected the first American publisher of a foreign work from competition within the trade, and also gave the author the opportunity of earning some remuneration even if he were unable to prevent the American publication of his work in the first place.

Indeed Dickens was one such beneficiary of courtesy copyright, and received large sums in respect of the American sales of his works.[44] Nevertheless courtesy copyright only operated in the US, and it soon became inoperative when newer publishing houses refused to honour the custom, especially with the emergence of cheap library editions.[45] Hence Dickens's concern with the lack of copyright protection.[46] Not all British authors were similarly opposed to plagiarism and piracy in the US. Thomas Macaulay, the famous writer and opponent of copyright law in UK, was much plagiarized in the United States but he was nonchalant as to these activities and remained very opposed to copyright law.

In 1842, Lord Palmerston, the British prime minister, attempted to initiate high-level contacts with the American government in an effort to induce the United States to agree to a copyright treaty, but failed.[47] In that same year, after finishing *Barnaby Rudge*, Dickens travelled to the United States – the primary reason, it has been argued by a few writers, was that he had gone to plead for the protection of British works and the acceptance of international copyright law.[48] Dickens, ignorant of the economic depression and political reality, was strongly advocating international copyright in his speeches and activities, as is evident from this after-dinner speech given in New England in 1842:

> Gentlemen, as I have no secrets from you, in the spirit of confidence you have engendered between us, and as I have made a kind of compact with myself that I never will, while I remain in America, omit an opportunity of referring to a topic in which I and all others of any class on both sides of the water are equally interested – equally interested, there is no difference between us – I would beg leave to whisper in your ear two words, International Copyright. I use them in no sordid sense, believe me, and those who know me best, best know that. For myself, I would rather that my children coming after me, trudged in the mud, and knew by the general feeling of society that their father was beloved, and had been of some use than I would have them ride in their carriages, and know by their banker's books that he was rich. But I do not see, I confess, why one should be obliged to make the choice, or why fame, besides playing that delightful reveille for which she is so justly celebrated, should not blow out of her trumpet a few notes of a different kind from those with which she has hitherto contented herself.[49]

Although he did not allude to this subject either before or after his visit to the United States, it appears from his novel *Martin Chuzzlewit* that he was deeply affected by the experience, including the vigorous attack of the press who accused him of seeking profit.[50] One press report characterized his mission as follows:

> If Mr. Dickens prefers dollars and cents to literary fame – selfish, sordid gratification to a position of commanding respect – and a flash waistcoat to a laurel wreath, it is his own misfortune – the result of traits inseparable from his character . . . Mr. D. has not strength of character and mind enough to prove the European axiom that a parvenue must betray himself by his vulgarity.[51]

Dickens recounted his unsuccessful trip thus:

> I spoke, as you know, of international copyright, at Boston; and I spoke of it again at Hartford. My friends were paralysed with wonder at such audacious daring. The notion that I, a man alone by himself, in America, should venture to suggest to the Americans that there was one point on which they were neither just to their own countrymen nor to us, actually struck the boldest dumb! It is nothing that of all men living I am the greatest loser by it. It is nothing that I have to claim to speak and be heard. The wonder is that a breathing man can be found with temerity enough to suggest to the Americans the possibility of their having done wrong. I wish you could have seen the faces that I saw, down both sides of the table at Hartford, when I began to talk about Scott. I wish you could have heard how I gave it out. My blood so boiled as I thought of the monstrous injustice that I felt as if I were twelve feet high when I thrust it down their throats.[52]

More on the subject he wrote:

> I have never in my life been so shocked and disgusted, or made so sick and sore at heart, as I have been by the treatment I have received here (in America I mean) in reference to the International Copyright question. I – the greatest loser by the exist-ing Law, alive – say in perfect good humour and disinterestedness(for God knows that I have little hope of its ever being changed in my time) that I hope the day will come when Writers will be justly treated: and straightway there fall upon me scores of your newspapers; imputing motives to me, the very suggestion of which turns my blood to gall . . .[53]

He returned frustrated, disillusioned and pessimistic in his final analysis of the situation, stating firmly that nothing would induce an American to give up the power he possesses of pirating British literature:[54]

> I do not expect that any alteration will take place in the Law of International Copyright, until I am past the sense of Justice or Injustice, and my children are fighting their own way in the World. Until the Law is altered nothing can be done through the General Honesty and Good Feeling. The absence of all Generosity, Honour, or Truth which distinguishes the gross assaults that have been made upon me, here, for alluding to the subject, sufficiently assures me of that.[55]

In this, he proved to have been naive as to the power of authors or public opin-ion in influencing national American politics, and he may have been misled in viewing American and international politics as being similar to British and European politics. What were his activities upon return to England six months later? He printed a circular addressed to influential friends urging them to join him in refusing to sell advance proofs or to otherwise cooperate with American publishers. This was his last act on behalf of authors and interna-tional copyright. The copyright agreement between UK and US did not come into being until 1891, 20 years after his death, and five years after the Berne Convention.

The Pecksniffian Hypocrite or Knight Errant?

Why the sudden drop in activities? One reason may have been that Dickens was greatly hurt by the criticisms. He wished to be thought of as the 'knight errant battling for Europe' in relation to the question of copyright, and not as someone pleading for his own personal needs and gains.[56] As one reviewer of *American Notes* states, this travel book of Dickens based on his study of America was weak due to his primary goal of visiting America – to be

> a kind of missionary in the cause of International Copyright; with the design of persuading the American public to abandon their present privilege, of enjoying the produce of all the literary industry of Great Britain without paying for it . . .[57]

However it has also been argued that Dickens was more greatly affected by his failure and he did allude to copyright problems in an obscure fashion – in Chapter 35 of *Martin Chuzzlewit* where Mr Pecksniff wins an architectural competition based on drawings plagiarized from his apprentice's drawings before the latter went off to the US. Interestingly Gerhard Joseph's account reminds us that Pecksniff's action and claim to ownership was strictly legal in the context of nineteenth-century law and practice: he was the intellectual owner of the plans of his apprentice by virtue of his status as 'master' to his apprentice, and by having made minor additions to the drawings (such as windows), contemporary standards would absolve him of the charge of plagiarism.[58]

Gerhard Joseph and Alexander Welsh insinuate that Dickens occupied the Pecksniffian position in the US – by arguing that copyright was important as a matter of natural rights principle, rather than a pecuniary one. Gerhard Joseph states:

[F]or Dickens the money seemed (or so he would have told himself) less important than the principle of a creator's 'natural rights' to his words subject to whatever contractual arrangements he might wish to make.[59]

Nevertheless Gerhard Joseph argues that Dickens, despite these pronouncements, was 'no stranger to Pecksniffian hypocrisy, rampant egoism, and mercenary calculation himself', and he did try 'to mask a self-serving advocacy of International Copyright behind the less strictly commercial, more high-minded motives of gathering materials for a book'. In other words Dickens the author was well aware of the fact that by pushing for international copyright protection and reciprocity, money was a primary motive, if not the only motive. Human rights and romantic rhetoric of the 'right of the author' or 'authorial personality' were served as a diversion and delusion – for both the public and the author.

A HAPPY ENDING?

The Emergence of Copyright Stakeholders in American Society

Despite a sustained effort by the American Senator Henry Clay to enact international copyright legislation, no position on international or bilateral copyright agreements was forthcoming to protect foreign authors. The 1837 Clay Report recommended legislation that would 'extend US copyright protection to British and French authors under rigorous conditions', mainly by maintaining some support for the local publishing industry.[60] Indeed the key may have been the lack of local stakeholders in terms of writers:

Nothing better characterised the years 1837–1842 than the lacklustre efforts of American authors. An inverse ratio seemed to function in the literary community: the more illustrious one was, such as Irving, Cooper, and Prescott, the less he was involved.[61]

At some point however during the late nineteenth century, American novels finally began to be read by readers on the European continent. A new breed of American authors emerged and over the next 100 years they became household names on both sides of the Atlantic: Ralph Waldo Emerson, Nathaniel Hawthorne, Henry Wadsworth Longfellow, Herman Melville, Edgar Allan Poe, Harriet Beecher Stowe, Walt Whitman and, of course, Mark Twain. American authors began to feel the growing discrimination against them, both abroad and at home.[62] Internationally they received no rights or royalties due to reciprocity clauses under national copyright laws in the UK and other European countries – as long as foreign authors were denied rights under US law, so would the Americans authors be denied rights.

Domestically, American authors had to compete with cheaper pirate copies or imports of foreign-authored books.[63] One key proponent of copyright law was Mark Twain who wrote in *Century Magazine* in 1886:

> The statistics of any public library will show that of every hundred books read by our people, about seventy are novels – and nine-tenths of them foreign ones. They fill the imagination with an unhealthy fascination with foreign life, with its dukes and earls and kings, its fuss and feathers, its graceful immoralities, its sugar-coated injustices and oppressions; and this fascination breeds a more or less pronounced dissatisfaction with our country and form of government, and contempt for our republican commonplaces and simplicities; it also breeds a longing for something 'better' which presently crops out in the diseased shams and imitations of the ideal foreign spectacle: Hence the 'dude.'[64]

Indeed recent research indicates that Twain may have overestimated the influence of foreign novels. Although the popular view was that native authorship would be disadvantaged as long as the average author had to compete with 'the great masters of England whose works were appropriated without cost',[65] statistical analyses seem to indicate that by 1850 most books in the US were written by Americans, though mostly in the field of schoolbooks, medical volumes and other non-fiction – such non-fiction titles remained non-substitutable and geography or country dependent. Thus although Americans did not produce any great works of literature during the latter part of the nineteenth century, it is doubted that this lacuna is due to the lack of copyright protection for foreign books. Indeed one has to consider not only the nature of books discussed (that is, novel versus non-fiction), but also the type of book (that is, gilt-edged volume of history bound in morocco with a detective story printed on cheap yellow paper). Furthermore where the 'quality' of literature is high, studies show that leading publishers offered foreign authors such as Dickens, Thackeray, Tennyson, side by side with American authors such as Hawthorne, Longfellow and Thoreau.[66]

The absence of international copyright legislation did not necessarily harm the development of indigenous literature or local markets – it only became harmful at such a time as there was an American literature which could be sold to an international market.

International Copyright Treaty – The Berne Union

In the meantime, a push was being made for an international copyright law treaty. France, a major publishing and book centre, was battling piracy at her borders with Belgium and the Netherlands, with the French government threatening Belgium with trade reprisals until it concluded a trade treaty which also assured copyright protection for French works. European countries then began to form a web of trade bilateral agreements with reciprocity clauses to protect works across borders.[67] However bilateral agreements were difficult to negotiate and conclude, and moreover, as France discovered, once a trade agreement was revoked or renegotiated, copyright protection was often affected. France solved this problem by issuing the Decree of 28 March 1852, which unilaterally extended copyright protection to all works regardless of their country of origin. First, the French believed that authors' rights were rooted in natural rights and 'should therefore not be subject to artificial restraints such as nationality and political boundaries'.[68] Second France was concerned about the length of time it was taking to negotiate bilateral treaties with Belgium and the Netherlands – the two principal hotbeds of French piracies.[69] They hoped that the unilateral grant of protection to authors from these countries in France would shame these two nations into responding in like manner.[70] Third, the French at that time believed that bargaining was not the best method of securing international protection of authors' rights, and that if France should begin declaring that piracy of a foreign work in France was a crime punishable by the law, the other governments would be more willing to take the same step.

Driven by the impetus of the French Decree, authors and artists met at the Congress on Literary and Artistic Property in Brussels in 1858 to discuss the international protection of authors' rights. More than 300 members attended, and 14 countries were represented. Three years later, a new Congress was called in Antwerp to induce countries to adopt uniform legislation. Important national meetings of authors and artists were held in several countries, particularly France and Germany, and the number of bilateral conventions that were made during this period increased rapidly.[71] Two decades later, artists met at another Congress in Antwerp to celebrate the tercentenary of the birth of another artist (and notable copyist) – Peter Paul Rubens. While the Congress was in session, the attendees adopted a unanimous resolution to call upon the recently established Institute of International Law 'to draft a project of world law on the protection of artistic works' – but no further progress was made. At the Universal Exposition of 1878 in Paris, the Literary Congress, presided over by French novelist Victor Hugo, met and decided to create an international association of literary societies and authors; the association extended its membership to include artists and expanded its role to cover both artistic and literary property. The Association Littéraire et Artistique Internationale, commonly known today as ALAI, met in 1882 in Rome, and Paul Schmidt of the German Publishers Association proposed to establish a Union to protect literary property.[72] The Association unanimously approved the proposal, and the conference met in Berne in September 1883. At the Berne meeting a draft convention, which consisted of ten articles, was proposed, and Switzerland agreed to communicate the project to 'all civilized countries'. For the next three years, intergovernmental conferences were held in Berne. Although the meetings were not well received in the very beginning and countries disagreed as to how they should protect authors' rights, the participant countries eventually became receptive to the idea of having a multilateral convention. When the final conference met on 5 September 1886, 12 countries participated in the conference. Except Japan (which joined in 1899) and the United States (which joined in 1989), which only attended the conference as observers, all the participant countries signed the final instrument.[73] Upon ratification, the Berne Convention for the Protection of Literary and Artistic Works entered into force on 5 December 1887. The Berne Convention created the first truly multilateral copyright treaty in history.

US Compromise – The 1891 Chace Act and the Manufacturing Clause

Contemporaneously with the development of the Berne Union, countries on the American continent were exploring the possibility of creating Pan-American copyright conventions. Backed by pressure from American authors and publishers, Congress enacted the International Copyright Act of 3 March 1891 – commonly referred to as the Chace Act. Under this Act, foreign authors received copyright protection when the President proclaimed that their home country provided American citizens with 'the benefit of copyright on substantially the same basis as its own citizens' or that such a country was a party to an international agreement that provided reciprocal copyright protection to its members and to which 'the United States may, at its pleasure, become a party'.[74]

Concerned about the threat from British publishers, the American publishing industry and printers' unions demanded, and obtained, a compromise.[75]

Firstly, authors could only secure copyright by registering the work in the United States before publication and by depositing two copies of the work on or before the date of publication anywhere. Secondly, as far as 'books, photograph, chromo or lithograph' were concerned, the Act included a manufacturing clause, requiring that the two deposit copies be

> printed from type set within the limits of the United States, or from plates made therefrom, or from negatives, or drawings on stone made within the limits of the United States, or from transfers made therefrom.

Such a requirement granted rights to foreign authors, but still denied foreign publishers any rights. These clauses resulted in US failure to qualify for admission to the Berne Convention until 1988, approximately 100 years after the initial Convention.

Dickens and Andersen

How to contrast the attitudes of Dickens and Hans Christian Andersen: the former, whilst ostensibly and very visibly vocal about good literature, was nevertheless very good at ensuring a steady stream of income from his writings; the latter, on the other hand, appears not to have been interested in monies as much as fame and glory – and not one jot in copyright. Initially Charles Dickens was an admirer of Andersen, and met him in 1847 after returning from his American trip. Dickens showered the Danish writer with signed copies of his collected works. Apart from mere interest in another fellow author, Dickens may also have been interested in Andersen during this period as he was in the midst of writing *Dombey and Son* which he imbued with elements of fable and fairy tale.[76] The two maintained a correspondence until, on Andersen's next journey, Dickens invited him to Gad's Hill Place, his country home in Kent. The visit started well, with Dickens personally arranging for Andersen's guest room to be furnished with an interesting selection of books and essays; he also went to the extent of giving Andersen advice on how to survive critical reviews when the latter was found sobbing on the lawn of Gad's Hill Place.[77]

During the brief honeymoon of the friendship, both of them discussed monies – as all authors invariably do. Authors may be bad diplomats or negotiators, and Dickens certainly was a public relations disaster for the cause of international copyright law, but he was good at negotiating his payments and 'working' his copyrights.[78] Dickens himself expressed considerable surprise when he compared his royalties with those of Andersen.[79] It was clear from his autobiography that Andersen was not paid well, or even at all for some exploitations of his works such as translations. Andersen's attitude to copyright is an irony compared to that of his biographer in the United States, many years later, who has only been too ready to draw upon twentieth-century copyright law to protect his own interest in exploiting Andersen's life.[80]

However Andersen's visit eventually turned into a disaster. First, the timing was atrocious, for the Dickens's matrimonial relationship was severely strained at this point. Second, Andersen never noticed the tension in the household and proved to be a needy guest, much to the chagrin of the other members of the Dickens household who nicknamed him the 'bony bore'.[81] Third, part of the problem was that Andersen spoke virtually no English. 'In English, he is the Deaf and Dumb Asylum', Dickens sneered to a friend, which led London society to view the writer as something of a simpleton. After Andersen's departure, Dickens placed a sign above the dressing room mirror which read:

> Hans Andersen slept in this room for five weeks – which seemed to the family AGES.[82]

Andersen himself never understood why he never heard from Dickens again despite Andersen having sent him several letters, books and photographs. Shortly thereafter Dickens published *David Copperfield*, in which the character Uriah Heep is said to have been modelled on Andersen – a back-handed compliment, to say the least.[83] Perhaps this antagonism reflects their different perspectives of life and their works – Dickens was always concerned as to monies and ever resentful of having to cater for a large family of ten children, whilst Andersen – never having married, and eternally in love with Swedish nightingales and fairies[84] – had no need for utilitarian, or any other, concept of copyright law.

NOTES

1. David Nimmer, *A Tale Of Two Treaties Dateline: Geneva-December 1996*, [1997] 22 Colum.-VLA J.L. & Arts 1.
2. Graham Dutfield and Uma Suthersanen, *Harmonisation or Differentiation in Intellectual Property Protection? The Lessons of History*, [2005] 23(2) Prometheus 131.
3. Ibid; and also UNCTAD-ICTSD, 'Policy Discussion Paper on Intellectual Property Rights: Implications for Development' (2003, available at http://www.iprsonline.org/unctadictsd/projectoutputs.htm#policy).
4. B. Zorina Khan, 'Does copyright piracy pay? The effects of U.S. international copyright laws on the market for books, 1790–1920', NBER Working Paper Series, Working Paper 10271, February 2004, http://www.nber.org/papers/w10271.
5. Ibid.
6. R.K. Webb, 'The Victorian Reading Public', in *From Dickens To Hardy* (Boris Ford ed., 1958), at 205; John Sutherland, *Victorian Fiction: Writers, Publishers, Readers* 151–2 (1995).
7. Diane Leenheer Zimmerman, *Authorship Without Ownership: Reconsidering Incentives in a Digital Age*, [2003] 52 DePaul L. Rev. 1121, at 1128.

8. See generally U. Suthersanen, *Copyright and Educational Policies – A Stakeholder Analysis* [2003] 4 *Oxford Journal of Legal Studies* 586.
9. The Statute of Anne, of course, was notorious in its practice of not assisting authorial rights, but rather promulgating publishers' control. Indeed, a primary purpose of the Statute was to promote competition among printers and booksellers. See generally Ray Patterson, *Copyright in Historical Perspective* (1968); Mark Rose, *Authors and Owners: The Invention of Copyright* (1993).
10. Martha Woodmansee, *The Author, Art and the Market: Rereading the History of Aesthetics*, at 53–4 (1994) (quoting Edward Young's conjecture that an original work 'may be said to be of a vegetable nature; it rises spontaneously from the vital root of genius; it grows, it is not made').
11. See Peter L. Shillingsburg, *Pegasus in Harness: Victorian Publishing and W.M. Thackeray* (1992), who compares this attitude of Dickens with the more realistic stance of writers such as William Thackeray, at 68.
12. M.H. Abrams, *The Mirror and the Lamp: Romantic Theory and the Critical Tradition* (1953), especially Chapter 9.
13. Indeed, this was a recurrent theme regarding authorial works, especially in the case of Coleridge – see Susan Eilenberg, *Strange Power of Speech: Wordsworth, Coleridge and Literary Possession* (1992).
14. Eilenberg, at 204. Note however Wordsworth's hypocrisy in denying the essential collaboration of his sister Dorothy, in the writing of his famous poem, *The Daffodils* (1807) – discussed in Peter Jaszi and Martha Woodmansee, *The Ethical Reaches of Authorship*, [1996] Volume 95:4, *South Atlantic Quarterly*, at 947, at 950 *et seq*.
15. Cited in David Saunders, *Authorship and Copyright* (1992), at 128. For an excellent and comprehensive discussion of Talfourd's struggles on behalf of copyright reform in the early nineteenth century, see Catherine Seville, *Literary Copyright Reform in Early Victorian England: The Framing of the 1842 Copyright Act* (1999), and also 'Talfourd and his contemporaries: the making of the Copyright Act 1842', in *The Prehistory and Development of Intellectual Property Systems* (ed. Alison Firth) (1997) at 1997.
16. S. Rep. No. 134, 24th Cong., 2d Sess. (1837), reprinted in R.R. Bowker, *Copyright, Its History and Law: Being a Summary of the Principles and Law of Copyright, with Special Reference to Books* 341 (1912) [hereinafter Clay's Report]; see also Paul Edward Geller, *Copyright history and the future: what's culture got to do with it?*, [2000] 47 Journal, Copyright Society of the USA, at 229.
17. Marjorie Plant, *The English Book Trade: An Economic History of The English Book Trade: An Economic History of the Making and Sale of Books* 57–8 (1939); see also Jonathan Rose, *The Intellectual Life of the British Working Class* (2003), who similarly charts the reading habits of the working class and suggests that their lack of education did not preclude a voracious appetite for classical literature such as Shakespeare, Scott and Milton.
18. Seville, Chapter 5.
19. Macaulay's view was that patronage was fatal to the integrity and independence of literary men, Seville, at 64.
20. John Feather, *A History of British Publishing* (1988), at 152–3.
21. Diane Leenheer Zimmerman, *Authorship Without Ownership: Reconsidering Incentives in a Digital Age*, [2003] 52 DePaul L. Rev. 1121, at 1129.
22. Chapman and Hall were progressive American publishers, who also acted as Thackeray's bankers as well as publishers and paid him monies even though his work was being lawfully published by three other companies, and pirated by another six publishers, Shillingsburg, at 69.
23. The business was run by a single person – Charles Edward Mudie, who had such an enormous purchasing power that publishers had to take account of his needs, Feather, at 154.
24. Feather, at 146.
25. Seville, at 5.
26. Seville, at 19–20.
27. Seville, at 21, 42–5.
28. *Hansard, Parliamentary debates* (3rd series), lvi, 346 (5 February 1840). The text of the

speech is also widely available on the Internet – see for example, http://homepages.law.
asu.edu/~dkarjala/OpposingCopyrightExtension/commentary/MacaulaySpeeches.html

29. Macaulay's speech heavily emphasized how copyright could have been used as a tool of
censorship, naming works such as *Clarissa* by Richardson, or religious works by John
Wesley.

30. Seville, at 8, 26–7, 28.

31. However, one of the first few cases under the 1842 Act was in relation to an abridgement of
Dickens's novel, *A Christmas Carol*, with Talfourd appearing as counsel for Dickens –
Dickens v. Lee (1844) 8 Jur 183.

32. Seville, at 184–5.

33. James J. Barnes, *Authors, Publishers and Politicians: The Quest for an Anglo-American
Copyright Agreement 1815–1854* (1974), at 95.

34. Stephen M. Stewart, *International Copyright and Neighbouring Rights* (2d ed. 1989), §
2.17, at 24.

35. Peter Yu, *The Copyright Divide*, 25 Cardozo L. Rev. 331 [2003] at 337.

36. The statute was modelled after the English Statute of Anne, and granted US authors and their
heirs and assigns 'the sole liberty of printing, publishing and vending' any new books,
pamphlets, maps, or charts within the State of Connecticut for two renewable terms of 14
years.

37. Resolution Passed by the Colonial Congress, Recommending the Several States to Secure to
the Authors or Publishers of New Books the Copyright of Such Books (2 May 1783), as
quoted in Yu, p. 339. The resolution recommended securing to US authors, publishers, their
executors, administrators, and assigns, copyright protection in books for a minimum term of
14 years and to grant a minimum renewal term of 14 years to authors, if then living, or their
heirs and assigns. In response to this recommendation, New Jersey, New Hampshire, Rhode
Island, Pennsylvania, South Carolina, Virginia, North Carolina, Georgia, and New York
passed legislation to protect literary property. Concerned about the divergent protection
offered by other states, more than half of the state copyright statutes contained reciprocity
clauses that limited copyright protection to authors from states offering similar protection.

38. The clause was derived from proposals introduced by James Madison and Charles Pinckney.
James Madison offered the following commentary in the *Federalist*: 'The utility of [the
copyright] power will scarcely be questioned. The copyright of authors has been solemnly
adjudged, in Great Britain, to be a right of the common law. The right to useful inventions
seems with equal reason to belong to the inventors. The public good fully coincides in both
cases with the claims of individuals. The States cannot separately make effectual provision
for either of the cases, and most of them have anticipated the decision of this point, by laws
passed at the instance of Congress', *Federalist*, 43, at 271–2 (James Madison) (Clinton
Rossiter ed., 1961), as cited in Yu, at 341. Also see Patterson, at 203–12; Karl Fenning, *The
Origin of the Patent and Copyright Clause of the Constitution*, 17 Geo. L.J. 109 (1929);
Ralph Oman, *The Copyright Clause: 'A Charter for a Living People'*, 17 U. Balt. L. Rev. 99
(1987).

39. E. Plowman and M. Hamilton, *Copyright: Intellectual Property in the Information Age*
(1980), at 16; Patterson, at 199 (noting the need to protect the new nation against the established trade in England); Yu, at 341.

40. Sam Ricketson, *The Birth of the Berne Union*, 11 Colum.-VLA J.L. & Arts 9, 12 (1986);
Henry G. Henn, *The Quest for International Copyright Protection*, 39 Cornell L.Q. 43, 43
(1953).

41. Siva Vaidhyanathan, *Copyrights and Copywrongs: The Rise of Intellectual Property and
How It Threatens Creativity* (2001), at 50 (noting that a 'London reader who wanted a copy
of Charles Dickens's A Christmas Carol would have to pay the equivalent of $2.50 in 1843
[while a]n American Dickens fan would have to pay only six cents per copy'); Stewart, at
25.

42. Ricketson, at 13–14; Vaidhyanathan, at 52; Barnes, at 84.

43. Seville, at 13; Feather, Chapter 3, Rose, Chapters 5 and 6. The system fell apart when the
Scottish booksellers refused to take notice of the customary London privileges.

44. Ricketson, at 14.

45. Vaidhyanathan, at 52–3 (discussing the emergence of cheap library editions).
46. Gerhard Joseph, *Charles Dickens, International Copyright, and the Discretionary Silence of Martin Chuzzlewit*, (1992) 10 Cardozo Arts & Ent. L.J. 523 (1992). Other irate authors included Gilbert and Sullivan – see *Carte v. Ford*, 15 F. 439 (C.C.D. Md. 1883) (The Iolanthe Case); *Carte v. Duff*, 25 F. 183 (C.C.S.D.N.Y. 1885) (The Mikado Case); *Carte v. Evans*, 27 F. 861 (C.C.D. Mass. 1886).
47. Vaidhyanathan, at 51.
48. See Alexander Welsh, *From Copyright to Copperfield* (1987), 12, 30–38, Gerhard Joseph, Charles Dickens, International Copyright, and the Discretionary Silence of Martin Chuzzlewit, in *The Construction of Authorship: Textual Appropriation in Law and Literature* (M.Woodmansee and P. Jaszi, eds), 1994, 259–70; and J.B. Priestley, *Charles Dickens and his World*, (Thames & Hudson, 1978).
49. *The Speeches of Charles Dickens*, (ed. K.J. Fielding), (1960), 21, 24–5, as cited in Welsh, at 32.
50. Welsh, at 30.
51. *Brother Jonathan*, quarto ed. II (6 August 1842), pp. 410–11, as cited in Barnes, at 29.
52. *Letter from Charles Dickens to John Foster* (24 Feb. 1842), cited in P. Yu, at 343.
53. *Letter to Jonathan Chapman*, 22 February 1842, *Letters of Dickens* (eds Madeleine House and Graham Storey, 1965–), III, 79, as cited in Welsh, at 33.
54. Not all authors were as pessimistic – Anthony Trollope was of the view that the problem lay with 'the book-selling leviathans, and . . . those politicians whom the leviathans [were] able to attach to their interests'. Anthony Trollope, *An Autobiography* 308 (Michael Sadleir and Frederick Page (eds) Oxford Univ. Press 1980, cited in Yu, at 343.
55. *Letter to John S. Bartlett*, 24 February 1842, Letters of Dickens, III, 79, as cited in Welsh, at 35.
56. Welsh, at 36.
57. *Edinburgh Review*, 76 (1843), 500–501, as cited in Welsh, at 37.
58. Joseph, at 266.
59. Joseph, at 269.
60. Clay's Report, as cited and discussed in Yu, at 343–5.
61. Barnes, at 76.
62. Some uncertainty existed as to whether foreign authors, including American authors, could secure a valid copyright in Britain – much depended upon the interpretation of the statutes by the Court of Chancery or the Common Law Courts. The vagaries of common law copyright exist till today. The Second Circuit court recently confirmed in *Capitol Records Inc. v. Naxos of America Inc.* (2nd Cir. April 5, 2005, 2005 WL 756591) that, irrespective of federal copyright law, the common-law copyright in the State of New York extended protection to sound recordings made (and which have expired) in Britain in the 1930s. This decision not only emphasizes the continuing arbitrary nature of the law, but also the importance of harmonized legal rules concerning the availability and extent of protection.
63. Max Kempelman, *The United States and International Copyright*, (1947) 41 Am. J. Int'l L. 413.
64. Vaidhyanathan, at 61 (quoting Mark Twain).
65. Aubrey J. Clark, *The Movement for International Copyright in Nineteenth Century America*, Wash, DC, Catholic University Press, 1960, at 49.
66. Khan, at 13–15.
67. Ricketson, at 15–16; Geller, at 233.
68. Ricketson, at 14.
69. Yu, at 347.
70. Ricketson, at 14.
71. Ricketson, at 9.
72. Ricketson, at 19–20.
73. These 12 countries included Belgium, France, Germany, Haiti, Italy, Japan, Liberia, Spain, Switzerland, Tunisia, the United Kingdom, and the United States.
74. Yu, at 352.
75. The situation regarding the printers' unions is slightly comical – one means by which the

publishers could cut costs was to abandon highly paid unionized men in favour of non-union women who were willing to accept low wages. Dismayed at the fact that non-allegiance to international copyright law was protecting jobs for the wrong type of person (that is, women), the printers' unions soon abandoned their opposition and joined the major publishers and authors in support of some measure of international copyright, Vaidhyanathan, at 55.

76. Peter Ackroyd, *Charles Dickens* (1999), at 554.
77. Ibid.
78. That he was obsessed with monies and income is clear from his biography – a lot of this had to do with his fear of descending into the poverty of his childhood. Dickens 'worked' his copyrights by republishing his works in different editions and formats, including the 'English people' edition (which were cheap weekly and monthly editions of his novels), the more expensive 'Library Edition of Dickens', the last and most exclusive 'Charles Dickens Edition', Ackroyd, at 437, 556, 823 and 1046.
79. Ackroyd, at 566; Han Christian Andersen, *The Fairy Tale of My Life* (1855), at 145.
80. See, for example, *Toksvig v. Bruce Publishing Co.* (181 F.2d 664, 7th Cir. 1950) where the plaintiff spent three years researching Andersen's life from Danish sources and wrote a biography. The defendant subsequently wrote a book based on Andersen's life after less than a year of researching English sources, including the plaintiff's biography. The US 7th Circuit court concluded that the defendant had breached the plaintiff's copyright by copying 24 specific passages, as well as certain general concepts about Andersen, his life, and his friends, that had first appeared in plaintiff's book. The court ignored the defendant's argument that these materials were in the public domain, and that she could have secured the same information from other works.
81. Ackroyd, at 823–6.
82. Ibid, at 826.
83. See Doris Alexander, *Creating Characters With Charles Dickens* (1991), as cited in Mary Frances Prechtel, *Classical Malice*, (1994) 55 Ohio St. L.J. 187, at note 45.
84. Note the latest biography of Andersen and the references to his almost homosexual friendship with the ballet dancer Harald Scharff in Jackie Wullschlager, *The Life of a Storyteller* (2001).

4. Adaptations with integrity

Leslie Kim Treiger-Bar-Am

INTRODUCTION

Adaptations abound. Versions of Hans Christian Andersen's tales are countless. In bookshops and libraries it is often easier to find 'The Little Mermaid' as retold by others, than to find Andersen's own tale. The variety of video versions, puzzles and toys based on that tale are astounding. The Disney version of Andersen's 'The Little Mermaid' is titled 'Disney's Masterpiece', and is already called a Disney 'classic'. Disney has since produced a follow-up, *Return to the Sea*.

This chapter discusses authors' rights to control modifications, including adaptations, of literary, visual and musical artworks. The author's moral right of integrity will be examined. Upon the Anglo-American divide between copyright and moral rights, it is the latter that will be in focus. The economic interest in copyright can be used to prevent modifications to artworks, and gives copyright owners control over derivative uses of the primary work. Yet this analysis examines authors' moral right of integrity.

The analysis will centre on UK law, and its enactment of section 80 of the Copyright, Designs and Patents Act 1988 (hereinafter 'Act'). Section 80 provides that an author has the right to prevent treatment that 'amounts to distortion or mutilation of the work or is otherwise prejudicial to the honour or reputation of the author or director'.[1] Section 80 implemented into UK law Article 6*bis* of the Berne Convention for the Protection of Literary and Artistic Works. Reference to US and Continental jurisdictions will be made as well, for a general comparative approach.

I have argued elsewhere that the integrity right protects an author's autonomy of expression.[2] A modification that distorts a primary author's expression violates the author's integrity right. This is in contrast with the common interpretation of the right as a protection of the author's reputation, personality or feelings, or of cultural heritage. Rather, the integrity right is a right of expression. It can be seen as arising directly from freedom of expression principles and case law.

In this chapter I will build from that premise, to evaluate when a primary author's expression is distorted. Certain types of modifications, whose place on the spectrum of modifications that may give rise to liability is sometimes put in doubt, will be examined: modifications to copies, contextual uses and the destruction of artworks. The inclusion of these various types of modifications within the scope of integrity right protection will be defended. It will be argued that such modifications may distort the primary author's expression.

The argument of this chapter is that modifications to all artforms, and of all types, ought potentially be actionable pursuant to the integrity right. While a broad understanding of the coverage of the right is offered, a broad reading of defences is proposed as well. The modifier's expression must also be protected. Transformative modifications, and modifications of what shall be termed 'public fora', must provide a defence to a claim of integrity right violation. The conflicting autonomies of expression must be balanced. It will be seen that the readers' autonomy of expression may enter the balance as well: in some situations the autonomy of expression of the reading, viewing or listening public will enter a court's evaluation of an integrity right claim.

A few notes as to terminology: The term 'author' will be used throughout to include artist and film director, as in section 80. The term 'treatment' will be avoided because of its connotations of physical treatment. I prefer the term 'modification' as in the Berne Convention's Article 6*bis*, to encapsulate various forms of changes to artworks that may or may not attract liability. Yet the phrase 'derogatory treatment' is often confused with defamatory treatment. 'Distortion' will be used to refer to a violative modification. 'Mutilation' may be viewed as extreme distortion, and complete mutilation is destruction. This chapter considers which modifications are distortive and hence may infringe an author's integrity right.

TYPES OF MODIFICATIONS: THE SPECTRUM

The inclusion of three types of modifications within the scope of integrity right protection is sometimes questioned. First, ought the right to protect against distortive modifications to copies of artworks? Second, ought the right to include actionability for contextual uses of works? Third, ought destruction to be actionable? I submit that liability may arise in each of the three areas.

Copies

Laws
Section 80 of the UK Act protects copies in addition to originals. Such coverage is not universal however. For example the US Visual Artist's Rights Act of 1990 (VARA) protects only original works of visual art.[3] The question arises: should the integrity right apply only to originals?

Copyright of course protects against copying. It also protects copies, by protecting against unauthorized modifications to copies in the form of derivative works. Derivative works include adaptations. Distortions of a work which may violate the author's exclusive right in copyright to derivative uses also may violate the author's integrity right:[4] derivative uses are precisely works that copy and change the primary work. In the UK Act, adaptations are specifically listed as a 'treatment' that may be violative.

The derivative rights doctrine has expanded copyright's scope excessively. There are calls to return copyright's prohibitions to approximate its early prohibition of exact reproductions.[5] It is submitted that while the excesses of copyright doctrine must be curbed, with the integrity right doctrine there is a place for protection against distortion of copies with changes, including adaptations.

An author's rights over copies ought to be protected alongside his or her rights over originals. Copies, as originals, reflect their author's expression. Yet the parameters will differ: protection that copies receive will be weaker, given their greater distance from the primary author's expression. Moreover copies must receive weaker protection from the perspective of the modifier and society's rights of expression: the modifier-as-author will be influenced by earlier works, and must be allowed to use and change copies of those works.

Examples
Creative works are ordinarily in some sense copies of prior works, where those works are adapted or serve as sources or inspiration. Those primary works themselves often use copies of prior artworks. The works of Hans Christian Andersen have been utilized by numerous writers and artists, with myriad modifications. Yet his works were themselves influenced by previous tales. Tales read to him as a child by his father, Danish folk tales he heard at the local workhouse with his grandmother, and German and other folk tales, were among his sources.[6]

Adaptations are made of all of the various artforms. With literary works, the numerous adaptations of 'The Little Mermaid' into theatre, film and now video are a prime example. So too with visual art: Marcel Duchamp's painting of a moustache on the *Mona Lisa* can be called a modification to a copy of Da Vinci's work, namely an adaptation of it. Picasso's studies of Velazquez's *Las Meninas* are another example.[7] Raphael and Marcantonio's *Judgment of Paris* took the assembly of figures from a Hellenistic sarcophagus; and Manet took the assembly as the centrepiece of his *Déjeuner sur l'herbe*.[8] Again with a musical work: while every performance may be an instance of it,[9] each of those instances varies and hence may be called an adaptation of the work. Further adaptations are then often made upon primary musical works, such as the variations on Bach's *Art of Fugue*.[10]

It is submitted that with the integrity right, the various artforms may be treated similarly. Historically, artforms were categorized differently than today.[11] Today works of different artforms are sometimes given different protection. For example performances are protected as neighbouring rights, and VARA's protection extends only to visual artworks. Yet today artworks of various forms are all considered artistic expression.

The terms 'original' and 'copy' take on different meanings with respect to the various artforms. With a literary work, unlike with visual artworks, any instantiation of the work is called a copy. Yet works of all the artforms have an incorporeal 'original', as well as instantiations of it.[12] I thus take a different view from Stina Teilmann's in this volume. With a literary work that instantiation is multiple; with a cast or lithograph it is often less numerous but still multiple; and with a painting or sculpture it is often singular. Yet 'copy' as used herein refers to 'reproduction' generally, with respect to all of the artforms, in contrast with an author's 'original' text. Reproductions with changes are 'adaptations', again with respect to all of the artforms.

Modifications to copies of works of all of the different artforms may be evaluated by the same standard. Again here I take a different view to that of Teilmann, who argues that the integrity right standard cannot be applied in the same way to the various artforms.[13] As Goodman and Elgin write:

> The object produced by the painter is the work itself . . . But variations are distinguished from nonvariations on a work in much the same way in painting as in music and etching.[14]

Yet as seen above, originals must receive stronger protection than copies; and so too original visual artworks must receive stronger protection than other original works.[15] We will see this below in particular with respect to the necessary protection of visual artworks against destruction. With visual art, the original is distinct in a way that an original of a literary or musical work cannot be. Original visual artworks bear a materiality that the others lack. Thus the same standard for originals and copies of all of the various artforms will be applied for evaluating modifications, but with different parameters.

Moreover with transfer of medium and adaptations a great deal of room for changes must be allowed, to allow others to offer diverse interpretations and transformations.[16] So too in French law different parameters govern modifications to originals and copies: the right of integrity is at its strongest with original works of visual art, where no modification is allowed; with a reproduction or public performance, a strict duty of fidelity is imposed; and with adaptation from one medium to another, where modification is inevitable, only distortions are prohibited.[17]

An additional artform has been introduced by the digital world. In current times, with the digitalization of works and the Internet, the exposure of works of art to copying and the opportunities for their modification is much expanded. Digital reproductions can be infinitely reproduced, and manipulated with ease. Such digitalization of artworks will be treated here as an example of copying, and thus on the spectrum of potentially actionable modifications. Yet where *digital artwork* is modifed, the parameters will differ for a consideration of the distortive effect of digitalized manipulations. The nature of the medium may generate low expectations of the parties as to non-modification. Thus a higher threshold for a finding of liability will apply.

Postmodern critique

Copies   The argument here that both originals and copies are to be protected must be distinguished from a different form of dissolution of the distinction between the two, namely the postmodern argument that originality is a flawed concept, and all works are copies. That argument will be rejected. Yet it will be seen that reflecting on the postmodern view will sharpen the issues for analysis.

Postmoderns (and poststructuralists, together termed here postmoderns) call original authorship a myth. They critique authors' rights of control over 'original' works. The postmoderns argue that all so-called 'originals' are copies.[18]

The argument herein acknowledges that original works are not created *tabula rasa*.[19] Authors and artists often work together. Also when working independently, an author's work responds to and is influenced by other works in artistic traditions. Yet the expressing self remains. Even if an author's work represents a small change to what came before, nevertheless the creative spark that the author adds must be recognized and protected as that author's original expression. In the digital age, the distinction between originals and copies seems to fade further, as duplicates can replicate the original perfectly; yet even in the digital age, individual expression must be recognized.[20]

Original expression exists then and must be protected. What of copies of that primary original work? The postmoderns argue that no work is original, everything is copied. Their conclusion is that therefore nothing ought be protected. And yet why not draw the opposite conclusion, that every work ought be protected?

The postmodern argument is perhaps not so new. The postmodern argument that all works are copies may be seen as a version of the classical pre-Romantic understanding of art. On the early mimetic view, art was a copy of nature or reality. For Plato, artworks are a reflection of objects in the world – which are themselves a reflection of forms, which have a higher level of reality.

Also later, when the originality of the artist came to be valued, original art continued to be understood as at some level a copy in two ways. An original visual work depicting nature was a reproduction – or copy – of nature.[21] Moreover a work (especially a literary work) was seen as a copy of what was in its author's mind: for the Romantics, the artist-genius was original, while his (with the artist generally perceived to be male) work was said to reflect the workings of his inner mind.[22]

The language in modern copyright statutes reflects this Romantic view. In the US Copyright Act, the intangible 'work' is the 'product of "authorship" ' in the mind of the creator. A 'copy' is the 'material object . . . in which it can be embodied'. A book then 'is a particular kind of "copy" '.[23] Both the US statute[24] and UK Act[25] distinguish between a work and its embodiment, thus reflecting the Cartesian subject–object view of creation whereby all works emanate from the authors' mind.[26]

Justice Holmes's opinion in *Bleistein v Donaldson* illustrates both views. A drawing from life or nature has something unique in it, and hence is original. Yet such an artwork is also a copy of nature. Thus: 'Others are free to copy the original. They are not free to copy the copy.'[27]

Thus the postmoderns react against the Romantic and modern view that all artworks are originals. Yet the postmodern view makes the classical argument, albeit in modified form, that all art is a copy. Even the modern view belies reliance on the earlier view that artworks crafted by the human hand are copies of the originals in nature.

On that earlier view, where all art was considered a copy, art nevertheless retained its value (except for Plato, who critiqued art for its mimesis).[28] So too in the instant analysis it is suggested that copies, together with originals, reflect their authors' expression.

Taking this position to the extreme, it could be argued that all copies are sacrosanct, similar to the Bible: With the Bible, every copy is considered original, and holy. Even given the variations of approach of different religious, each reproduction of the Bible is revered as 'The Bible', and in that sense an original. On some views, art may be seen this way as well. Vasari writes of sketches being kept as holy relics. That is not the approach I argue for here. I submit that the expression of authors, be it in the form of originals or copies, justifies protection. Yet the protection afforded to copies will be weaker: copies are more distant from the author as source, namely less original.[29]

While this discussion of the postmodern argument underscores the need to protect both originals and copies of the primary author's expression, it illuminates the necessity to protect the modifier as well. As the postmoderns argue, to some degree all so-called original works contain or rely on copied elements. Thus every so-called primary author is at some level a secondary author as well. Creation depends upon borrowing, copying and then transforming prior works. Modification is an important part of the creative process. The transformative creative spark added by the modifier must be defended as its author's expression, as discussed further in the final section of this chapter.

Forgeries Postmoderns place forgeries together with copies. Umberto Eco notes that 'fake' is defined as 'any copy or likeness'.[30] We have seen that post-moderns argue that originals and copies are not meaningfully distinguished; the argument is also made that originals and forgeries are often not aesthetically distinguishable, but the original is valued out of snobbery.[31] The ease of modifying works with digitalization exacerbates this issue as well. Again this argument will be rejected, but will be seen to illuminate points of analysis.

An original and a forgery can be distinguished by their histories. Original works and forgeries derive from different points in time and locations. As Dutton writes, the 'nominal authenticity' of a work refers to empirical facts concerning the correct identification of its origin.[32] UK copyright law recognizes the significance of a work's point of origin, or source, in determining a work's originality.[33] The postmodern debate is helpful in putting into focus that every artwork has a history.

A work's history entails a series of changes. Up to and including the time of its execution, its history includes who inspired it and influenced it, who commissioned it, and who created it. Going forward from the point of its creation, a work's history includes who bought it and sold it, who viewed it and signed it (such as by adding a colophon), and even who held it. A book's history, Eco writes, includes the number of times it was opened and leafed through in a bookstore. Eco continues:

> [W]e see as original and authentic ancient works which have been substantially altered by the course of time and by human intervention: we have to allow for loss of limbs, restoration, and fading colors. In this category belongs the neoclassical dream of a 'white' Greek art, where in fact the statues and temples were originally brightly colored . . . [As] any material is subject to physical and chemical alteration, from the very moment of its production, every object [c]ould be seen as an instant forgery of itself.[34]

Also with the integrity right, modifications may be understood broadly. This supports the liberal reading of the primary author's right. Thus under section 80, 'treatment' of a work may be conceived of broadly, including for example contextual uses, as discussed below.

Yet the ubiquity of modifications supports a liberal reading of defences as well. Modifications are an inevitable part of an artwork's history. As artworks will necessarily undergo a certain amount of change, not all modifications can support liability. An example is a modification made during an act of conservation of an artwork. Nor ought minor modifications be grounds for liability. It is to the range of modifications that the discussion shall now return.

Contextual Uses

The above discussion supported integrity right protection against distortive modifications to copies of artworks, in addition to originals. Here it will be seen that the spectrum continues further: the right also ought to be understood to protect against uses of artworks that by their context distort the primary authors' expression.

Laws

Many commentators have taken the position that contextual use may not ground liability under the UK statutory language. Section 80's prohibition on 'derogatory treatment' is sometimes taken to refer only to physical treatment of a work.[35] Yet commentators describe the integrity right generally as including contextual uses, as for example in France.[36] The broad language of the Berne Convention's Article 6*bis* presumably includes contextual use, given its protection against 'other modification of, or other derogatory action in relation to, the said work'.[37]

It is submitted that contextual use is covered by the language of the UK Act, as such use may be 'distortion' or 'otherwise prejudicial'. Moreover 'treatment' in the Act includes 'adaptation' of a work, and as such cannot be understood to refer only to physical changes to the actual work.

Context can distort. As Vaver writes: 'A work might be distorted by the company it keeps.'[38] Contextual use should be recognized in some situations to be grounds for liability.

Meaning or message?

It is often assumed that the injury in cases of alleged contextual distortion is to the author's reputation. I submit that by contrast, it is the author's autonomy of expression that suffers upon distortion, including with contextual misuse. Nor is the injury in contextual misuse to the meaning of a work.[39] Rather, the right protects the work's message.

Meaning is beyond an author's control. The meaning of a work is determined by its reader (or viewer or audience). Here I accept the postmodern understanding of meaning. A single work may have different meanings for different readers.

Rather than offering a monopoly on meaning, the integrity right protects the author's intention as to presentation of the work. It is the presentation of the author's message that may be distorted by a contextual use and hence ground liability. Contemporary artists may deny that their work has a 'message' or an intended 'meaning' altogether; yet it is the author's presentation of form and content that the integrity right protects. A change in meaning of a work, for the reader and also for the modifier, must be allowed.

Examples

Cases in which a modifier's contextual use allegedly has been distortive include De Chirico's objection to an exhibition of his work that the artist claimed disproportionately represented his earlier work.[40] Shostakovich argued that the use of his work in an American spy movie during the Cold War gave the music a distortive connotation due to the movie's anti-Soviet theme.[41] An Israeli court found that the re-publication of an author's article in an extreme right-wing leaflet violated the author's integrity right.[42] The hypertext linking of an artwork on one website to that on another might be called distortion by contextual use.[43]

The issue of contextual use may be one of semantics. In many situations an alleged infringement may be termed distortion alternatively by contextual use, or by other treatment. In *Morrison Leahy Music Ltd v Lightbond Ltd* the court found it a triable issue of fact whether the change of context of musical selections distorted the primary work.[44] Laddie (2000) prefers a different reading of the case, writing that the megamix required 'treatment' of each portion of the work, namely deletion of all but a few bars of each piece of music.[45]

In *Bernard-Rousseau v Galeries Lafayette*,[46] a French department store was held to have violated painter Henri Rousseau's integrity right by displaying reproductions of his work that differed in colour and form from the original. This case has been described as presenting the issue of contextual use of a work,[47] and alternatively as a case about modifications to copies of an artwork.[48] The UK case of *Tidy v Trustees of the Natural History Museum*[49] also involved reproductions changing the colour and size of the originals, and could be described in the same alternative ways.

Other characterizations are possible. In the US case of *Mirage Editions, Inc v Albuquerque ART Co*,[50] art prints were removed from a book and mounted on ceramic tiles with a border. The case has been described as an adaptation.[51] Yet as the prints were placed in a different setting the modification could be described as contextual misuse. Further, the removal or relocation of a site-specific work may be called use of a work in a different context; alternatively it may be considered a destruction of the work.

The distinctions between categories on the spectrum of modifications thus may be dissolved. I submit that distortive contextual uses may be actionable along with other modifications. They have a place on the spectrum of modifications. Yet as with other forms of modifications as well, where changes in context bring about a transformation of the primary work, the expression of the modifier must be protected. Laddie (2000) writes that removing material from its context may effectively destroy its originality, so that no substantial part is taken.[52] Duchamp's readymades show us that context can itself be artistic expression. Duchamp's *Fountain* took on the significance it did because the artist changed the context of the urinal.

Destructions

We now look to the end of the spectrum. This section will explore liability for the destruction of artworks. 'Offences of destruction are at the terminal point of a passage which begins with an original work, then passes through adaptations.'[53]

In this section I refer to artists rather than authors. With destructions, it is visual artworks that are under discussion. Given the distinction between work and copy, an author's literary work cannot be destroyed, but only copies of it. Even a ban on the publication of a work is not equivalent to its destruction, as access may be had to it via other means. By contrast, visual artworks depend upon their materiality for their aesthetic efficacy, more than literary works do. Visual works cannot easily be separated from their physical instantiation.[54] The destruction of visual works is thus irreversible.[55]

Moreover this section will look to originals, or singular and important copies. 'Destruction' is taken to mean destruction of an original work. It also refers to significant destruction. A primary artist may say that a minor alteration destroys her work. Indeed any level of distortion, including a contextual change, can be called destruction of an artwork. Yet here I discuss substantial destruction, or other physical treatments of original visual artworks.

Laws

The UK Act does not directly indicate whether the destruction of artworks can sustain liability. The Act is often considered not to protect against destructions.[56] The language of the Berne Convention's Article 6*bis* is also silent on the subject. Ricketson believes that the Berne Convention's provision does not cover destruction.[57]

The laws of other jurisdictions vary. In France, different interpretations arise of the law and courts' judgments.[58] Under VARA, the destruction of works of recognized stature is actionable.[59] The California Art Preservation Act prohibits only the intentional destruction of a work of fine art.[60]

I submit that destruction is within the purview of section 80. The statute protects against 'mutilation'. I take 'mutilation' to be an extreme form of 'distortion'. I would argue that destruction is a further extreme, where mutilation is complete. It is the furthest point on the spectrum of modifications. As Vaver notes, a lack of protection against destruction parallels the 'cynical but regrettably often accurate observation in the field of damages for personal injuries that a defendant is better off monetarily if he kills rather than merely maims his victim'.[61] Whereas other modifications may distort the primary artist's expression, destruction distorts that expression completely.

Examples

The variety and motivations of destructions are numerous. Conklin discusses the destruction of artworks for political and ideological goals, from Parisian mobs pulling down statues of kings to the demolishing of Diego Rivera's mural in NYC's RCA Building when he refused to remove from the painting a portrait of Lenin.[62] Works may be destroyed due to offended morality,[63] or with religious motives.[64] Art is destroyed where works are seen to hinder development in line with taste, such as with the Art Project during the Great Depression. Destructions are undertaken with financial goals, for example with the development of buildings, or where a painting by Picasso was cut up into postage-stamp size pieces for sale by Australian entrepreneurs.[65] Other pragmatic motives include the protection of public safety.[66]

An artistic motive also may support an intent to destroy a primary artwork. A modifier may claim that her destruction of a primary work should be considered transformative of that work. Does an artistic motivation justify the modifier-destroyer's act? I suggest that even acts done with artistic motivation, where destructive, are violative of the integrity right. A destruction defended as transformation of a copy of a primary artwork may well be defensible. Yet the supposed transformation of an original work of art through its destruction would be very difficult to defend.

Consider the artist M. Pierre Pinoncely's urination in Duchamp's *Fountain* (a urinal) at an exhibition in Nîmes. Pinoncely argued that his act transformed Duchamp's work back into an industrial object. The French court found Pinoncely civilly liable. I submit that this destructive act distorted Duchamp's expression.

Recently, original Goya etchings entitled *Disasters of War* that the Chapman Brothers had covered in ink with caricatures were exhibited at Modern Art Oxford.[67] A viewer at the exhibit splattered red paint on the works. I submit that both acts, by the Chapman Brothers and the viewer, would have been violative of Goya's integrity right.

A defendant's motivation should not matter where the modifier has intended (or by negligence has acted) to destroy an original work. Whatever their motivation, destructions of artworks distort the primary artists' expression.[68]

The freedom of expression principle supports political expression as well as artistic expression, and in many instances political expression receives stronger protection.[69] Nevertheless, whether the slashing of Picasso's *Guernica* was motivated by politics or artistic expression, in neither case should the motivation provide a defence.

Over the years, the *Little Mermaid* sculpture has been knocked off of her stone, had her head and arm cut off and been drenched with paint. At least one of those acts was done by an artist; I submit that nevertheless those acts were violative of the sculptor's integrity right. Nor ought religious or commercial motivations justify a destruction.

Yet in evaluating relief for destructions of original visual artworks, for example assessment of damages, a court may take the defendant's artistic motivation into account. A modifier's destruction of a work done with intent to transform it may mitigate the damages due. In the case described above, as Pinoncely's act was one of artistic expression, he was charged only 60 per cent of the cost of restoration of Duchamp's work.[70]

Further, determining defendant's intention may aid a court in determining whether a modification (including destruction) to a copy of a work has transformed it.[71] But intentional or negligent destruction of an original visual artwork must be considered beyond the scope of defensible modifications.

The argument from reputation disputed

Many commentators presume that the integrity right is at its heart a protection of an artist's reputation. The argument follows that where a work is destroyed, no reputational harm can fall, as there would be 'no existing work to convey a misimpression'.[72] The destruction of a work is said not to 'present [an artist] to the public as the creator of a work not his own, and thus make him subject to criticism for work he has not done'.[73]

I fail to see the logic in this argument. Destruction might reflect poorly on an artist, by implying that his or her work was not worth preserving. More important, I submit that the integrity right is not about authorial reputation, but rather about authorial expression. Destruction is a complete distortion of that expression. Destruction also eradicates the public's right to enjoy the primary artwork.

Destruction by the artist's own act

An exception to the proposed protection against the destruction of original visual artworks is where the artist consents to a work's destruction, or destroys the work him or herself. Actionability against the artist for destroying his or her own artwork would violate the artist's autonomy of expression. The California Act recognizes this: while intentional destruction is actionable, the artist can modify or destroy his or her own work.

Yet at the same time, an artwork may become an element of the public's cultural expression. An original visual artwork such as the *Little Mermaid* sculpture, or the *Mona Lisa*, may become an integral part of culture and indeed a cultural icon. Destruction, even by the artist herself, of the original of such an artwork may be actionable.[74] The artist's destruction of it would harm perhaps not his or her own right of expression, but that of the public.

An exception to this exception however, would be where an artwork is intended by the artist to be temporary. Such would be the case with a work by Christo, such as the temporary 'wrapping' of a bridge, or of Central Park. These are works which 'can only express what their artists intend if they are dismantled after a period of time'.[75] They are complete only once they are destroyed. To interfere with their destruction would be to interfere with their artists' freedom of expression.

Maintenance

On the edge of the spectrum of modifications – just before destruction – lies the issue of maintenance and preservation of artworks. Under UK law, courts would be cautious to allow actions for maintenance.[76] Yet some courts have recognized actionability for failure to maintain artworks. Israeli law requires preservation and maintenance of artworks under certain circumstances.[77] A right to preservation in French law is implied, it has been argued, from the right to completion.[78]

The lack of maintenance or preservation is distortion, and indeed sometimes destruction, even if by negligent omission rather than by intentional act.[79] The standard in the California statute which makes only grossly negligent or intentional destruction actionable is thus inadequate. VARA's distinction that only works of 'recognized stature' are protected from destruction is also inadequate. Rather, destructions of all originals should be actionable, whether intentionally or negligently.

Yet the expectations of the parties play a role in this situation. As seen above with respect to digitalization, where expectations of non-modification are low, the liability threshold will be high. So too where an artist creates a work using materials that he or she knows will disintegrate, or sets up a sculpture in an environment which he or she knows will allow wear on the work, the artist cannot then expect his or her integrity right to require that the work be maintained.[80]

THE SCOPE OF DEFENCES

It has been argued that copies, including adaptations, as well as contextual uses, destructions and maintenance, come within the purview of the integrity right. A broad spectrum of actionable modifications is proposed. Yet where modifications to works represent the modifier's autonomy of expression, the protection of those modifications also must be broad. The nature of the necessary balancing of such autonomies will be considered. Defences pursuant to the integrity right will then be discussed. It will be seen that the autonomy of expression of the public may enter the balance as well.

Broad–broad Balancing

The proposed broad protection of works under the integrity right and also of
defences is in contrast with frequent characterizations of the Anglo-American
copyright system as having specific, narrow protection and broad defences,
while the French system of *droit d'auteur* has broad protection and specific,
narrow defences.[81] In any event the Anglo-American system today arguably
has become broad–broad. Copyright has expanded, such that claimants' rights
are broad. Defendants' rights are broad given the fair use defence. While under
the UK copyright fair dealing doctrine exceptions are specifically listed and
narrow, as are the exceptions to the integrity right,[82] UK law recognizes the
broad doctrine of fair use.[83]

Moreover the broad–broad balancing of rights is appropriate for the
integrity right where it is understood as a freedom of expression. The
European Convention for the Protection of Human Rights and Fundamental
Freedoms ('European Convention') Article 10, incorporated into English law
with the Human Rights Act 1998, recognizes that the freedom of expression
may be restricted by, and balanced with, the rights of others. An integrity right
claimant's freedom of expression likewise will be balanced with the freedom
of expression of the modifier. Liberal readings of the expression rights of both
are necessary.

Defendant's Freedom of Expression

Under the integrity right, defences are necessary to safeguard the modifier's
autonomy of expression. Transformative modification, and modification of a
public forum, are among those that must be protected to ensure the defendant's
freedom of expression.

Transformative modification
The fair use and fair dealing doctrines protect comment, criticism and review
from copyright infringement claims. A comment on a primary work, such as
an interpretation or review of it, may use modification as its method. Fair use
is not specifically applicable to the UK integrity right but broadly applies (and
is specifically provided for as a defence to a VARA claim under US law).[84]
Moreover, comments that modify primary works must be protected as within
the freedom of expression of the modifier.

Some of Hans Christian Andersen's rewriting of earlier folk tales may be
considered comments on those earlier tales. For instance Andersen wrote in an
explanatory note to 'The Wild Swans' that the tale on which it was based, 'The
Proud Maid', contained features 'which could not decently be retold in the
manner in which they were told to me as a child'.[85]

A comment on a primary work may be called a transformation of it, given the comment's different object and purpose. Transformative uses are broader as well. Andersen's tales are of course not only comments, but take a step further in the creative process. Visual and musical artworks comment and develop upon earlier works as well.[86] Transforming earlier works is the way the creative process works. Creativity works via building blocks; even genius breakthroughs react to tradition. Thus borrowing from the past must be protected. Also the creative spark added, namely the transformation of the past, must be protected as the modifier's expression.

Transformative use is more clearly protected in the US than in the UK. Under UK law, courts may look not at how much was changed, but how much was taken from the primary work. If a substantial part was taken, then infringement may well be found.[87] Yet the subject of a section 80 claim is the modification, and it is the modification that may well transform the primary work. With the integrity right, the question is not how much was taken but how much was changed from the primary work. It is submitted that where a defendant has transformed a primary work, the transformative modification must find protection against a section 80 claim as within the modifier's freedom of expression.

Parodies present a case in point. Under UK copyright doctrine, parodies are given 'latitude',[88] and under US law parody is protected as transformative use.[89] Similarity between the parody and the primary work is permitted as the parody needs to 'conjure up' the primary work in order to parody it.[90] Thus a good deal of copying is allowed.

But what of modifications? The parody will distort the primary work, for comic and ironic effect. The distortive modification may attract an integrity right claim. It is on the basis of the parody's object and purpose that it is protected against copyright infringement claims;[91] on the same basis it should be protected against integrity right claims. Yet it is submitted that a parody also must find protection from (a copyright infringement or) an integrity right claim as the modifier's freedom of expression.[92]

Two recent US copyright infringement cases involving parodies may be illustrative. In *Suntrust Bank v Houghton Mifflin Co.*,[93] the novel *A Wind Done Gone* followed a similar story line as in the Margaret Mitchell novel *Gone with the Wind*, but as seen through the eyes of the slaves. The new novel was protected as a parody. In *Mattel Inc v Walking Mountain Productions*,[94] an artist's use of images of Barbie dolls in ironic positions and situations was again protected as a parody.

In both cases, integrity right claims could not have been brought under US law, where VARA protects only visual artists. Yet it is submitted that the transformations made by both parodies to the earlier works would have found protection against hypothetical integrity right claims. The copying and use of the primary works in both cases were justified by the transformations of the primary works; so too the changes wrought by both defendants were justifiable by the transformations made. Both transformations were within the modifier's freedom of expression. Further, both cases involved works – *Gone with the Wind* and Barbie dolls – that have become public fora, to which the discussion will now turn.

Public fora

A further defence to an integrity right claim must lie where a primary work has so entered the cultural language that it has become a cultural icon. Modification of a cultural icon must be protected as within the defendant's freedom of expression. Freedom of expression generally may not be restricted in a public forum.[95] Where artworks are cultural icons, the works themselves have become public fora. Modifications to public fora works are analogous to speech in public fora, and must be protected. On a property model for copyright, works in the public domain may be used without violating copyright; so too on a freedom of expression model for the integrity right, a primary work that has become a public forum may be modified.

'The Little Mermaid' arguably has achieved this cultural status, having become a cultural icon, and thus itself a public forum. A modification of that Andersen tale ought then to find protection. Such would be the case where a modification is transformative of Andersen's tale, but even where it is not. Similarly, Duchamp's painting of a moustache on the *Mona Lisa* would find protection against a hypothetical integrity right claim, for its transformative nature, but also given the integral part that the *Mona Lisa* plays in our cultural expression.

The Modifier's Spectrum of Defences

Another element that may limit the rights of the primary author is the public's autonomy of expression. For instance the protection of modifications of works that have become public fora protects not only the modifiers; it also protects our cultural language. Hence it protects all of us. Use of our language and culture must remain free, to respect the public's autonomy of expression.

Thus copies of public forum images may be modified, even more freely than other works. Yet at the same time, the originals of those works must be protected, arguably even more than other works, due to their part in our cultural expression. Here again the public's autonomy of expression is engaged, but in defence of the primary author rather than the modifier. The public's right to receive ideas and information,[96] that is, the public's autonomy of expression, must be respected. Accordingly, original visual artworks that make up our cultural heritage must be protected against distortion.

Further, we saw above that destructions, which present the complete distortion of the artist's expression, must ground liability. A modifier's claim that the destruction of a primary artwork is a transformative act must be rejected. Here the endpoints of the two spectrums meet: the destruction of original visual artworks is at the end of the spectrum of modifications that ground liability, and the endpoint of the spectrum of defences to modifications. Not only does the protection of the author's autonomy of expression require protection against destruction; also the protection of the public's autonomy of expression supports the preservation of original visual works against destruction.

CONCLUSION

The integrity right protects the author's autonomy of expression. It thus calls for a broad interpretation encompassing the spectrum of modifications. Both originals and copies ought be protected, yet with originals receiving stronger protection. The primary author should be safeguarded against distortion of his or her expression in adaptations, contextual uses, and destructions of his or her artwork as well.

While the primary author must be protected in his or her expression, the modifier must be protected as well. He or she too is an author. Freedom of expression is both the justification for the author's integrity right and for defences to claims pursuant to the right. The approach espoused here advocates a liberal reading of both the right and its limitations.

Also, the autonomy of expression of the public, as reader, viewer or audience of the artwork, must be protected. Prevention of the destruction of original visual works protects the primary artist and the public as well. Further, where a modification is made to a primary work that has so entered our cultural language as to become a public forum, the modifier is not only an author, but also a reader. He or she is a member of the public using our shared language. Protection of the modification of a public forum work protects not only the modifier but the public as well. The analysis thus comes full circle, with the modifier seen as an author and also a reader. The integrity right spectrums require a balancing of autonomies of expression of author, modifier and reader.

NOTES

1. The fuller work of which this chapter takes part addresses that notion of prejudice.
2. That argument I develop in Treiger-Bar-Am (2005).
3. And works of limited editions, 17 USC sec 106A (supp II 1991).
4. 17 USC sec 106. See Goldstein (1983), pp. 49, 53.

5. Rubenfeld (2002), p. 55; Netanel (2001), p. 17 and nn. 61–3.
6. Bredsdorff (1975), pp. 308–13.
7. See Goodman and Elgin (1988), pp. 66–82 (termed there 'variations').
8. See Pon (2004), pp. 1–2.
9. Goodman and Elgin (1988), pp. 73–4.
10. See for example The Brentano String Quartet's *Bach Perspectives: Ten Composers React to the Art of Fugue.*
11. Beardsley (1966), pp. 105, 159–61.
12. See text at nn. 23–6, 54.
13. Teilmann (2005a). It is submitted that the same standard can be applied, but with different parameters, for instance with regard to destructions, as to which she and I take the same approach, see n. 55.
14. Goodman and Elgin (1988), p. 74.
15. Here Teilmann and I agree. Teilmann suggests that the plaintiff-artists in the UK cases of *Tidy v Trustees of the Natural History Museum*, 39 IPR 501 Ch D, and *Pasterfield v Denham* [1999] FSR 168, lost because their claims regarded copies rather than original works of visual art. Teilmann (2005a).
16. This need is recognized in aesthetic theory as well as law. See Zangwill (2001), p. 131.
17. Damich (1988), pp. 15–16.
18. Foucault (Harari (ed.) 1980).
19. I have discussed and rejected the postmodern arguments in Treiger-Bar-Am (2005). The view proposed is not a Romantic argument that the original author must be guarded in her individual genius; a more democratic, universal approach is taken. The instant analysis need not enter the debate as to the nature of originality except as to transformative works, see text at nn. 84–94.
20. Kaplan (1967), pp. 117–21.
21. As to the complexities of the concept of nature in relation to art, see Beardsley (1966).
22. The biography of the author and artist was thus paramount to an understanding of the work. Beardsley (1966), p. 249.
23. Notes of Committee on the Judiciary, House Report No. 94-1476 on sec 102.
24. 17 USC sec 101.
25. Act sec 3(2).
26. See Geller (1994), p. 179. On the authorship norm, the artwork is then conceived of as an extension of the author's personality, Geller (1994), p. 178; perhaps on both the authorship and copyright norms, it can be called a copy of what is in the author's mind.
27. 188 US 239, 249 (1903).
28. *Republic* X.
29. See text at n. 33.
30. *Webster's Dictionary*, cited by Eco (1990), p. 175.
31. Koestler (1964), pp. 400–409.
32. Dutton (2003). For Dutton, the 'expressive authenticity' of a work refers to the work's meaning. It is submitted that determining a work's meaning is not a part of the integrity right analysis, as discussed below, text at n. 39. A forgery also involves deceptive intentions.
33. *University of London Press v Universal Tutorial Press* [1916] 2 Ch 601, 608.
34. Eco (1990), p. 184.
35. Laddie (2000), at 13.18 (s80 covers modification to and not other treatment of a work). See Laddie on *Morrison Leahy*, n. 45.
36. For example, Netanel (1994), p. 38, n. 190 (presentation); Kwall (1985), pp. 95–6 (contextual uses).
37. Article 6*bis* continues: 'which would be prejudicial to his honour or reputation'.
38. Vaver (1983), pp. 358 9. Yet Vaver writes that in Canada, contextual use would not ground liability.
39. Spence points to a change in meaning as violative of an author's integrity right. Spence (2002), p. 399. On some views the French standard requires an objective determination of the author's intended meaning. Netanel (1994), pp. 54–5.
40. The court denied relief. See DaSilva (1980), p. 34 (citation omitted).
41. *Shostakovich v Twentieth Century-Fox Film Corp.*, 80 NYS2d 575 (1948), aff'd, 87 NYS2d

430 (1949). The American courts denied the composer relief, but the French court ruled differently, see Kwall (1985), at n. 157 (citation omitted).

42. *Baltiansky v Kach*, CC 19213/86 (Magistrate, Tel-Aviv) (unpublished).
43. Stokes (2002), at 4.22.
44. *Morrison Leahy Music Ltd v Lightbond Ltd* [1993] EMLR 144, 150.
45. Laddie (2000), at 13.18.
46. Judgment of Mar 13 1973 Trib gr Inst [1974] 48 JCP 224.
47. Netanel (1994), at n. 194.
48. Damich (1988), p. 22.
49. 39 IPR 501 Ch D.
50. 856 F2d 1341, 1343 (9th Cir 1988), cert denied, 489 U.S. 1018 (1989).
51. See Netanel (1994), at n. 194.
52. Laddie (2000), at 3.139.
53. Julius (2002), p. 476.
54. See n. 15. Yet visual works can be detached insofar as they engage intertextual discourse, see nn. 8, 10, such that some distinction must stand between the 'work' and its physical embodiment.
55. Teilmann (2005a) argues that because copyright doctrine was developed with literary works in mind, legal protection against destruction of visual artworks is inadequate.
56. Laddie (2000), at 13.18. Laddie writes that destruction of the physical embodiment of a work is not the same as destruction of the work itself. This argument fails to note the difference in materiality between visual and literary works.
57. Ricketson (1990), p. 474.
58. Compare DaSilva (1980), p. 33; Damich (1988), pp. 18–19, nn. 80, 87–8; Teilmann (2005b).
59. VARA, 17 USC sec 106A(a)(3)(B). See *Carter v Helmsley-Spear, Inc.*, 71 F.3d 77, 81–82 (2d Cir. 1995) cert. den. 517 US 1208 (1996) (destruction in that instance held not actionable).
60. Cal. Civ. Code 987(c) (West Supp. 1983).
61. Vaver (1983), p. 357.
62. Conklin (1994), p. 245.
63. For example, the burning by Ruskin of Turner drawings, Conklin (1994), p. 248.
64. See for example *Crimi v Rutgers Presbyterian Church*, 194 Misc. 570, 89 NYS2d 813 (Sup. Ct. 1949); Damich (1988), at n. 88, citing the French case of *Lacasse v Quenard* Cour d'Appel, Paris, 27 avr 1934, DH1934.385, where a church whitewashed the walls with a fresco that it found did not mesh with the sanctity of the site; Conklin (1994), pp. 250–51.
65. 136 Cong.Rec. H3111-02, H3115 (daily ed. 5 June 1990) (statement of Rep Markey).
66. See Damich (1988), p. 19, on the French cases from Rennes and Grenoble.
67. If the Goya works had been unique originals rather than etchings, the violation would have been more severe.
68. This is so even where the destruction is reversible (through cleaning and restoration such as with Duchamp's work), or even if the destruction is only of a portion of a work (as with Goya's works).
69. *Campbell v MGN* [2004] EMLR 15, at para. 117.
70. Teilmann (2004). Yet Pinoncely was also reported to have smashed the Fountain (Teilmann 2004). That irreversible destructive act should have met with more severe legal consequence.
71. See n. 92.
72. Damich (1988), p. 33; ibid p. 25, n. 159.
73. Roeder (1940), p. 569. See also Kwall (1985), p. 9.
74. Under French law, an artist can destroy her work until publication, as a necessary analogue to the right of disclosure. DaSilva (1980), p. 17.
75. Young (1989), p. 373.
76. Cornish and Llewelyn (2003), at 11–77.
77. *Fabian v Municipality of Ramat Gan*, CC (Magistrate. Tel-Aviv) 73028/97 (unpublished).
78. Netanel (1994), p. 39, discussing *Dubuffet v Renault* (citation omitted).
79. Conklin (1994), pp. 231–3.

80. VARA recognizes this, at 17 USC 106A c(1). See also Damich (1988), p. 19 (on the *Grenoble* case); Nemser (2002), p. 18 (Hesse remarking that she feels 'a little guilty' when people want to buy a work made out of rubber; 'I want to write them a letter and say it's not going to last . . . Life doesn't last; art doesn't last.').
81. Geller (1994), p. 170; Strowel (1994), pp. 249–50.
82. Laddie critiques the narrowness of the range of non-infringing acts of modification, Laddie (2000), at 13.28.
83. Laddie (2000), at 3.134 (literary works), 4.54 (artistic works).
84. On UK law, see n. 83, n. 91. Fair use under the US Copyright Act, 17 USC sec 107, including comment, is a defence to integrity right claims under VARA, sec. 106A.
85. Bredsdorff (1975), p. 310.
86. See nn. 8, 10.
87. *Schweppes Ltd v Wellingtons Ltd* [1984] FSR 210; *Williamson Music Ltd v P Carson Partnership Ltd* [1987] FSR 97. Yet where the material taken is altered or the context changed, no substantial part is incorporated into the second work. Laddie (2000), 3.139.
88. Laddie (2000), at 3.142 (the law 'smiles on' parodies and may indulge them by the device of holding that a parodist has not taken a substantial part).
89. *Campbell v Acuff-Rose Music, Inc.*, 510 U.S. 569, 590 (1994). Compare French law, *Code de la propriete intellectuelle*, Art L 122-5, and Germany's Alcolix case [1995] 7 EIPR D-198.
90. *Williamson Music* [1987] FSR 97; *Campbell v Acuff-Rose Music, Inc.*, 510 U.S. 569, 590 (1994).
91. Under UK law, Laddie (2000) at 4.54 (courts look to object and purpose). Under US law, Copyright Act 1976 sec 107 (fair use doctrine includes evaluating the 'purpose and character of the use'); *Campbell v Acuff-Rose*, 510 U.S. at 586–7 ('the extent of permissible copying varies with the purpose and character of the use').
92. Even with intentional distortion, the parodist's object and purpose is defensible expression. Treiger (1989), p.1219.
93. 252 F.3d 1165 (11th Cir. 2001).
94. 353 F.3d 792 (9th Cir. 2004).
95. Such is the rule under Article 10 of the European Convention but also previously under UK law, see Feldman (2002), p. 1015.
96. Article 10 of the European Convention; *Campbell v MGN* [2004] EMLR 15 at para. 116.

REFERENCES

Beardsley, Monroe C. (1966), *Aesthetics from Classical Greece to the Present: A Short History*, Tuscaloosa and London: University of Alabama Press, reprinted New York: Macmillan.

Bredsdorff, Elias (1975), *Hans Christian Andersen: The Story of His Life and Work 1805–75*, London: Phaidon Press.

Conklin, J.E. (1994), *Art Crime*, London and Westport, CT: Praeger.

Cornish, William and David Llewelyn (2003), *Intellectual Property: Patents, Copyright, Trademarks and Allied Rights*, 5th edn, London: Sweet & Maxwell.

Damich, E. (1988), 'The Right of Personality: A Common Law Basis for the Protection of the Moral Rights of Authors', *Georgia Law Review*, **23**, 1–96.

DaSilva, R.J., (1980), 'Droit Moral and the Amoral Copyright: A Comparison of Artists' Rights in France and the United States', *Bulletin, Copyright Society of the USA*, **1** (34), pp. 1–58.

Dutton, Denis (2003), 'Authenticity in Art', in J. Levison (ed.), *The Oxford Handbook of Aesthetics*, New York: Oxford University Press, pp. 258–74.

Eco, Umberto (1990), *The Limits of Interpretation*, Indianapolis, IN: Indiana University Press.

Feldman, David (2002), *Civil Liberties and Human Rights in England and Wales*, 2nd edn, Oxford: Oxford University Press.

Foucault, Michel (1980), 'What is an Author?', in J.V. Harari (ed.), *Textual Strategies: Perspectives in Post-Structuralist Criticism*, London: Methuen, pp. 141–60.

Geller, Paul Edward (1994), 'Must Copyright be Forever Caught between Marketplace and Authorship Norms?' in Brad Sherman and Alain Strowel (eds), *Of Authors and Origins*, Oxford: Clarendon Press, pp. 159–201.

Goldstein, P. (1983), 'Adaptation Rights and Moral Rights in the United Kingdom, the United States and the Federal Republic of Germany', *International Review of Industrial Property and Copyright Law*, **14**, 43–59.

Goodman, Nelson and Catherine Z. Elgin (1988), *Reconceptions in Philosophy and Other Arts and Sciences*, London: Routledge.

Julius, Anthony (2002), 'Art Crimes', in Daniel McClean and Karsten Schubert (eds), *Dear Images: Art, Copyright and Culture*, London: Ridinghouse, pp. 473–503.

Kaplan, Benjamin (1967), *An Unhurried View of Copyright*, New York: Columbia University Press.

Koestler, Arthur (1964), *The Act of Creation*, London: Hutchinson & Co.

Kwall, R. (1985), 'Copyright and the Moral Right: Is an American Marriage Possible?' *Vanderbilt Law Review*, **38**, 1–97.

Laddie, Sir Hugh, Peter Prescott and Mary Vitoria (2000), *The Modern Law of Copyright and Designs*, 3rd edn, London: Butterworths.

Nemser, Cindy (1970), 'A Conversation with Eva Hesse', in Mignon Nixon (ed.), *Eva Hesse (October Files)*, Cambridge, MA and London: MIT Press, pp. 1–24.

Netanel, N. (1994), 'Alienability Restrictions and the Enhancement of Author Autonomy in United States and Continental Copyright Law', *Cardozo Arts and Entertainment Law Journal*, **12**, 1–78.

Netanel, N.W. (2001), 'Locating Copyright within the First Amendment Skein', *Stanford Law Review*, **54**, 1–86.

Plato, *Republic* X.

Pon, Lisa (2004), *Raphael, Durer, and Marcantonio Raimondi: Copying and the Italian Renaissance Print*, New Haven and London: Yale University Press.

Ricketson, S. (1990), 'Is Australia in Breach of its International Obligations with respect to the Protection of Moral Rights?', *Melbourne University Law Review*, **17**, 462–83.

Roeder, M.A. (1940), 'The Doctrine of Moral Right: A Study in the Law of Artists, Authors and Creators', *Harvard Law Review*, **53**, 554–78.

Rubenfeld, J. (2002), 'The Freedom of Imagination: Copyright's Constitutionality', *Yale Law Journal*, **112**, 1–60.

Spence, Michael (2002), 'Justifying Copyright', in Daniel McClean and Karsten Schubert, eds, *Dear Images: Art, Copyright and Culture*, London: Ridinghouse, pp. 389–403.

Stokes, Simon (2002), *Digital Copyright: Law and Practice*, London: Butterworths.

Strowel, Alain (1994), 'Droit d'auteur and Copyright: Between History and Nature', in Brad Sherman and Alain Strowel (eds), *Of Authors and Origins*, Oxford: Clarendon Press, pp. 235–53.

Teilmann, Stina (2004), *British and French Copyright: A Historical Study of Aesthetic Implications*, PhD thesis, University of Southern Denmark.

Teilmann, S. (2005a), 'Framing the Law: The Right of Integrity in Britain', *European Intellectual Property Review*, **27** (1), 19–24.

Teilmann, Stina (2005b), 'Justifications for Copyright: The Evolution of le droit moral', in Fiona Macmillan (ed.), *New Directions in Copyright Law*, Vol. 1, Cheltenham, UK and Northampton, MA: Edward Elgar, pp. 68–82.

Treiger-Bar-Am, Leslie Kim (1989), 'Protecting Satire Against Libel Claims: A New Reading of the First Amendment's Opinion Privilege', *Yale Law Journal*, **98**, 1215–34.

Treiger-Bar-Am, L.K. (2005), 'The Moral Right of Integrity: A Freedom of Expression', in Fiona Macmillan (ed.), *New Directions in Copyright*, Vol. 2, Cheltenham, UK and Northampton, MA, US: Edward Elgar, pp. 127–58.

Vaver, D. (1983), 'Authors' Moral Rights in Canada', *International Review of Industrial Property and Copyright Law*, **14**, 329–71.

Young, J.O. (1989), 'Destroying Works of Art', *Journal of Aesthetics and Art Criticism*, **47** (4), 367–73.

Zangwill, N. (2001), 'Aesthetic Functionalism', in E. Brady and J. Levinson (eds), *Aesthetic Concepts*, Oxford: Clarendon Press, pp. 123–48.

5. What might Hans Christian Andersen say about copyright today?

Fiona Macmillan

INTRODUCTION

To ask what Hans Christian Andersen might say about copyright today tends to suggest that he waxed loquacious on the subject in the mid- to late nineteenth century. This is patently not the case. It is likely that along with other European writers of this period[1] he was concerned about the international protection of his literary works.[2] Certainly, his relationship with Charles Dickens, a famous campaigner for bilateral copyright treaties (see Welsh 1987), is well documented – it was even somewhat spiky.[3] Whether their conversations ever roamed over the subject of international harmonization of copyright protection is not known (or at least not documented).

To attempt, as this chapter does, to address the question of Andersen's attitude to today's copyright regime is a risky business. Aside from what we know of his own literary and publishing practice, the only evidence we have of Andersen's likely views on this topic is the moral and ethical positions and opinions that apparently underlie his famous and extensive collection of stories. In this chapter I attempt to glean these positions and opinions and to reconsider the critique of the copyright system contained in my earlier work (for example Macmillan 2002a, 2002b, 2005) in the light of them. The inherent subjectivity, and scope for error, of this approach is acknowledged from the outset. There is also an obvious potential for temporal distortion. In the light of the realities of the twenty-first century and, in the context of this chapter, the twenty-first century copyright regime, perhaps Andersen would have modified his views. On the other hand, to the extent that we place value on Andersen's stories in other contexts, we often seem to believe that they speak to the human condition generally and without particular temporal constraint. If this is because we reinterpret them to suit the tenor of our times, then this chapter is consistent with current reading practice. More sceptical readers should feel free however to regard it as a flight of imaginative fancy.

COPYRIGHT, CULTURE AND TRADE

Originality

As a matter of rhetoric, copyright (and intellectual property as a whole) has associated itself with concepts of genius, creativity and culture.[4] A closer look however reveals that copyright has often failed these concepts (Macmillan 1998). An example of this at the general level might be the very low threshold of the 'originality' requirement in relation to literary, dramatic, musical and artistic works (Macmillan Patfield 1997). It is relatively clear that the content of this requirement[5] derived from concerns that copyright should confer a monopoly over the form of, rather than the ideas in, a work and accordingly the notion of originality attached itself to differences in form (Chartier 1994). Nevertheless copyright law has been left in a situation where it grants monopoly protection to works that have little to do with any accepted notions of creativity.[6] It is likely that Hans Christian Andersen would have found this somewhat unpalatable. It is clear from many of his stories that he placed a great premium on talent and artistic creativity,[7] which is hardly surprising. In 1837 he wrote, 'A great poet in this world and an even greater one in the next, that's what I dream of being'.[8] Consistently with this, he was somewhat contemptuous of the volumes of what he believed to be very inferior 'poetry' that poured onto the market (Crone Frank and Frank 2004a, p. 269) and asides like the following, in his story 'The Nightingale', reflect this: 'And poets – those who could write – wrote the most beautiful poems, all about the nightingale in the woods by the deep sea' (Crone Frank and Frank 2004a, 128).

Preserving the Cultural Commons

Another example of copyright failing creativity and culture lies in the weakness of the fair dealing laws. In the famous Koons's 'String of Puppies' case,[9] Koons's use of an image in a photograph of a couple holding eight puppies as the basis of a sculpture failed to escape copyright infringement on the basis of the fair use defence. Koons argued that he was entitled to the protection of the fair use doctrine on the basis that his work was a parody for the purpose of criticizing the banality of popular cultural images.[10] It was held however that the fair use defence only applies where the infringing work has used a copyright work for the purpose of criticizing that copyright work and not where it has been used for the purpose of criticizing society in general. The fact that the fair use doctrine did not entitle Koons to engage in an act of cultural pastiche and parody is of concern if one thinks that copyright law should be about the promotion of cultural activity and diversity. It is of serious concern if one subscribes to the postmodernist view that modern cultural products are all about pastiche or parody or both,[11] whether consciously referential or not. What is happening here is that copyright is failing to secure what has been described as the cultural or intellectual commons.[12] This is because one way of safeguarding the intellectual commons is by strong fair dealing or fair use laws.[13] It is arguable that a diverse and vigorous cultural development cannot occur without safeguarding the intellectual commons (Macmillan 1998, 2002a).

Certainly both his own practice as a writer, and the content of some of his stories, make it clear that Andersen regarded tranformative use of the cultural commons as creatively important. Andersen used the commons extensively as source material for his stories.[14] In both 'Auntie Toothache' and 'The Shadow' he refers directly to the practice of using the stories of others. His reference to this literary practice in 'The Shadow' makes it clear that he was aware of the distinction between imitating and some more transformative use.[15] In the light of this, it is interesting that this story, which concerns the separation of a learned man and his shadow, plays upon the idea of something that sounds a little like a poetic commons. The shadow tells his originator that when they parted company he discovered that Poetry lived across the street:

> 'Do you know who lived in the house across the street?' the shadow asked. 'The most beautiful of all: Poetry. I was there for three weeks, and it was like being there for three thousand years, reading everything that has ever been written. Believe me, I'm telling you the truth. I've seen everything and know everything' . . . 'What was it like in the room farthest inside?' the learned man asked. 'Was it like a fresh forest? Was it like a holy church? Was it like the clear starry sky when you stand on a tall mountain?' 'It was everything' the shadow said . . . (Crone Frank and Frank 2004a, 211–12)

Instrumentalism and Fundamentalism

Copyright's failure to secure the commons is one indication of the fact that it has not supported creativity and culture at a fundamental level. Rather, it may be argued, its relationship to these concepts is instrumental.[16] That is, copyright has been well used as an instrument for promoting trade in the cultural output that comes within its purview. Accordingly copyright deals with works in relation to which it subsists as products or commodities, the importance of which are reflected in their impact on trade rather than in any value they may enjoy in their own right. A fundamental relationship between copyright, culture and creativity, on the other hand, would result in copyright stimulating and protecting cultural output on the basis that it has a non-economic value in itself as an expression of human creativity.

The negotiation and conclusion of the World Trade Organization's Agreement on Trade Related Aspects of Intellectual Property Rights (the

TRIPs Agreement) is not only one of the best examples of the ascendancy of the instrumental approach, but it has also introduced a shift in intellectual property discourse that further consolidates this approach. The conclusion of the TRIPs Agreement, as one of the multilateral trade agreements of the World Trade Organization (WTO), was formally driven by the United States. However lying behind the government of the United States as formal actor was a formidable coalition of US-based multinational corporate interests (see Sell 2003, especially Chapters 5 and 6). Acting in concert with these corporate interests, the US used two tools in particular to drive the TRIPs negotiations (Blakeney 1996, Chapter 1). First, it took on the burden of convincing the GATT Council that intellectual property rights were relevant to GATT,[17] by citing evidence of massive trade losses as a consequence of the non-enforcement or absence of intellectual property laws.[18] The second tool used by the US to drive the TRIPs process was the amendment in 1984 to section 301 of the Trade Act of 1974 to make intellectual property protection explicitly actionable under section 301 (Blakeney 1996, 4). This was followed by the introduction in the Omnibus Trade and Competitiveness Act of 1988 of 'Special 301', enabling the US Trade Representative to put countries that failed to protect US intellectual property on a watch-list with a view to investigation and possible trade retaliation (Blakeney 1996, 5). The ensuing TRIPs Agreement might be argued to be the central normative force in global copyright law.[19]

For those who would want to see copyright bolstering the fundamental rather than the instrumental role of culture, some comfort might be taken from the fact that the TRIPs Agreement refers to the trade-related aspects of intellectual property and thereby suggests that there may be some other aspects – but it is cold comfort. The truth is that, at least in the Anglo-Saxon model of copyright law, we had already gone a long way down the instrumental and trade-related road before the US did us the favour of bringing it all out into the open. In my earlier work (Macmillan 2002a, 2002b, 2005), I have argued that there are five interdependent aspects of Anglo-American copyright law that have been essential to the commodification process and to copyright's consequent instrumental approach to culture and creativity. The first and most basic tool of commodification is the alienability of the copyright interest. A second significant aspect of copyright law making it an important tool of trade and investment is its duration. The long period of copyright protection increases the asset value of individual copyright interests (Towse 1999, 98–9). Thirdly, the progressive horizontal expansion of copyright to cover a wider range of works has increasingly sucked cultural production into the purview of copyright law. Fourthly, vertical expansion in the form of strong commercial distribution rights,[20] especially those which give the copyright holder control over imports and rental rights, have put copyright owners in a particularly strong market position, especially in the global context. Finally, the power of the owners of copyright in relation to all those wishing to use copyright material has been undermined by a contraction of some of the most significant defences to copyright infringement. Of particular note in this respect are the repeated assaults on the cogency and practical utility of the fair dealing and public interest defences to copyright infringement.

The trade-related nature of the instrumental approach to culture and creativity manifested in modern copyright law might have been as much of a surprise to Andersen as it would have been to the well-known nineteenth-century literary advocates of an international copyright regime. However there is reason to think that a somewhat different type of instrumental approach to literature was familiar to Andersen. 'Auntie Toothache', the last story in Andersen's last published collection (Crone Frank and Frank 2004a, 282), begins with a wry passage that is apparently a narration by Andersen himself (Crone Frank and Frank 2004a, 282):

> Where did we get this story?
> Do you want to know?
> We got it from the rubbish bin – the one with old scraps of paper in it.
> Lots of good rare books have gone to the general store and the grocer's – not to be read but as paper to wrap flour and coffee beans, salt herring, butter, and cheese. Literature, after all, has its uses.
> Things are often tossed into the rubbish that shouldn't be.
>
> (Crone and Frank 2004a, 247)

Perhaps Andersen would have regarded instrumentalism as inevitable and, if so, might even have preferred the modern version, which at least does not necessarily result in the destruction of the work.

COMMODIFICATION AND THE 'AUTHOR'

Perhaps copyright's instrumentalism does not cause nineteenth-century authors to spin in their graves. But one wonders whether their spirits (and cadavers) would be quite so calm about the way in which copyright's process of commodification deals with the author. The fact that famous nineteenth-century authors were at the vanguard of the movement for improved international copyright protection suggests that they regarded the author as being at the centre of the copyright system. Perhaps, like some modern writers, they viewed the parallel emergence of the author as a romantic concept and the author as a construct of copyright law as demonstrating an inherent connection (see for example Rose 1993). However copyright's commodification of creativity casts some doubt upon this. Clearly there is some basis for the argument that the relationship between copyright and the 'author' is more than merely coincidental. For example the development in copyright law of the moral rights of authors, as distinct from their transmissible economic rights, owes more than a passing debt to the romantic idea of the author (see for example Woodmansee and Jaszi 1994). There are also a number of ways in which the scope of the economic rights comprised in copyright appear to have been extended as a result of the influence of romantic conceptions of authorship and the author's right to control the work. Lionel Bently (Bently 1994, 979) argues that increases in the duration of copyright protection,[21] restrictions on the fair dealing defence,[22] and the extension of the exclusive rights of the copyright holder to rights over adaptations and derivations of the work (for example screenplays or performances), are all manifestations of this influence. In this sense romantic notions of the author have been significant in creating a copyright climate that has allowed the process (and consequences) of commodification to flourish.

This appears to be a counter-intuitive proposition. The moral rights of authors, being non-transmissible and (largely) non-economic, might have some reasonable claim to being regarded as a counterweight to both the process and consequences of commodification, in the sense that the ability of copyright owners to deal with the work is constrained by the moral rights attached to it. If moral rights are the epitome of the influence of romantic literary property notions on the development of copyright law, how can responsibility for stoking the fires of commodification also be levelled at the romantic concept of the author? In approaching an answer to this question it is important to remember that while copyright's concept of the author has been influenced by the romantic literary concept, the relationship between these two concepts has never been inherent or absolute (see Saunders 1992). What made the notion of literary property so open to commodification through copyright was the alienability of the copyright interest. It seems likely that copyright developed as an alienable property interest because the law's concept of property is, by and large, attached to concepts of alienability. Copyright's development of the concept of authorship therefore accommodates romantic ideas within the law's concept of the meaning of property as an alienable interest. Thus, as Bently argues, the concept of the author in copyright law operates as a point of attachment and divestment:

> While copyright may be built on an image of creative authorship, copyright uses that image as a point of attachment – a point at which to ascribe a property right and by which that right can be determined. But the essence of that ascription is that it is a divestible or alienable right. In law, authorship is a point of origination of a property right which, thereafter, like other property rights, will circulate in the market, ending up in the control of the person who can exploit it most profitably. Since copyright serves paradoxically to vest authors with property only to enable them to divest that property, the author is a notion which needs only to be sustainable for an instant. (Bently 1994, 980–81)[23]

In modern copyright law therefore the concept of authorship is no more and no less than the essential first step in the process of commodification. This means that copyright law, at times, recognizes 'authors' that would not be accommodated by romantic theories of authorial creativity. An important example of this phenomenon is the recognition of producers as authors of sound recordings[24] and as authors or joint authors[25] of films. In these cases, financial investment takes the place of creativity as the touchstone of authorship. So far as copyright law is concerned, films and sound recordings are born as commodities, rather than as creative works.[26] At other times copyright law denies the status of 'author' to those who have participated in the creative process. Those excluded range from significant stylistic influences, such as the forerunners in a musical genre, to actual participants in the creation of the work in question, such as musical collaborators or film editors. The process of exclusion is often remarkable for its (one-eyed and myopic) focus on the moment of fixation of the work in material form (see for example Vaidhyanathan 2001, Chapter 4). But as Bently says, in copyright law 'the author is a notion which needs only to be sustainable for an instant' (Bently 1994, 981). It is this uninspiring and unromantic notion of authorship that gives rise to copyright's alienable property right and that thus constitutes the essential building block of the copyright's commodification of creativity. The other tools of commodification, commercial distribution rights, duration, weak fair dealing or fair use defences, would be of hardly any value in the commodification process without the author and its alienable property right over the work. Built upon the alienable property right however, they create a sturdy edifice for the commodification process.

Hans Christian Andersen might very well have accepted the idea that the work, once put into the public domain, is severed from the author and takes on a life of its own independent of authorial control. One could read 'The Shadow' as reflecting this type of relationship with the products of one's own mind.[27] However, it is difficult to read into this an acceptance of the marginalization of the author in favour of another controller in the form of a new copyright owner. One suspects that Andersen would have decried the marginalization of the author in modern copyright law.[28] Nevertheless he might have been critical of the extent to which at least some authors were complicit in this process. In 'The Tinderbox' the young soldier breaks his promise to the old witch and refuses to hand the apparently worthless tinderbox to her, and this despite the fact that he has been well rewarded for undertaking the mission to retrieve the tinderbox.[29] This turns out to be a wise choice for the soldier since he discovers later that the tinderbox has an infinite ability to provide for his needs and desires, and thus is far more valuable than money in the hand. One reading of this story is that if something apparently worthless is highly prized by another, then it may be that it has a value yet to be revealed. Andersen might have noted, had he been asked about it, that many authors have failed to appreciate this point when assigning away their copyright, often for very little. The fact that the commodifiers (publishers, film production companies, television and other broadcasting companies, entertainment conglomerates, and so on) have been so keen to acquire copyright interests should perhaps have alerted authors to their value. It is even possible that Andersen would have a grudging admiration for those media and entertainment corporations that have so astutely built up their vast copyright portfolios. Stories such as 'Little Claus and Big Claus' and 'The Emperor's New Clothes' are not particularly condemnatory of those who take advantage of the stupidity of others. However an argument may be made that the law sometimes needs to protect people from their own folly or naivety. This is especially so when, as in this case, the consequences of a failure to do just that have an impact on the way in which society engages with creativity and cultural production. The critique of the commodification of creativity in this chapter recognizes that at least some 'authors' may have connived in their own loss of status within the copyright system, but it is more concerned with the impact of copyright's tendency to commodification on society at large.

Unless we regard copyright as being just about trade or economics, then there is no overwhelmingly compelling reason why the integrity of copyright law requires this structural tendency to commodification. Justifications of commodification generally seem to hinge around the need to protect the interests of the commodifiers and to encourage them to invest in the exploitation of copyright works. Something about this sounds fishy:

> Where else do we say that it is a matter of equity that investors should make a profit? Usually our view is that investors venture out into any market at their own risk. If a given market happens to be structured in such a way as to yield poor returns, that may be a matter of utilitarian or economic concern, but it is hardly a matter of intervention on grounds of fairness to cover investors' costs. (Waldron 1993, 854)

On the other hand, it might be possible to justify a degree of commodification by reference to the need for creators to be remunerated in order to encourage them to create[30] and by reference to the need for cultural works to be disseminated in order to reap the benefits of their creation. This latter point would fit in with the argument that an important aspect of copyright is its communication role (van Caenegem 1995; Netanel 1996). Whether some degree of commodification is essential to the integrity of copyright law or not, the point is that we have allowed the process of commodification to take over copyright without really asking what the costs and consequences of this commodification are.

THE ACQUISITION OF PRIVATE POWER

Global Rights, Global Distribution, Global Dominance

One consequence of the commodification of creativity through copyright is the build-up of private power over cultural output (Bettig 1996; Towse 1999). The way in which the distribution rights attaching to copyright might be used by a multinational corporation to carve up the international market (Macmillan 1998) is a small part of a much bigger story about the way in which commodification can lead to global domination of a market for cultural output. The capacity to achieve a position of global power is a combination of the international nature of intellectual property rights, the fact that many of the corporations owning the rights operate on a multinational level, and the fact that many of the media and entertainment corporations are conglomerates that display a high degree of horizontal integration by operating in a number of different areas of cultural output (Towse 1999, 97–8). Some are also vertically integrated with a high degree of control over the entire distribution process.[31] The oligopolistic nature of the media and entertainment sector is accentuated through the prevailing pattern of horizontal and vertical mergers.

The fashion for horizontal and vertical mergers and acquisitions in the media and entertainment sector began in the 1970s. It seems that one force driving these mergers is the desire to increase the level of corporate ownership over copyright interests. As Smiers puts it:

> The best way to acquire rights on huge quantities of entertainment and other artistic materials is through mergers. Synergy is the rationale for media conglomerates snatching up as much copyrighted material as they can. (Smiers 2002, 120)[32]

Such activity is not only stimulated by the significant asset value of copyright interests,[33] it also reflects the strategic business concerns. Bettig describes mergers and acquisitions in the media and entertainment sector as 'a process of reorganization around core and related lines of business along with an effort to establish alliances across national boundaries with market dominant firms in other countries' (Bettig 1996, 37). This process has been reflected in the activities of media and entertainment corporations such as Viacom Inc. (which owns Paramount Communications Inc.), Time Warner Inc., News Corporation Ltd and Walt Disney so that the activities of these corporations involve diversified lines of business including film and television production and distribution, international ownership of cinema chains, broadcasting, cable networks, music and book publishing.[34] Beginning in the late 1980s there has also been a trend on the part of corporations that were primarily engaged in the production of technology used in the distribution of media and entertainment content to merge with or acquire interests in corporations producing that content. So for example Sony Corporation acquired Columbia Pictures Entertainment in 1989, and Matsushita Electric Industrial Company acquired MCA, the parent company of universal pictures, in 1991. The most significant recent example of this tendency towards the integration of corporations owning rights over content and distribution of filmed entertainment, and those owning rights over the technology of distribution, is the merger of AOL and Time Warner. Not only do these mergers increase the concentration of copyright ownership in the media and entertainment sector, but they also place the ownership of the patent rights over the distribution technology in the same hands.[35] This process of concentration seems to be leading inexorably to the conclusion that 'a handful – six to ten vertically integrated communications companies – will soon produce, own and distribute the bulk of the culture and information circulating in the global marketplace' (Bettig 1996, 38).

Copyright has been an essential tool in the orchestration of this type of global oligopoly because of the long period of control that it gives its owner over the distribution of content (Towse 1999). The market for filmed entertainment provides a particularly good example of this. In this market the copyright monopoly, allied with the vertical integration of the market, has allowed the major media and entertainment corporations to dominate, not only the market for first-run cinema, but also the markets that have been created as a consequence of the development of new technologies for the distribution of filmed entertainment. That is, the same oligopolistic market structure controls the market for television feature films, cable transmission of films, videos and now DVDs (Bettig 1996, 39–42). The video market, now being superseded by the market for DVDs, has been a particularly significant market for the major media and entertainment corporations (Macmillan 2002b).

The modern vertically integrated multinational business enterprise is essentially a product of the twentieth century. Specifically, it ascended spectacularly after the Second World War when the US, as the dominant capitalist power, effectively 'internalized' (Arrighi 2002, 72–3, 281ff) international trade within the domains of its large trading corporations. It is almost impossible to work out what Andersen, who was used to personal dealings with national publishing houses,[36] would have made of the twenty-first century multinational media and entertainment empires. Would he have objected to the power of capital, and the subjugation of other values, represented by these entities? Stories like 'Kids' Talk'[37] seem to reflect on a certain vulgarity inherent in the pursuit of money: 'The merchant had brains and heart too, but people talked less about that than about all his money' (Crone Frank and Frank 2004a, 230). On the other hand, the story is triumphalist about the way in which the excluded low-born and poor child grows up to be extremely rich. In the end, it is hard to read much more into this story than its reflection of Andersen's own insecurity about his financial, intellectual and social status.

The Role of Technology

Technological developments tend to cause crises for the media and entertainment oligopolies by threatening their control over distribution. Copyright law, which is the key to the control of distribution, is intimately bound up with these technological developments because they raise questions about either the scope or the enforceability of copyright. Thus the major music labels and music publishers leapt to the defence of their market control in a series of copyright cases in the US directed at preventing the distribution of music on the Internet by the use of MP3 files. The upshot of at least some of these proceedings is that the major record labels have entered (or are negotiating to enter) into distribution arrangements with online music providers (Macmillan 2002a).

Another recent controversy, which has created alarm in the ranks of the filmed entertainment industry and has seen the majors jumping to the defence of their distribution monopoly, was the release of the DeCSS (Decrypted Content Scrambling System) source code. This source code allows the copying of DVDs and their transmission via the Internet. Not only did the eight US majors of the filmed entertainment industry take an action against the publishers of sites that had disclosed the code, they also commenced proceedings against the campaigning group Copyleft for reprinting the code onto a T-shirt.[38] Of the three Internet site publishers pursued by the film industry majors, two negotiated consent decrees. The third, who goes by the underground name of Eric Corley,[39] had published the code in his online journal, *2600: The Hacker Quarterly*, and chose to defend the case. On 17 August 2000 US District Court Judge Lewis Kaplan handed down a decision preventing *2600* from continuing to publish the DeCSS code on its website.[40] This decision, which may resonate in European jurisdictions as a result of Article 6 of the Copyright in the Information Society Directive, has now been affirmed on appeal.[41]

Judge Kaplan's original decision was based on a provision of the Digital Millennium Copyright Act.[42] This Act forms part of the amended US Copyright Act of 1976. The Act, in section 1201(a)(1), prohibits the circumvention of technological measures controlling access to a copyright work. Section 1201(a)(2) prohibits a person, amongst other things, offering to the public or providing 'any technology, product, service, device, component or part thereof' that:

1. is primarily designed for the purpose of circumventing a technological measure,
2. has limited commercially significant purpose other than circumvention of a technological measure, or

3. is marketed with personal knowledge of use in circumventing a technological measure.

Corley was held to have breached this section. This was despite the fact that section 1201(c) of the Act provides that nothing in the section limits the rights of free speech for activities using consumer electronics, telecommunications or computing products, nor the rights of fair use with respect to copyright works. Taking the matter of free speech first, there is a reasonable argument to be made that merely posting and linking the DeCSS code, as opposed to making use of it, is purely expressive. If this is so, then injuncting such behaviour raises serious free speech concerns.[43] The US Court of Appeals for the Second Circuit accepted that the decryption code was constitutionally protected speech. However it held that the right of the copyright holder to protect its property must be balanced against the right to free speech and that, as a result, the restraint imposed by the circumvention provisions of the Digital Copyright Millennium Act was not an undue restraint on speech.

So far as the issue of fair use and fair dealing is concerned, the consequences of the case are also serious. The Court of Appeals noted that Corley was not claiming to have made a fair use of the copyright material. However it did observe that fair use does not involve a right to access to copyright material 'in order to copy it by the fair user's preferred technique or in the format of the original'.[44] Overall, the Court of Appeals seems to have brushed aside the combined result of its determinations on the free speech and fair dealing issues. If the publication and use of the DeCSS code is not permitted it will not be possible to copy any part of a film on DVD. Consequently, the right to engage in a fair use or fair dealing with the film, for example for criticism or review, is meaningless. Thus the effect of this case is to strengthen considerably the rights of the filmed entertainment corporations over their output and fatally undermine the cogency of the fair use and fair dealing defence. The case does more than merely maintain the exclusive distribution rights of the majors.

Coming hot on the heels of the decision of the Court of Appeals in the DVD case is a case that looks very much as though it will be the film industry's Napster. The complaint in *Metro-Goldwyn-Mayer Studios Inc v Grokster Ltd*[45] was filed on behalf of the film studios making up the Motion Pictures Association of America (MPAA) in November 2001. It makes up one part of two closely associated actions, the other filed as a class action on behalf of all music publishers represented by the Harry Fox Agency, against the same defendants in respect of the same activities. The activities complained of relate to peer-to-peer file sharing software provided by the defendants, which it is alleged amounts to 'a 21st century piratical bazaar where the unlawful exchange of protected materials takes place across the vast expanse of the Internet'[46] or 'a cybernetic Alice's Restaurant [where] the menu is our protected content'[47] – either way, a copyright infringement. The software in question, variously known as KaZaA, Grokster or Morpheus (but referred to as Morpheus hereafter), can be downloaded by the user from the defendant's website. Once the user has logged on to the defendant's server, it is connected to a so-called 'supernode', a more powerful computer operated by another user. Search requests are sent to the supernode, which searches the computers of other users in the Morpheus network and compiles search results. The user then selects and downloads the files that it wants directly from the other user.

The plaintiffs in the Morpheus case appear to have accepted that the issue is not about the software per se,[48] but rather about the behaviour of the defendants in relation to the use of the software.[49] That is, they argue that the defendants are 'knowingly and systematically, participating in, facilitating, materially contributing to, and encouraging'[50] infringing behaviour of the users. Concerns that the entertainment industry is not attempting to use copyright law in a fashion that is anti-innovation should not however be regarded as being allayed. The line between accepting the lawfulness of the programme, but not of its distribution, is a rather blurry (if not completely meaningless) one. This is particularly so when there is a good argument to be made that distribution is the only thing the defendants have actually done. The defendants draw the attention of the users to their obligations under copyright law. Unlike the famous Napster programme, the Morpheus programme does not rely on a central server system to hold an index of all available files on the network.[51] This was crucial to the decision of the Central District Court of California[52] granting partial summary judgment to the defendants and denying it to the plaintiffs. This decision was affirmed by the US Court of Appeal for the Ninth Circuit, but on appeal the US Supreme Court handed down a decision in favour of the plaintiff studios.[53] The decision of the Supreme Court is very narrowly tailored to the facts of the case and the jury (of public, legal and academic opinion) is still out on the question of whether innovations in the use of the Internet have to be approved by the entertainment industry before the rest of us can enjoy them. However, some may think that the mere fact that the entertainment industry uses its deep pockets to take such overreaching actions in order to protect its distribution monopoly means that we already live under that regime.

THE SIGNIFICANCE OF PRIVATE POWER

Cultural Filtering and Homogenization

What are the consequences of this copyright-facilitated aggregation of private power? First, the complete control that is conferred upon copyright owners means that the media and entertainment corporations are able to act as a cultural filter, controlling what we can hear. This ability to control and manipulate markets also means that the range of cultural products on offer often has 'about as much cultural diversity as a Macdonald's menu' (Capling 1996, 22).[54] Reflecting on the Australian popular music market, Anne Capling remarks:

> The domination by these global entertainment corporations of the Australian market facilitates the globalisation of a mass culture of mediocrity in a number of ways. It ensures, for instance, the prevalence of the top sellers to the detriment of other less mainstream overseas music ... The import restrictions also make it much more difficult for local Australian performers and composers to get airplay within Australia. Pop and rock account for close to ninety per cent of the Australian music market and, with the exception of a handful of Australian acts which have won an international following, this market is overwhelmingly dominated by North American and British artists. (Capling 1996, 22)[55]

And, of course, Australia is hardly likely to be the only market where this happens. The processes that produce cultural homogeneity and mediocrity are global. It is interesting in this respect to note that one of the arguments that is made on behalf of the activities of MP3 Internet music file trading services, such as Napster, is that they give exposure and airplay to smaller artists and small independent labels. If this is so, then it is a benefit likely to be lost if the major labels gain a distribution grip over the online music providers.

It is not just the music industry where the corporate sector controls what filters through to the rest of us. For example the control over film distribution that is enjoyed by the major media and entertainment corporations means that these corporations can control to some extent what films are made, what films we can see, and our perception of what films there are for us to see. The expense involved in film production and distribution means that without access to the deep pockets of the majors and their vertically integrated distribution networks, it is difficult, but not impossible, to finance independent film-making and distribution. This naturally reduces the volume of independent film-making. The high degree of vertical integration that characterizes the film industry, especially the ownership of cinema chains, means that many independent films that are made find it difficult to make any impact on the film-going public. This is mainly because we don't know they exist. The control by the media and entertainment corporations of the films that are made is also a consequence of their habit of buying the film rights attached to the copyright in novels, plays, biographies and so on. There is no obligation on the film corporations to use these rights once they have acquired them, but of course no one else can do so without their permission. Similarly the film corporations may choose not to release certain films in which they own the exclusive distribution rights or only to release certain films in certain jurisdictions or through certain media. All these things mean that the media and entertainment corporations are acting as a cultural filter.[56] The problem of cultural filtering with respect to films appears to have received recent acknowledgement in the UK in the form of the UK Film Council's Digital Screen Network under which grants will be made to cinemas for the installation of digital cinema technology on the condition that they show a wider variety of specialized films.[57] It seems a pity that public money raised for good causes through the National Lottery must be used to remedy a privately created distortion.

A further example of this filtering function, if one is needed, is provided by the publishing industry. The economic power of publishers has, in its wake, conferred a broader power on publishers to determine what sort of things we are likely to read. Richard Abel is eloquent on this topic:

> Book publishers decide which manuscripts to accept; form contracts dictate terms to all but best-selling authors; editors 'suggest' changes; and marketing departments decide price, distribution and promotion. Sometimes publishers go further ... The Japanese publisher Hayakawa withdrew a translation of *The Enigma of Japanese Power* because the Dutch author had written that the Burakumin Liberation League 'has developed a method of self-assertion through "denunciation" sessions with people and organizations it decides are guilty of discrimination'. Anticipating feminist criticism, Simon and Schuster cancelled publication of Bret Easton Ellis's *American Psycho* a month before it was to appear. (Abel 1994a, 52)[58]

There are a number of other current examples of the same phenomenon in publishing. For example it was reported that HarperCollins (UK), a member of the Murdoch Group, declined to publish Hong Kong Governor Chris Patten's memoirs in breach of contract because it was alleged the memoirs included commentary on the Beijing government that might threaten Murdoch's substantial business interests in China.[59] It has also been suggested that the takeover of the British publisher Fourth Estate by HarperCollins (UK) was in some way related to a biography of Rupert Murdoch contracted to be published by Fourth Estate. The biography was not published by Fourth Estate.[60] On the other hand, a development that may have the effect of breaking down some of the power of publishers is the advent of electronic self-publishing. It seems however that any inroads that this makes in the power of publishers will be confined to publications by the very few authors who command sufficient market power to dispense with the promotional services of the publishers.[61]

So the media and entertainment industry controls and homogenizes what we get to see, hear and read. In so doing it is likely that it also controls the way we construct images of our society and ourselves (Coombe 1998, 100–129; Macmillan 2002b). In 'The Swineherd', Andersen seems to warn against the dangers of abandoning 'reality' and allowing ourselves to be seduced by synthetic, and somewhat debased, cultural charms. In this story, as in so many others, the handsome prince wishes to marry the Emperor's beautiful daughter. The Emperor's daughter is however something of a philistine and rejects the prince's rare gifts – a rose that bloomed only every five years but 'smelled so sweet that you forgot all your worries and cares' (Crone Frank and Frank 2004a, p. 119) and a nightingale 'which sang as if it kept every lovely melody in its throat' (Crone Frank and Frank 2004a, 119) – complaining that they are 'real'. The prince then disguises himself as a swineherd and creates ingenious toys, which are much desired by the Emperor's daughter. He, however, will only sell these to her in return for kisses. Commenting, 'One must encourage the arts' (Crone Frank and Frank 2004a, 124), she agrees to the price asked. When the Emperor catches her in the act of payment he throws both his daughter and the swineherd-prince out of his kingdom:

> 'Oh, I'm so miserable,' the princess said. 'If only I'd married the handsome prince. I'm so unhappy.'
> The swineherd went behind a tree, wiped the black and brown off his face, threw his filthy clothes away, and stepped forward in his princely outfit. He looked so handsome that the princess had to curtsy at the sight of him.
> 'I've got nothing but contempt for you,' he said. 'You didn't want an honest prince. You didn't understand the rose and the nightingale, but you were willing to kiss the swineherd for a plaything. You're on your own.'
> (Crone Frank and Frank 2004a, 126)

A talented nightingale also makes an appearance in 'The Nightingale'. In this story a mechanical nightingale is constructed that imitates the beautiful song of the real thing. While being greatly prized, those of perception knew that it lacked the quality of the real thing. For one thing, it always sang the same song, although the tasteless masses appeared to value this quality: 'They could sing along, and they did' (Crone Frank and Frank 2004a, 134).[62] The attempt to capture and homogenize talent and creativity had of course also stultified it. Perhaps the essence of true creativity is its ability to develop and diversify, drawing on both internal inspiration and the richness of the commons. If this is so, the prognosis for cultural and intellectual creativity is looking a little grim – internal inspiration may be compromised by the processes of cultural filtering and homogenization, while the commons is under increasing threat.

Loss of the Commons

The scope of the power to control and homogenize large swathes of cultural production is reinforced by the media and entertainment industry's assertion of control over the use of material assumed by most people to be in the intellectual commons. The irony is that the reason people assume such material to be in the commons is that the copyright owners have force-fed it to us as receivers of the mass culture disseminated by the mass media. The more powerful the copyright owner, the more dominant the cultural image, but the more likely that the copyright owner will seek to protect the cultural power of the image through copyright enforcement. The result is that not only are individuals not able to use, develop or reflect upon dominant cultural images, they are also unable to challenge them by subverting them.[63] This is certainly unlikely to reduce the power of those who own these images.

As an example of this type of concern Waldron (1993) uses the case of *Walt Disney Prods v Air Pirates*.[64] In this case the Walt Disney Corporation successfully prevented the use of Disney characters in *Air Pirates* comic books. The comic books were said to depict the characters as 'active members of a free thinking, promiscuous, drug-ingesting counterculture' (Waldron 1993, 753).[65] Note however that the copyright law upon which the case was based does not prevent this depiction only; it prevents their use altogether. Waldron comments:

> The whole point of the Mickey Mouse image is that it is thrust out into the cultural world to impinge on the consciousness of all of us. Its enormous popularity, consciously cultivated for decades by the Disney empire, means that it has become an instantly recognizable icon, in a real sense part of our lives. When Ralph Steadman paints the familiar mouse ears on a cartoon image of Ronald Reagan, or when someone on my faculty refers to some proposed syllabus as a 'Mickey Mouse' idea, they attest to the fact that this is not just property without boundaries on which we might accidentally encroach . . . but an artifact that has been deliberately set up as a more or less permanent feature of the environment all of us inhabit. (Waldron 1993, 883)[66]

Coombe describes this corporate control of the commons as monological and, accordingly, destroying the dialogical relationship between the individual and society:

> Legal theorists who emphasize the cultural construction of self and world – the central importance of shared cultural symbols in defining us and the realities we recognize – need to consider the legal constitution of symbols and the extent to which 'we' can be said to 'share' them. I fear that most legal theorists concerned with dialogue objectify, rarefy, and idealize 'culture', abstracting 'it' from the material and political practices in which meaning is made. Culture is not embedded in abstract concepts that we internalize, but in the materiality of signs and texts over which we struggle and the imprint of those struggles in consciousness. This ongoing negotiation and struggle over meaning is the essence of dialogic practice. Many interpretations of intellectual property laws quash dialogue by affirming the power of corporate actors to monologically control meaning by appealing to an abstract concept of property. Laws of intellectual property privilege monologic forms

against dialogic practice and create significant power differentials between social actors engaged in hegemonic struggle. If both subjective and objective realities are constituted culturally – through signifying forms to which we give meaning – then we must critically consider the relationship between law, culture, and the politics of commodifying cultural forms. (Coombe 1998, 86)

If copyright has any hope of answering a criticism this cogent, then a key aspect of copyright law is the fair use, fair dealing defence. It is this aspect of copyright law that permits resistance and critique (Gaines 1991, 10). Yet the fair dealing defence is a weak tool for this purpose and becoming weaker. The determination in *Rogers v Koons* that the fair use defence only applies where the infringing work has used a copyright work for the purpose of criticizing that copyright work, rather than for the purpose of criticizing society in general, exposed a crucial flaw in the use of the defence as a tool of resistance and critique. Recent developments in the context of the digital reproduction,[67] which are well illustrated by *Universal Studios v Corley*,[68] the DVD case, tend to remove the utility of the defence altogether.

Copyright and Development?

The utilitarian or development justification for copyright is overwhelmingly familiar. The general idea underlying this rationale is that the grant of copyright encourages the production of the cultural works, which is essential to the development process.[69] However the consequences of copyright's commodification of creativity, as described above, seem to place some strain on this alleged relationship between copyright and development. This argument may be illustrated by reference to the World Commission on Development and Culture's concept of development as being about the enhancement of effective freedom of choice of individuals (World Commission on Culture and Development 1996).[70] Some of the things that matter to this concept of development are 'access to the world's stock of knowledge . . . access to power, the right to participate in the cultural life of the community' (World Commission on Culture and Development 1996, Introduction).[71] The edifice of private power that has been built upon a copyright law that seems to care more about money than about the intrinsic worth of the cultural product it is protecting has deprived us all to some extent of the benefits of this type of development. As Waldron comments, '[t]he private appropriation of the public realm of cultural artifacts restricts and controls the moves that can be made therein by the rest of us' (Waldron 1993, 885). Andersen might have gone further and noted the possibility of adverse effects on individual development. His eponymous shadow reports that his opportunity to spend time in the house of Poetry allowed him to become 'more human . . . I learned to understand my inner self – what I was born with, my connection to Poetry' (Crone Frank and Frank 2004a, 212).

Things look no better if we focus on the World Commission on Development and Culture's fundamental approach to culture, which is the handmaiden of its wide concept of development. A fundamental approach to culture means valuing cultural output as an end in itself, a commitment to diversity and multiculturalism, and the control of power in the form of cultural domination (World Commission on Culture and Development, Analytical Chapter 9). Not only has copyright failed to effect these things in relation to cultural output, but it is also arguable that it has effected their opposite. In other words, copyright law's approach to culture is not fundamentalist. Since copyright law dominates the production and distribution of many forms of creativity, its failure to take a fundamentalist approach to the cultural products that fall within its purview may be regarded as a factor in our failure to achieve development in the wide sense. What is more, the unaccountable and self-reinforcing power of the media and entertainment conglomerates suggests that this process of development failure is accelerating.

THE VERDICT?

One somehow doubts that Hans Christian Andersen would have been sanguine about the picture of cultural homogenization and domination painted above. It is likely that he would have found the devaluation of creativity and talent unappealing. He surely would have remarked negatively on the contraction of the intellectual commons and the foreclosure of the public domain. He may have even worried that we are turning into the sort of society in which dissent, subversion and debate is effectively silenced (Macmillan 2005). We cannot doubt his views about the vacuity of such a society, as he made them clear in one of his most well-known stories. In this story, the most powerful person is blinded by vanity and love of empty (or even, naked) ostentation, those who should be wise are silenced by their own fear of exposure and desire for self-advancement, and unscrupulous swindlers operate with effectiveness and impunity. In this society everyone finds it more convenient to stay silent and avoid the obvious – or at least nearly everyone. A child disrupts the consensus however when he famously says, 'But he hasn't got anything on!'[72] Some disruption of the current copyright consensus might very well be a fitting tribute to Hans Christian Andersen.

NOTES

1. Emile Zola, as president of ALAI, for example was a leading campaigner for multilateral copyright protection: see Blakeney (2004).
2. See n. 28.

3. Apparently, Andersen never understood why, after Dickens' enthusiastic invitation, his protracted stay with Dickens in 1857 resulted in Dickens' avoiding all further contact with Andersen: see Crone Frank and Frank (2004b), p. 21. According to Crone Frank and Frank (2004a), p. 283, this was the explanation for the following mention of Dickens in Andersen's story 'Auntie Toothache' (published 1872), Crone Frank and Frank, 2004a, 247, at 254:
   > 'You're a poet!' Auntie exclaimed. 'Just write down your story, and you'll be as good as Dickens. But you're much more interesting to me – you paint pictures when you talk.'
4. '[T]he life of the law is not logic, and the fact that there is no *test* of talent or genius does not prevent the resonance of those ideas from influencing the rhetoric which sustains intellectual property doctrine as a whole', Waldron (1993), p. 853.
5. As laid down in for example *University of London Press v University Tutorial Press* (1916) 2 Ch 601, 608 per Peterson J.
6. While at the same time arguably denying protection to other works that display creativity and/or innovation: see for example *Norowzian v Arks Ltd (No 2)* [2000] FSR 363 (CA).
7. See for example 'The Swineherd' (published 1842), Crone Frank and Frank (2004a), p. 119; 'The Nightingale' (published 1844), Crone Frank and Frank (2004a), p. 127; 'The Shadow' (published 1847), Crone Frank and Frank (2004a), p. 206; 'The Gardener and the Aristocrats' (published 1872), Crone Frank and Frank (2004a), p. 239; 'Auntie Toothache' (n. 3 supra); and maybe even, in a backhand way, 'The Emperor's New Clothes' (published 1837), Crone Frank and Frank (2004a), p. 95.
8. Letter to Madame Iversen, 4 January 1837, quoted in Crone Frank and Frank (2004a), p. 283.
9. *Rogers v Koons*, 751 F Supp 474 (SDNY 1990), *aff'd*, 960 F 2d 301 (2d Cir), *cert denied*, 113 S Ct 365 (1992).
10. On the issues and problems posed for copyright law by Koons' artistic contribution, see Bowrey (1994), esp pp. 311–16.
11. This is somewhat of an oversimplification. See further for example Hutcheon (1989) and Polan (1993).
12. The concept of subconscious copying may be another good example of copyright's failure to secure the intellectual commons: see Waldron (1993), pp. 882ff; and Vaidhyanathan (2001), Chapter 4, esp pp. 126–31.
13. It is doubtful that our fair dealing laws can be described as strong: see further, Macmillan Patfield (1997), pp. 123–5; and Macmillan Patfield (1996), pp. 222–32. See also Waldron (1993), pp. 859–60. *Campbell v Acuff-Rose*, 114 S Ct 1164 (1994) may be regarded as a step in the right direction. On the need for strong fair dealing exemptions in the digital environment, see van Caenegem (1995).
14. For example the following stories were all based on folk tales or existing literary works: 'Little Claus and Big Claus' (published 1835), Crone Frank and Frank (2004a), pp. 41, 262; 'Thumbelisa' (published 1835), Crone Frank and Frank (2004a), pp. 57, 264; 'The Emperor's New Clothes', n. 7 supra, pp. 95, 266; 'The Wild Swans' (published 1838), Crone Frank and Frank (2004a), 100, 267; 'The Swineherd', n. 7, 119 and 268. 'The Little Match Girl' (published 1845), Crone Frank and Frank (2004a), pp. 197, 275, was based upon an illustration by the Danish artist, J. Th. Lundbye.
15. 'It annoyed him, not so much because his shadow was gone but because he knew the old tale about a man without a shadow – and everyone in the cold countries knew that story. If he came home and told his own story, people would say that he was an imitator, which was the last thing he needed to hear. So he was not going to talk about it at all and that was very sensible of him', Crone Frank and Frank (2004a), p. 209. See also Crone Frank and Frank (2004a), p. 277.
16. The fundamental/instrumental distinction drawn here is drawn from the World Commission on Culture and Development (1996). For a further discussion and application of that distinction in the context of copyright, see Macmillan (1998).
17. GATT is the General Agreement on Trade Tariffs, which was a free standing agreement regulating world trade in goods from 1 January 1948 until 1 January 1995 when it was folded into the newly created World Trade Organization.
18. Possible Renewal of the Generalised System of Preferences – Hearing Before the

Subcommittee on Trade of the US House of Rep Comm on Ways and Means, 98th Cong 1st Sess (1983); and Unfair Foreign Trade Practices, Stealing American Intellectual Property: Imitation is Not Flattery, 98th Cong 2nd Sess (1984): both cited in Blakeney (1996), 2n.

19. Although the Berne Convention made a comeback with the WIPO Copyright Treaty 1996 and the WIPO Performances and Phonograms Treaty 1996.

20. See especially the TRIPs Agreement, Articles 11 and 14(4), which enshrine rental rights in relation to computer programmes, films and phonograms; WIPO Copyright Treaty 1996, Article 7; and WIPO Performances and Phonograms Treaty 1996, Articles 9 and 13.

21. Bently (1994), 979n., refers here to Wordworth's support for Sergeant Talfourd's famous campaign to extend the duration of copyright. See also Vaidhynathan (2001), Chapter 2.

22. Bently (1994), 979n., cites *Sayre v Moore* (1785) in *Cary v Longman* (1801) 1 East 358, 359n., 102 ER 138, 139n.; *West v Francis* 5 B & Ald 737, 106 ER 1361; and *Bramwell v Halcomb* (1836) 2 My & Cr 737, 40 ER 1110, as examples of a transition in the application of the fair dealing defence from focusing on what the defendant had added to what the defendant had taken.

23. Footnote omitted.

24. See for example Copyright Designs and Patents Act 1988 (UK), s 9(1) and (2)(aa).

25. See for example Copyright Designs and Patents Act 1988 (UK), s 9(1) and (2)(ab).

26. Although the fact that moral rights are commonly granted to the authors of films (see for example Copyright Designs and Patents Act, 1988 (UK), ss 77(1), 80(1), 84(1)(b)) suggests that film may have something more akin to a hybrid status as both creative work and commodity. The commodity status of films and sound recordings is reflected in, for example, the Australian Copyright Act 1968 (Cth) by the fact that the Act does not bother to identify an author of these works for the purpose of establishing copyright ownership, but rather merely identifies the relevant 'maker' as the owner: see ss 97(2) and 98(2).

27. Admittedly, it is more likely that 'The Shadow' is a meditation on the nature of celebrity. Cf Crone Frank and Frank (2004a), p. 276, who read in it a reflection of Andersen's bitter relationship with Edvard Collin.

28. When, in 1868, the US publisher Hurd & Houghton approached Andersen with a proposal for publishing his work in English, he appears to have concerned himself with the question of the absence of protection in the US for English translations of his work. He agreed to try and prevent competing English translations, although it is unclear what he could have done about these. Perhaps it was partially by way of reparation for his inability to give any guarantees in this respect, that he later agreed to give Hurd & Houghton 'a true literary coup: the sequel to *The Fairy Tale of My Life* [his first volume of memoirs] – the years between 1855 and 1867 – and the first crack at some new stories, all of which would be published in the United States before they appeared in Denmark': Crone Frank and Crone (2004b), p. 25.

29. 'The Tinderbox' (published 1836), Crone Frank and Frank (2004a), p. 33.

30. See however Towse (2001), especially Chapters 6 and 8, in which it is argued that copyright generates little income for most creative artists. Nevertheless Towse suggests that copyright is valuable to creative artists for reasons of status and control of their work.

31. For further discussion of the way in which the filmed entertainment industry conforms to these industry features, see Macmillan (2002c).

32. See also Bettig (1996), pp. 40–42.

33. It was reported for example that Chrysalis, the music and broadcasting group, raised £60 million against its music publishing catalogue, which comprised 50 000 copyrights valued for the purpose of the securitization at £150 million and generating a revenue stream of £8 million per year: 'Chrysalis in £60m fundraising', *The Times*, 9 February 2001.

34. For an example of this, see Bettig's description of the process of integration by Paramount Communications Inc.: Bettig (1996), pp. 37–8.

35. Thus returning us, strangely enough, to the origins of the filmed entertainment industry, which grew out of a need to exploit patents over cinematograph technology: see further for example Vaidhyanathan (2001), pp. 87–93.

36. See for example n. 28.

37. 'Kids' Talk' (published 1859), Crone Frank and Frank (2004a), p. 230.

38. See *The Wizard*, 7 August 2000, http://www.wizardfkap.com/page6.html and http://www.copyleft.net.
39. In homage to the character of the same name in George Orwell's, *Nineteen Eighty Four*.
40. *Universal City Studios, Inc v Shawn C Reimerdes*, 111 F Supp 2d 294 (2000, SDNY).
41. *Universal City Studios, Inc v Corley*, 273 F 3d 429 (US Court of Appeals (2nd Cir), 2001).
42. Section 1201, Title 17 of the US Code.
43. 'Studios Score DeCSS Victory', *Wired News*, 17 August 2000.
44. Note 41, 459.
45. 259 F Supp 2d 1029 (CD Cal, 2003).
46. Complaint in *MGM v Grokster*, n 45, para. 1, http://www.eff.org/IP/P2P/NMPA_v_MusicCity/ 20011002_mgm_v_grokster_complaint. html.
47. Hearing Transcript in *MGM v Grokster*, n. 45, 8, http://www.eff.org/IP/P2P/NMPA_v_MusicCity/20020304_mgm_hearing_transcript.html.
48. The legality of which would appear to be protected on the basis that it has substantial non-infringing uses pursuant to the authority of *Sony Corp v Universal City Studios, Inc*, 464 US 417 (1984).
49. See Hearing Transcript in *MGM v Grokster*, n. 45, 6–9, http://www.eff.org/IP/P2P/NMPA_v_MusicCity/20020304_mgm_hearing_transcript.html.
50. Complaint in *MGM v Grokster*, n. 45, para 52, http://www.eff.org/IP/P2P/NMPA_v_MusicCity/20011002_mgm_v_grokster_complaint.html.
51. The plaintiffs are, of course, downplaying this difference between Napster and Morpheus, referring to it as being merely 'architectural': Hearing Transcript in *MGM v Grokster*, n. 45, 10, http://www.eff.org/IP/P2P/NMPA_v_MusicCity/20020304_mgm_hearing_transcript. html.
52. *Metro-Goldwyn-Mayer Studios Inc v Grokster Ltd* (Order on Motions, 25 April 2003), http://www.eff.org/IP/P2P/NMPA_v_MusicCity/030425_order_on_motions.php. This Order on Motion relates only to the Grokster and Morpheus software, no order was made in relation to the KaZaA software.
53. *Metro-Goldwyn-Mayer Studios Inc v Grokster Ltd* (United States Court of Appeals for the Ninth Circuit, 19 August 2004), http://www.eff.org/IP/P2P/MGM_v_Grokster/20040819_mgm_v_grokster_decision.pdf, and *Metro-Goldwyn-Mayer Studios Inc v Grokster Ltd*, (Supreme Court of the United States, 27 June 2005), http://www.eff.org/IP/P'2P/MGM_v_Grokster/04-480.pdf.
54. The issue of release and promotion of recorded music is a big issue for many popular composers and performers. For example popular music composer Michael Penn is quoted as saying: 'People disappear in this business not through drug abuse but because record companies sign them and then mess them around . . . They're very vengeful people. If you protest, like George Michael & Prince did, you're a whining rock star. In our case you're simply a loser . . . Epic put my album out but they won't spend a cent on promotion. The business is incredibly narrow now. The opportunities for flukes are zero. To escape this multinational hell, your only recourse is stuff like MP3', *The Evening Standard*, 12 July 2000.
55. The import restrictions to which Capling makes reference were removed from Australian copyright law in 1998 (Copyright (Amendment) Act (No 2) (1998 Cth)), but this has done little to alter the patterns of control and distribution in the Australian recorded music market.
56. For further discussion of the issue of cultural filtering and homogenization in the film industry, see Macmillan (2002b).
57. See UK Film Council, Digital Screen Network, http://www.ukfilmcouncil.org.uk/funding /distributionandexhibition/dsn/, accessed 10 September 2004.
58. Footnote omitted. Ironically, in attempting to publish the monograph in which this passage appears, Abel himself was to feel the brunt of his publisher's attempt at censorship. He has subsequently defined this as an attempted exercise of private power to control speech: see Abel (1994b), 380.
59. 'Londoner's Diary', *Evening Standard*, 11 July 2000.
60. Ibid.
61. In 2000 Stephen King decided to by-pass the electronic publishing division of his publishers, Simon & Schuster, and self-publish his novel, *The Plant*, on the Internet: see 'King

writes off the middleman', *Weekend Australian*, 22–23 July 2000. King later abandoned this project: see *Metro* (London), 30 November 2000.
62. For a different reading of these stories in the context of a copyright critique, see Teilmann (2005).
63. See also, the discussion of *Rogers v Koons* in the text acc nn. 9–13; Chon (1993); Koenig (1994); Macmillan Patfield (1996), pp. 219–22.
64. 581 F 2d 751 (9th Cir, 1978), *cert denied*, 439 US 1132 (1979).
65. Quoting Wheelwright (1976), p. 582.
66. Footnote omitted.
67. These developments now appear endemic: see for example the Digital Millennium Copyright Act, the Australian Copyright Amendment (Digital Agenda) Act 2000, and European Parliament and Council Directive on the harmonization of certain aspects of copyright and related rights in the Information Society, COM (1999) 250 final.
68. Note 41.
69. For a good example of a statement of this rationale, see the Preface to WIPO (1978). For discussion of this rationale, see for example Waldron (1993), pp. 850ff; and Macmillan Patfield (1997), p. 113.
70. For a detailed and persuasive account of this approach to development, see Sen (1999).
71. See further, Macmillan (1998, 2002a).
72. 'The Emperor's New Clothes' (of course), Crone Frank and Frank (2004a), p. 99.

REFERENCES

Abel, R.L. (1994a), *Speech and Respect*, London: Stevens & Son/Sweet & Maxwell.
Abel, R.L. (1994b), 'Public Freedom, Private Constraint', *Journal of Law and Society*, 21, 374–91.
Arrighi, G. (2002), *The Long Twentieth Century: Money, Power and the Origins of Our Times*, London and New York: Verso.
Bently, L. (1994), 'Copyright and the Death of the Author in Literature and in Law', *Modern Law Review*, 57, 973–86.
Bettig, R.V. (1996), *Copyrighting Culture: The Political Economy of Intellectual Property*, Boulder, Co: Westview Press.
Blakeney, M. (1996), *Trade Related Aspects of Intellectual Property Rights*, London: Sweet & Maxwell.
Blakeney, M. (2004), 'Part I – Commentary', in A. Ilardi and M. Blakeney (eds), *International Encyclopaedia of Intellectual Property Treaties*, Oxford: Oxford University Press, pp. 3–183.
Bowrey, K. (1994), 'Copyright, the Paternity of Artistic Works, and the Challenge Posed by Postmodern Artists', *Intellectual Property Journal*, 8, 285–317.
Capling, A. (1996), 'Gimme shelter!', *Arena Magazine*, February/March, pp. 21–4.
Chartier, A. (1994), 'Figures of the Author', in B. Sherman and A. Strowel (eds), *Of Authors and Origins: Essays on Copyright Law*, Oxford: Clarendon Press, pp. 15–43.
Chon, M. (1993), 'Postmodern "Progress": Reconsidering the Copyright and Patent Power', *DePaul Law Review*, 43, 97–146.
Coombe, R. (1998), *The Cultural Life of Intellectual Properties*, Durham, NC and London: Duke University Press.
Crone Frank, D. and J. Frank (2004a) (eds), *The Stories of Hans Christian Andersen*, London: Granta Books.
Crone Frank, D. and J. Frank (2004b), 'The Real HC Andersen', in D. Crone Frank and

J. Frank (eds), *The Stories of Hans Christian Andersen*, London: Granta Books, pp. 1–30.

Gaines, J. (1991), *Contested Culture: The Image, the Voice and the Law*, Chapel Hill, NC and London: University of North Carolina Press.

Hutcheon, L. (1989), *The Politics of Postmodernism*, London and New York: Routledge.

Koenig, D.M. (1994), 'Joe Camel and the First Amendment: The Dark Side of Copyrighted and Trademark-Protected Icons', *Thomas M Cooley Law Review*, 11, 803–38.

Macmillan, F. (1998), 'Copyright and Culture: A Perspective on Corporate Power', *Media and Arts Law Review*, 10, 71–81.

Macmillan, F. (2002a), 'Corporate Power and Copyright', in R. Towse (ed.), *Copyright and the Cultural Industries*, Cheltenham, UK and Northampton, MA: Edward Elgar, pp. 99–118.

Macmillan, F. (2002b), 'The Cruel ©: Copyright and Film', *European Intellectual Property Review*, 483–92.

Macmillan, F. (2002c), 'Morpheus in the Undergrowth: Copyright and Film', *Intellectual Property Forum*, 49, 12–37.

Macmillan, F. (2005), 'Commodification and Cultural Ownership', in J. Griffiths and U. Suthersanen (eds), *Copyright and Free Speech: Comparative and International Analyses*, Oxford: Oxford University Press, pp. 35–65.

Macmillan Patfield, F. (1996), 'Towards a Reconciliation of Free Speech and Copyright', in E. Barendt (ed.), *The Yearbook of Media and Entertainment Law 1996*, Oxford: Clarendon Press, pp. 199–233.

Macmillan Patfield, F. (1997), 'Legal Policy and the Limits of Literary Copyright', in P. Parrinder, W. Chernaik and W. Gould (eds), *Textual Monopolies: Literary Copyright and the Public Domain*, London: Office for Humanities Communication, pp. 113–32.

Netanel, N.W. (1996), 'Copyright and a Democratic Civil Society', *Yale Law Journal*, 106, 283–387.

Polan, D. (1993), 'Postmodernism and Cultural Analysis Today', in E.A. Kaplan (ed.), *Postmodernism and Its Discontents*, London: Verso, pp. 45–58.

Rose, M. (1993), *Authors and Owners: The Invention of Copyright*, Cambridge, MA and London: Harvard University Press.

Saunders, D. (1992), *Authorship and Copyright*, London: Routledge.

Sell, S. (2003), *Private Power, Public Law: The Globalization of Intellectual Property Rights*, Cambridge: Cambridge University Press.

Sen, A. (1999), *Development as Freedom*, New York: Anchor Books

Smiers, J. (2002), 'The Abolition of Copyrights: Better for Artists, Third World Countries and the Public Domain', in R. Towse (ed.), *Copyright and the Cultural Industries*, Cheltenham, UK and Northampton, MA: Edward Elgar, pp. 119–39.

Towse, R. (1999), 'Copyright Risk and the Artist: An Economic Approach to Policy for Artists', *Cultural Policy*, 6, 91–107.

Towse, R. (2001), *Creativity, Incentive and Reward: An Economic Analysis of Copyright and Culture in the Information Age*, Cheltenham, UK and Northampton, MA: Edward Elgar.

Vaidhyanathan, S. (2001), *Copyrights and Copywrongs: The Rise of Intellectual Property and How it Threatens Creativity*, New York and London: New York University Press.

van Caenegem, W. (1995), 'Copyright, Communication and New Technologies', *Federal Law Review*, 23, 322–47.

Waldron, J. (1993), 'From Authors to Copiers: Individual Rights and Social Values in Intellectual Property', *Chicago-Kent Law Review*, 69, 841–87.

Welsh, A. (1987), *From Copyright to Copperfield: The Identity of Dickens*, Cambridge, MA: Harvard University Press.

Wheelwright, K. (1976), 'Parody, Copyrights and the First Amendment', *US Federal Law Review*, 564–626.

World Commission on Culture and Development (1996), *Our Creative Diversity*, 2nd edn, Paris: UNESCO.

World Intellectual Property Organization (WIPO) (1978), *Guide to the Berne Convention for the Protection of Literary and Artistic Works*, Geneva: WIPO.

Woodmansee, M. and P. Jaszi (1993), *The Construction of Authorship*, Durham, NC and London: Duke University Press.

6. Hans Christian Andersen and the protection of traditional cultural expressions

Michael Blakeney

THE PROTECTION OF TRADITIONAL CULTURAL EXPRESSION IN THE INTERNATIONAL INTELLECTUAL PROPERTY ARENA

Probably the first step towards establishing a political agenda for the protection of traditional cultural expressions was an African Study Meeting on Copyright, held in Brazzaville in August 1963, which had advocated copyright concessions for developing countries including reductions in the duration of protection and the protection of folklore.[1] At the time of the Stockholm Conference for the Revision of the Berne Convention, which was convened in June 1967, there were ten African states[2] included in the 58 members of the Berne Union.

The Stockholm Conference witnessed the first significant agitation from developing countries for an acknowledgement of their particular circumstances. In the preparations for the Stockholm Conference, it was proposed that the concerns of developing countries could be accommodated in a separate protocol. This question was the subject of some fairly acrimonious debates at Stockholm.[3] The critical issues for developing countries were the definition of developing-country translation rights and compulsory licensing. The establishment of a protective regime for folklore was a burgeoning consideration. Although a Protocol was grudgingly adopted by the final plenary session of the Stockholm Conference, it did not come into force as it failed to secure the requisite number of ratifications. This Protocol became an Appendix to the Paris Act, which was adopted by the Paris Revision Conference of 1971.

The current significance of the Berne Convention derives from the fact that its first 19 articles are incorporated into the TRIPS Agreement, but this incorporation does not include the Appendix.

The failure of developing countries to secure an effective protection of folklore within the regime administered by the World Intellectual Property Organization explains initiatives undertaken within other international organizations. In April 1973 the Government of Bolivia had sent a memorandum to the Director-General of UNESCO requesting that the organization examine the opportunity of drafting an international instrument on the protection of indigenous creative works in the form of a protocol to be attached to the Universal Copyright Convention, which is administered by UNESCO. Following that request a study was prepared in 1975 by the Secretariat of UNESCO on the desirability of providing for the protection of the cultural expressions of indigenous peoples on an international scale. Because of a perception of the broad scope of this analysis, in 1977 the Director-General of UNESCO convened a Committee of Experts on the Legal Protection of Folklore, which in a report in 1977 concluded that the subject required sociological, psychological, ethnological, politico-historical studies 'on an interdisciplinary basis within the framework of an overall and integrated approach'.[4]

Pursuant to a resolution adopted by the General Conference of the United Nations Educational, Scientific and Cultural Organization (UNESCO) in Belgrade in September–October 1980, and a decision taken by the Governing Bodies of the World Intellectual Property Organization (WIPO) in November 1981, a Committee of Governmental Experts on the Intellectual Property Aspects of the Protection of Expressions of Folklore was convened. After a series of meetings the committee formulated Model Provisions for National Laws on the Protection of Expressions of Folklore Against Illicit Exploitation and Other Prejudicial Action which were adopted by the two organizations in 1985.

The General Conference of UNESCO at its 25th session in 1989 adopted a Recommendation on the Safeguarding of Traditional Cultures and Folklore, which proposed a programme of measures to be taken at the national level for the identification, conservation, preservation and dissemination of the cultural works of indigenous peoples.

THE PEJORATIVE CONNOTATIONS OF 'FOLKLORE'

Since the mid-1980s, when WIPO and UNESCO had convened a Group of Experts on the Protection of Expressions of Folklore by Intellectual Property, there has been a lively debate about the terminology which should be used to describe the creations of a cultural community. The representatives of the Spanish-speaking countries at the 1985 meeting of the Group of Experts took the position that 'folklore' was an archaism, with the negative connotation of being associated with the creations of lower or superseded civilizations. However, over that objection, the 1985 meeting adopted the following definition:

> Folklore (in the broader sense, traditional and popular folk culture) is a group-oriented and tradition-based creation of groups or individuals reflecting the expectations of the community as an adequate expression of its cultural and social identity; its standards are transmitted orally, by imitation or by other means. Its forms include, among others, language, literature, music, dance, games, mythology, rituals, customs, handicrafts, architecture and other arts.

This definition was elaborated in the resultant WIPO/UNESCO Model Provisions for National Laws for the Protection of Folklore Against Illicit Exploitation and Other Prejudicial Actions. The misgivings expressed about the negative connotations of the term 'folklore' were deflected by participants at the 1985 meeting who pointed out that 'in recent times the term "folklore" obtained a new meaning and is widely accepted as a term suitable for the purposes of a relevant international treaty'.[5]

This terminological approach persisted until the conclusion of the World Forum on the Protection of Folklore, convened by WIPO and UNESCO in Phuket in April 1997. That forum was convened in response to the recommendations in February 1996 of the WIPO Committee of Experts on a Possible Protocol to the Berne Convention, and the Committee of Experts on a Possible Instrument for the Protection of the Rights of Performers and the Producers of Phonograms, that arrangements be made for the organization of an international forum to explore 'issues concerning the preservation and protection of expressions of folklore, intellectual property aspects of folklore and the harmonisation of different regional interests'.[6]

At the forum, a number of speakers referred to the negative connotations and Eurocentric definition of the term 'folklore'. For example Mrs Mould-Idrissu, in a paper on the African experience on the preservation and conservation of expressions of folklore,[7] observed that the Western conception of folklore tended to focus on artistic, literary and performing works, whereas in Africa it was much more broad, encompassing all aspects of cultural heritage.[8] For example she noted that under the Ghanaian Copyright Law of 1985, folklore included scientific knowledge.[9] Speakers criticized the Western attitude to folklore as something dead to be collected and preserved, rather than part of an evolving living tradition.[10] In a statement issued by indigenous Australian representatives at the forum, exception was taken to the use of 'folklore' as being too narrowly defined and implying an inferiority of the cultural and intellectual property of indigenous peoples to the dominant culture.[11] The Indigenous Australian representatives expressed a preference for the term 'indigenous cultural and intellectual property', which had been coined by Ms Erica Daes, Special Rapporteur of the Sub-Commission on Prevention of Discrimination and Protection of Minorities.[12]

The expressions 'traditional cultural expressions' or 'traditional knowledge' accommodate the concerns of those observers who criticize the narrowness of 'folklore'. However the latter term significantly changes the discourse. Folklore was typically discussed in copyright, or copyright-plus terms.[13] Traditional knowledge, on the other hand, also embraces traditional knowledge of plants and animals in medical treatment and as food. In this circumstance the discourse would shift from the environs of copyright to patents law[14] and biodiversity rights.[15] This shift is, in part, an explanation of the suggestions for *sui generis* solutions to the protection of traditional knowledge. Thus Simpson adopts Daes's view that it is inappropriate to subdivide the heritage of indigenous peoples 'as this would imply giving different levels of protection to different elements of heritage'.[16]

INDIGENOUS PEOPLES' DECLARATIONS

A significant initiative during the UN International Year for the World's Indigenous Peoples was the First International Conference on the Cultural and Intellectual Property Rights of Indigenous Peoples which was convened by the Nine Tribes of Mataatua in the Bay of Plenty Region of Aotearoa, New Zealand in June 1993. The resultant Mataatua Declaration on the Cultural and Intellectual Property Rights of Indigenous Peoples insisted that the protection of the rights of indigenous peoples in their traditional knowledge was an aspect of the right of indigenous people to self-determination. The Mataatua Declaration recommended in Article 1 that in the development of policies and practices, indigenous peoples should:

1.1 Define for themselves their own intellectual and cultural property.

1.2 Note that existing protection mechanisms are insufficient for the protection of Indigenous Peoples' Intellectual and Cultural Property Rights.

1.3 Develop a code of ethics which external users must observe when recording (visual, audio, written) their traditional and customary knowledge.

1.4 Prioritise the establishment of indigenous education, research and training centres to promote their knowledge of customary environmental and cultural practices.

. . .

1.6 Develop and maintain their traditional practices and sanctions for the protection, preservation and revitalization of their traditional intellectual and cultural properties.

. . .

1.8 Establish an appropriate body with appropriate mechanisms to:

(a) preserve and monitor the commercialism or otherwise of indigenous cultural properties in the public domain;

(b) generally advise and encourage indigenous peoples to take steps to protect their cultural heritage;

(c) allow a mandatory consultative process with respect to any new legislation affecting indigenous peoples, cultural and intellectual property rights.
1.9 Establish international indigenous information centres and networks.

The Mataatua Declaration in Article 2.1 recommended that in the development of policies and practices, states and national and international agencies 'should recognise that indigenous peoples are the guardians of their customary knowledge and have the right to protect and control dissemination of that knowledge'. In Article 2.2 it urged the recognition that 'indigenous peoples also have the right to create new knowledge based on cultural traditions'. The insufficiency of existing protection mechanisms was asserted in Article 2.3. Article 2.5 provided for the development:

> . . . in full cooperation with indigenous peoples an additional cultural and intellectual property rights regime incorporating the following:
> * collective (as well as individual) ownership, and origin and retroactive coverage of historical as well as contemporary works;
> * protection against debasement of culturally significant items;
> * co-operative rather than competitive framework;
> * first beneficiaries to be the direct descendants of the traditional guardians of that knowledge;
> * multi-generational coverage span.

The conference delegates recommended that the UN incorporate the Mataatua Declaration in its Study on Cultural and Intellectual Property of Indigenous Peoples.

The Statement issued by the International Consultation on Intellectual Property Rights and Biodiversity organized by the Coordinating Body of the Indigenous Peoples of the Amazon Basin (COICA), held at Santa Cruz de la Sierra, Bolivia in September 1994 reiterated the assertion of the Mataatua Declaration that:

> All aspects of the issue of intellectual property (determination of access to natural resources, control of the knowledge or cultural heritage of peoples, control of the use of their resources and regulation of the terms of exploitation) are aspects of self determination.

The COICA Statement was extremely critical of the current intellectual property regime. Article 8 declared that:

> Prevailing intellectual property systems reflect a conception and practice that is:
> * colonialist, in that the instruments of the developed countries are imposed in order to appropriate the resources of indigenous peoples;
> * racist, in that it belittles and minimises the value of our knowledge systems;
> * usurpatory, in that it is essentially a practice of theft.

The COICA Statement in Article 9 pointed to the danger of distortion to indigenous systems in adjusting them to the prevailing intellectual property regime. The statement formulated short- and medium-term strategies to deal with these problems. In the short term it identified intellectual property principles and mechanisms which were either inimical to or useful for indigenous peoples. For example Article 12 recognized that 'there are some formulas that could be used to enhance the value of our products (brand names, appellations of origin), but on the understanding that these are only marketing possibilities, not entailing monopolies of the product or of collective knowledge'.

The Statement in Article 14 proposed the design of a protection and recognition system in the short and medium term of mechanisms which 'will prevent appropriation of our resources and knowledge'. These would include 'appropriate mechanisms for maintaining and ensuring rights of indigenous peoples to deny indiscriminate access to the resources of our communities or peoples and making it possible to contest patents or other exclusive rights to what is essentially indigenous'. Although the COICA statement was largely concerned with indigenous people's rights in biodiversity,[17] it called for the training of indigenous leaders in aspects of intellectual property.

In Australia, the Julayinbul Statement on Indigenous Intellectual Property Rights was adopted by a Conference on Cultural and Intellectual Property held at Jingarrba on 25–27 November 1993. The Julayinbul Statement affirmed the unique spiritual and cultural relationship of indigenous peoples with the Earth which determined their perceptions of intellectual property. The statement asserted that 'Aboriginal intellectual property, within Aboriginal Common Law, is an inherent inalienable right which cannot be terminated, extinguished or taken'. The statement called on governments to review legislation and non-statutory policies which did not recognize indigenous intellectual property rights and to implement such international conventions which recognized these rights. The Conference also issued a Declaration Reaffirming the Self Determination and Intellectual Property Rights of the Indigenous Nations and Peoples of the Wet Tropics Rainforest Area. This declaration was primarily concerned with bioprospecting and the intellectual property rights of indigenous peoples to traditional knowledge.[18]

In April 1995 the South Pacific Regional Consultation on Indigenous Peoples' Knowledge and Intellectual Property Rights was held in Suva, Fiji. The Final Statement issued by the Regional Consultation declared 'the right of indigenous peoples of the Pacific to self-governance and independence of our lands, territories and resources as the basis for the preservation of indigenous peoples' knowledge'. Article 7 urged the strengthening of indigenous networks and encouraged the UN and regional donors to continue and support discussions on indigenous peoples' knowledge and intellectual property rights. Article 8 pointed out the importance of strengthening 'the capacities of indigenous peoples to maintain their oral traditions, and encourage initiatives by indigenous peoples to record their knowledge in a permanent form according to their customary access procedures'. Finally, the Final Statement urged 'universities, churches, governments, non-governmental organizations and other institutions to reconsider their roles in the expropriation of indigenous peoples' knowledge and resources and to assist in their return to their rightful owners'.

One of the results of the United Nations International Year for the World's Indigenous Peoples was the promulgation of a Draft Declaration on the Rights of Indigenous Peoples. Article 12 of the Draft Declaration recognized the right of indigenous peoples to 'practice and revitalize their cultural traditions and customs', including the right:

> to maintain, protect and develop the past, present and future manifestations of their cultures, such as . . . artefacts, designs, ceremonies, technologies and visual and performing arts and literature, as well as the right to the restitution of cultural, intellectual, religious and spiritual property taken without their free and informed consent or in violation of their laws, traditions and customs.

Article 29 recognized the entitlement of indigenous peoples 'to the full ownership, control and protection of their cultural and intellectual property'. This article also asserted the right of indigenous peoples 'to special measures to control, develop and protect their . . . cultural manifestations, including . . . oral traditions, literatures, designs and visual and performing arts'.

The growing self-realization of indigenous peoples that the international recognition of their intellectual property rights in their cultural expressions would depend upon their own efforts, has resulted in the development of international solidarity through international conferences of indigenous peoples. These conferences have promulgated intellectual property declarations, formulating norms for the protection of traditional knowledge.[19]

HANS CHRISTIAN ANDERSEN, TRADITIONAL CULTURAL EXPRESSION AND INTELLECTUAL PROPERTY

The criticism that the concept of 'folklore' was derived from Eurocentric precepts is equally applicable to the concept of intellectual property itself. The propertization of traditional knowledge implies rights such as authorship, ownership, alienation and exploitation.

The work of Hans Christian Andersen illustrates the inappropriateness of this property paradigm to traditional cultural expression. In *The True Story of My Life*, Andersen relates how he learned Danish folk tales in his youth from old women in the spinning room of the insane asylum where his grand-mother worked. 'They considered me a marvelous clever child,' he recalls, 'too clever to live long, and they rewarded my eloquence by telling me fairy tales, and a world as rich as that of *The Thousand and One Nights* arose before me.'

His first four tales ('The Tinder Box', 'The Princess and the Pea', 'Little Claus and Big Claus' and 'Little Ida's Flowers') were published in May 1835. These earliest stories were clearly inspired by Danish folk tales. However they were not unadorned retellings of Danish folk stories, but were original fictions using Danish folklore as their starting point with eclectic borrowing from *The Thousand and One Nights*, one of the few books owned by his father, and from the German tales collected by the Brothers Grimm, who became personal friends of the young author. Unlike the folk tales collected by the Grimms, set in fictional distant lands once upon a time, Andersen set his tales in Copenhagen and other familiar, contemporary settings. He combined fantast-ical descriptions with common ordinary ones, and invested everyday house-hold objects (toys, dishes and so on) with personalities and magic. The raw and unpolished Danish of these first stories was as radical as Mozart's intro-duction of vernacular German to the Italianate world of the opera. Also inno-vative, even revolutionary was Andersen's abandonment of the conventional motivation of authors to teach and inculcate moral values. Despite the Christian imagery recurrent in his tales, which characterized nineteenth-century fiction, Andersen's tales were anarchic, comical, cynical and fatalistic rather than morally instructive.

The folkloric borrowings which form the basis for Hans Christian Andersen's early works illustrate a universal characteristic of cultural creativ-ity in which ancient themes and ideas are reworked in contemporary contexts. James Joyce's *Ulysses* is merely an explicit example of this genre. Indeed a number of the literary creations of Hans Christian Andersen, such as 'The Ugly Ducking', 'The Little Mermaid' and 'The Little Match Girl' have them-selves been reworked in subsequent works. It is probably the case that in Hans Christian Andersen, there is no author in which folklore and autonomous creativity are more closely interwoven.

An intellectual property regime which provides for the protection of tradi-tional cultural creativity should also permit the natural development of culture through permissible borrowings.

A particularly problematic instance of cultural borrowing is the use of sacred beliefs in apparently profane contexts. Salman Rushdie's *Satanic Verses* is an example of this genre. It is interesting to note in this regard that English copyright law began life as a system for the political censorship of works.

IDENTIFYING THE BENEFICIARIES OF TRADITIONAL CULTURAL EXPRESSION PROTECTION

In the debate about the protection of traditional cultural expression, the implied beneficiaries of this protection are traditional peoples. Invariably, these are referred to as 'indigenous peoples'. A definitional issue, related to the delineation of the content of traditional knowledge, is defining the groups or communities who can assert property rights over this knowledge.

The definition which appears to enjoy widest support is that of Dr Martinez Cobo,[20] who describes indigenous communities, peoples and nations as 'those which, having historical continuity with pre-invasion and precolonial societies that developed on their territories, consider themselves distinct from other sectors of the society now prevailing in those territories or parts of them'. However it should be acknowledged that a number of representatives of these groups have asserted that the diversity of the world's indigenous peoples renders problematic an all-embracing definition, and that efforts by the international community to develop a binding, all-inclusive definition are a diversion of energies.

Dr Erica-Martin Daes identifies four factors[21] which provide practical definitional guidance:

1. priority in time with respect to the occupation and use of a specific territory;
2. the voluntary perpetuation of cultural distinctiveness, which may include the aspects of language, social organization, religion and spiritual values, modes of production, laws and institutions;
3. self-identification, as well as self-recognition by other groups; and
4. an experience of subjugation, marginalization, dispossession, exclusion, or discrimination, whether or not these conditions persist.

A perceived corollary to an acceptable definition of the concept of 'indigenous peoples' is the expectation that as peoples they will be able to avail themselves of the protections conferred by international instruments such as the UN Charter, which in Article 1 refers to 'the principle of equal rights and self determination of peoples' and the International Covenant on Civil and Political Rights and the International Covenant on Economic, Social and Cultural Rights which similarly refer to the 'right of all peoples to self-determination'. However as General Assembly Resolution 1514 (XV) on the Granting of Independence to Colonial Countries and Peoples subsequently provided, the rights of peoples are subordinated to the sovereignty of states. This statist interpretation of the rights of peoples has been a barrier to the recognition of various political and property rights, including intellectual property rights, of indigenous peoples and traditional communities.

WHY PROTECT TRADITIONAL CULTURAL EXPRESSIONS?

Alan Jabbour suggested a taxonomy of four 'inchoate' concerns or anxieties which have led to international proposals for the protection of folklore.[22] Firstly, a concern for the authentication of folklore in the face of the economic, psychological and cultural threat from alien sources. Secondly, the expropriation, not only of physical objects, but also the documentary and photographic record of traditional societies. Thirdly, the issue of compensation for appropriation and cultural harm. Fourthly, the issue of nurture, or cultural health.

In Australia, these concerns have been manifested in five main areas: (1) the infringement of the copyright of individual artists; (2) the copying of works not authorized by aboriginal groups and communities; (3) the appropriation of Aboriginal images and themes; and (4) the culturally inappropriate use of Aboriginal images and styles by non-Aboriginal creators.

Each of these problems is addressed below, together with a consideration of the efficacy of existing intellectual property law to provide a remedy.

Copyright Infringements

There are numerous instances of the designs of Australian Aboriginal artists being reproduced without their permission. The Australian Copyright Act 1968 provides a remedy to artists whose works have been copied without authorization. The first case which attracted significant attention concerned the 1989 action brought by John Bulun Bulun and 13 other artists to obtain compensation concerning the unauthorized reproduction of their works on T-shirts.[23] The case attracted some attention as it came immediately after the Bicentennial celebrations, and injunctions and an out-of-court settlement of $150 000 was obtained in this matter.[24] A more recent reported case concerning the unauthorised copying of the designs of Aboriginal artists was *Milpurrurru v Indofurn Pty Ltd.*[25] This concerned the importation by a Perth-based company of carpets manufactured in Vietnam, upon which were reproduced the designs of George Milpurruru, Banduk Marika, Tim Payungka Tjapangati and five deceased Aboriginal artists. These designs had been copied from a portfolio of artworks produced by the Australian National Gallery. The defendants in this case were obliged to pay substantial damages.[26]

Copying not Authorized by Aboriginal Groups and Communities

Although the Australian Copyright Act provides a remedy in relation to the unauthorized copying of the works owned or licensed by individual creators, it does not recognize the communal harm which may result from the unauthorized reproduction of Aboriginal designs.

The claim of communal proprietorship in sacred images was rejected by the Federal Court in *Yumbulul v Reserve Bank of Australia*.[27] That case concerned an attempt by representatives of the Galpu Clan to prevent the reproduction by the Reserve Bank of the design of a Morning Star Pole on a commemorative banknote. The pole had been created by a member of the clan who had obtained his authority and knowledge to create the pole through initiation and revelatory ceremonies. The Galpu asserted that the communal obligation of the artist was such that he owed an obligation to the clan to prevent the design of the pole from being used in any way which was culturally offensive. Although sympathetic to this argument, the trial judge considered that the artist who had created the pole had successfully disposed of his intellectual property rights in it through a legally binding agreement. He lamented that 'Australia's copyright law does not provide adequate recognition of Aboriginal community claims to regulate the reproduction and use of works which are essentially communal in origin',[28] and concluded by recommending that 'the question of statutory recognition of Aboriginal communal interests in the reproduction of sacred objects is a matter for consideration by law reformers and legislators'.[29]

A related issue to the failure of the courts to recognize communal proprietorship of traditional works is their failure to compensate communal harm.[30] In *Milpurrurru*, mentioned above, the court awarded damages for breach of copyright to a number of Aboriginal artists whose designs were wrongfully reproduced on carpets. The court agreed that this was a particularly egregious breach of copyright, involving a culturally demeaning use of the infringed works. However the court considered itself unable to compensate the communities whose images were used in culturally inappropriate ways, as 'the statutory remedies do not recognise the infringement of ownership rights of the kind which reside under Aboriginal law in the traditional owners of the dreaming stories'.[31]

Indeed a major problem which has been identified in analysing traditional knowledge and cultural expression in conventional intellectual property terms is the observation that 'indigenous peoples do not view their heritage in terms of property at all . . . but in terms of community and individual responsibility. Possessing a song, story or medical knowledge carries with it certain responsibilities to show respect to and maintain a reciprocal relationship with the human beings, animals, plants and places with which the song, story or medicine is connected'.[32]

The most recent Australian case concerned with the communal rights of an Aboriginal people in Australia, *Bulun Bulun & Anor v R & T Textiles Pty Ltd*,[33] arose out of the importation and sale in Australia of printed clothing fabric which infringed the copyright of the Aboriginal artist, Mr John Bulun Bulun, in his work *Magpie Geese and Water Lillies at the Waterhole*. The proceedings were commenced on 27 February 1997 by Mr Bulun Bulun and by Mr George Milipurrurru. Both applicants were members of the Ganalbingu people. Ganalbingu country is situated in Arnhem Land in the Northern Territory of Australia. Mr Bulun Bulun sued as legal owner of the copyright in the painting and sought remedies for infringement under the Australian Copyright Act 1968. Mr Milpurrurru brought the proceedings in his own name and as a representative of the Ganalbingu, claiming that they were the equitable owners of the copyright subsisting in the painting.

Upon commencement of the proceedings, the respondents admitted to infringement of Mr Bulun Bulun's copyright and consented to permanent injunctions against future infringement. In its defence to Mr Milpurruru's actions the respondent pleaded that as Mr Bulun Bulun's claim had been satisfied, it was unnecessary to consider the question of the equitable ownership of the copyright. Mr Milpurrurru sought to continue the action as a test case on the communal intellectual property rights of indigenous Australian peoples arising from the copyright infringement.

The principal questions for the court to address were whether the communal interests of traditional Aboriginal owners in cultural artworks, recognized under Aboriginal law, created binding legal or equitable obligations on persons outside the relevant Aboriginal community. This depended upon there being a trust impressed upon expressions of ritual knowledge. The court acknowledged that amongst African tribal communities, tribal property was regarded as being held on trust by the customary head of a tribal group.[34] However in the instant case the court considered there to be no evidence of an express or implied trust created in respect of Mr Bulun Bulun's art. This was an issue of intention and the court found no evidence of any practice among the Ganalbingu whereby artworks were held in trust.

In an extensive *obiter dictum* in this test case, the court was prepared to impose fiduciary obligations upon Mr Bulun Bulun, as a tribal artist, to his people. The factors and relationships giving rise to fiduciary obligations under equity law do not admit of easy definition.[35] In the instant case, the Court found the subsistence of a fiduciary relationship between Mr Bulun Bulun and his people, arising from the trust and confidence reposed in him, that his artistic creativity would be exercised to preserve their integrity, law, custom, culture and ritual knowledge. The fiduciary obligation imposed on Mr Bulun Bulun was 'not to exploit the artistic work in such a way that is contrary to the laws and customs of the Ganalbingu people, and, in the event of infringement by a third party, to take reasonable and appropriate action to restrain and remedy infringement of the copyright in the artistic work'.

Simulation of Aboriginal Images by Non-Aboriginal Creators

A controversial issue in recent years in Australia has been the creation of works or products: (1) which are claimed to be produced by Aboriginal creators or which are got up in the style of Aboriginal schools of art; (2) by people who think that they are Aboriginal creators; (3) or which are allegedly inspired by Aboriginal spirits or muses.

In relation to works which are falsely claimed to be produced by Aboriginal persons, trade descriptions remedies would seem to provide an adequate remedy. Because of these remedies, some traders pass their work off as 'Aboriginal style' or 'Aboriginal inspired'. This sort of qualification may well avoid liability, but it remains as a dilution of the repute of genuine Aboriginal creations. A particular problem which has arisen in a couple of instances in Western Australia is that of works produced by persons who assert that they are of Aboriginal descent, or who claim to be inspired by an Aboriginal muse. In the first category are the books of Colin Johnson, written under the name of Mudrooroo Nyoongar, and the books of Leon Carmen, written as those of an Aboriginal woman, Wanda Koolmatrie. Similarly the Western Australian artist Elizabeth Durack, painting under the pseudonym Eddie Burrup, claims to be inspired by an Aboriginal spirit. These impostures range from the malicious to the misguided, but each has been criticized as offensive to Aboriginal Peoples.[36] On the other hand, in Western eyes, the reinterpretation of classical stories is often considered to stand at the heart of some modern literature.

Culturally Offensive Use of Aboriginal Images and Themes

The adoption of Aboriginal themes and motifs in products has sometimes caused harm to those Aboriginal peoples for whom those matters have great spiritual and cultural significance. The National Indigenous Arts Advocacy Association, Inc. (NIAAA) reported the use of the Wandjina spirit as a logo for a surfboard company.[37] The Wandjina are the Creation Ancestors of the Kimberley Aboriginal People and their painted images are found in the rock galleries in that region. The question of authorship is impossible to resolve as it is believed that the paintings were done by the Wandjina.[38] In any event, the antiquity of these images means that their authorship is unknown. Wandjina images may be retouched or painted today, provided that appropriate deference is given to the ancient spirits. The Kimberley Aborigines believe that inappropriate treatment of these images will cause death and devastation.[39] However there is currently no law to prevent the use of these images by commercial enterprises.[40]

In *Foster v Mountford*[41] an anthropology text, *Nomads of the Desert*, which was written to document the life of the Pitjantjatjara people, reproduced images which were forbidden to uninitiated members of the Pitjantjatjara. The court in this case was prepare to grant an injunction to prevent the book being distributed in the Northern Territory because the author had been shown these sacred matters in confidence.[42]

However Aboriginal peoples have no right equivalent to those which are conferred under the action of blasphemy. The NIAAA report refers to a story used in the television series *Heartlands* which belonged to a Western Australian Aboriginal community, but which was represented as coming from New South Wales.[43] Because the story was in the public domain, the relevant community had no rights to prevent the transmission of this programme. The law does not currently recognize the proprietary interests of Aboriginal peoples in their Dreamings, stories, sacred images or dances.

Related to the culturally offensive use of Aboriginal themes is the misrepresentation of Aboriginal cultural life. A recent spectacular instance of this concerns the publication in 1990 of the book *Mutant Message Down Under*, by American author Marlo Morgan. This book contained an account of Morgan's alleged travels among 'cannibalistic' Western Australian Aboriginal tribes. The book was on the US bestsellers list for 25 weeks and was short-listed for the 1995 American Booksellers Book of the Year, and the author merchandised CDs and videos to promote the work and her form of new age spiritualism. Following a detailed investigation for the Kimberley Law Centre, it was revealed that the author had never visited Australia. And she confessed that the work was a hoax.

Another factor which has played an important role in agitation for the protection of traditional cultural works is economics. As in other areas of piracy and counterfeiting, Ralph Oman has highlighted the developments in communications and reprographic technologies which have exposed formerly isolated cultures to digital imitation and to global transmission, without compensation.[44] As with the exploitation of developing countries through bioprospecting, the exploitation of traditional cultural resources without exploitation raises similar issues.[45] Indeed Chengsi has suggested that folklore protection has become a trade-related issue.[46]

MODALITIES FOR THE PROTECTION OF TRADITIONAL KNOWLEDGE

Proposals of mechanisms for the protection of traditional knowledge have ranged across two axes. Along one axis are various suggestions to improve the private law rights of the creators or custodians of traditional knowledge. These suggestions range from proposals to modify existing copyright law through to the creation of *sui generis* traditional knowledge rights. Along another axis are suggestions to deal with the protection of traditional knowledge as a public law right. These suggestions range from the creation of a public protection authority, through *domaine public payant* proposals, to the empowerment of indigenous peoples' protective agencies. These various suggestions are considered below.

At the minimalist end of discussions concerning the protection of traditional knowledge are suggestions to deal with the perceived inadequacies of existing intellectual property laws by supplementary legislation. It should be noted at the outset that a number of commentators have questioned whether traditional knowledge is amenable to private law remedies. For example Rosemary Coombe has raised the issue of the applicability of private law concepts to cultural expressions.[47] Puri questions whether property concepts are cognizable under customary Aboriginal law.[48] Daes explains:

> indigenous peoples do not view their heritage as property at all – that is something which has an owner and is used for the purpose of extracting economic benefits – but in terms of community and individual responsibility. Possessing a song, story or medicinal knowledge carries with it certain responsibilities to show respect to and maintain a reciprocal relationship with the human beings, animals, plants and places with which the song, story or medicine is connected. For indigenous peoples, heritage is a bundle of relationships rather than a bundle of economic rights.[49]

However bearing these reservations in mind, the various private and public law suggestions for the protection of traditional knowledge are canvassed below.

Copyright

As has been indicated, in the survey of Australian cases above, existing copyright law does not easily recognize communal authorship, and to a lesser extent communal ownership. Both of these matters can be dealt with by statutory amendment. For example a form of representative or class action could be brought by indigenous and communal groups.

Another ownership issue is the matter canvassed in the *Yumbulul* case, discussed above, whether notwithstanding an assignment of copyright, a communal group retains the underlying right to the folklore. It has been suggested that this could be dealt with by the recognition of an underlying equitable right in the communal group.[50] This right would seem to have a similar quality to the moral rights which are recognized in civil law jurisdictions.

A major limitation of Western copyright law is its insistence upon material fixation as a precondition for protection. The Tunis Model Law on Copyright for Developing Countries, 1976, in s1(5*bis*) provides a useful precedent of the fixation requirement being waived for folklore.

The limited duration of copyright protection has been perceived as a problem for traditional works, some of which may have originated many thousands of years ago. Again this is a problem which could yield to appropriate legislative drafting.

It has been suggested that the unauthorized appropriation of the styles of indigenous peoples could be dealt with by the concept of copyright in derivative works.[51]

In general, the view of many commentators and committees of review is that the legal structure of copyright, with its emphasis on private proprietorial rights, is ill suited to protect traditional works.[52]

Moral Rights

Another copyright possibility for the protection of traditional knowledge is within the rubric of moral rights. Each of the moral rights of publication, paternity and integrity has an applicability to the protection of traditional knowledge. The right of publication allows a creator to decide whether a work should be made public. This would permit the creators of spiritually sensitive works to control their dissemination. The right to have paternity acknowledged would be useful in securing the authentication of traditional works. Most important is the right of integrity, which protects works from distortion, alteration or misrepresentation.

Domaine Public Payant

To deal with the fact that copyright works fall into the public domain after a finite time, a number of states have introduced legislation to prevent or sanction the use of such works, which would prejudice their authenticity or identity.[53] Additionally, a fee may be imposed for the use of such works. The moneys thereby received can be diverted to the promotion of cultural activities. This scheme is particularly suited for the nurturing of traditional works. The Tunis Model Law on Copyright encourages the use of *domaine public payant* to assist developing countries to 'protect and disseminate national folklore'.[54] However the extent to which this sort of law can protect traditional works has been questioned.[55]

Authentication Marks

A suggestion emanating from IP Australia, the Australian intellectual property office, is the appending of an authentication mark to works of indigenous creativity. This will be in the nature of a certification mark,[56] although of course it will be limited to certain manifestations of traditional knowledge.

Public Protection Models

The approach to protection which was adopted in the Model Provisions for National Laws on the Protection of Expressions of Folklore Against Illicit Exploitation and Other Prejudicial Action envisaged a system of prior authorization to be administered by a competent authority representing the relevant traditional community's interest in protecting its folklore. Authorization was required for commercial uses of folklore other than in the traditional and customary context, subject to the supervision of the competent authority.

Where folklore was used in a traditional context, an authorization was needed for publication, recitation, performance or distribution. Use of folklore outside its traditional context would have to seek the prior consent of the community or an authorized person. Authorization was not required for uses of expressions of folklore if the purpose relates to research, conservation and archiving. Furthermore, there is no need for authorization, outside of the traditional or customary context, when an expression of folklore was used: for educational purposes; by way of illustration; for creating an original new work; for reporting of a current event; and where folklore is permanently situated in a public place.

The Model Law prohibited unauthorized commercial use of expressions of folklore. It provided that where the competent authority granted authorization, it could set the level of remuneration and collect fees. The fees would be used for the purpose of promoting or safeguarding national culture or folklore. The commentary on the Model Law suggested that it would be advisable to share this fee with the community from which the folklore originated. The Model Law provided for offences relating to distortions of expressions of folklore. The offence provisions required the element of 'wilful intent', with fines and imprisonment imposed as punishment. There were also civil sanctions and seizure provisions.

The Model Law was anticipated in Australia by the 1981 *Report of the Working Party on the Protection of Aboriginal Folklore*, which envisaged the appointment of a Commissioner of Aboriginal Folklore to exercise a protective jurisdiction. The commissioner, rather than indigenous peoples, would initiate litigation against infringing activities. This report was commended in the 1982 WIPO/UNESCO meeting of experts on folklore,[57] but it was not implemented. The notion of a protective jurisdiction would certainly not find favour today. Certainly in Australia, the notion of a government-administered, protective jurisdiction has been thoroughly discredited, particularly because of the disastrous consequences of other paternalistic policies of protectivism.

However in countries which have not endured this sort of colonial experience, the protective model is considered unobjectionable. For example the folklore provisions of the Nigerian Copyright Act 1988 are based extensively on the WIPO/UNESCO Model Law and the supervision of the exploitation of cultural works is conferred upon the Nigerian Copyright Council.[58]

TRADITIONAL CULTURAL EXPRESSION AND SELF-DETERMINATION

The discourse about the protection of traditional knowledge assumes the necessity for this protection and also assumes that the primary beneficiaries of this protection will be indigenous peoples and community groups. However the state, as guardian of its people's cultural heritage, also has an interest in the preservation of the traditional knowledge which exists within it.[59] The various African laws which seek to protect folklore stress its significance as part of the national heritage.[60] Multiculturalism has begun to replace nationalist uniformity as the new orthodoxy. An incidental beneficiary will be the nation state: first, from the vigour of cultural health, and second, from the commercial exploitation of traditional knowledge.

A corollary to the assumption of the necessity to protect traditional knowledge is the assertion of the right of indigenous peoples and traditional communities 'to determine the appropriateness of the use being made of their culture'.[61] Thus Erica-Irene Daes declared that 'each indigenous community must retain permanent control over all elements of its own heritage. It may share the right to enjoy and use certain elements of its heritage under its own laws and procedures, but always reserves a perpetual right to determine how shared knowledge is used'.[62]

The increasing involvement of indigenous peoples in models for the protection of traditional knowledge can be seen in the Australian experience. In 1981 the *Report of the Working Party on the Protection of Aboriginal Folklore* proposed the establishment of a Commissioner for Aboriginal Folklore, who would exercise a protective jurisdiction on behalf of traditional peoples. Further reports in 1987,[63] 1989[64] and 1994[65] made recommendations which envisaged an increasing role for indigenous peoples in the protection of traditional knowledge. In 1998–99 Australian indigenous peoples conducted their own inquiry, based on a discussion paper 'Our Culture, Our Future: Proposals for the Recognition and Protection of Indigenous Cultural and Intellectual Property'.[66]

Today in Australia, indigenous peoples regard the protection of traditional knowledge as an issue of self-determination.[67] For other countries, with a less unfortunate colonial history, the issue of who controls the protection and conservation of traditional knowledge might be less politicized.

Among the political issues which have been raised in Australia are whether Eurocentric intellectual property law can be trusted with the subject of traditional knowledge.[68] Similarly, it has been suggested that 'a suspicious eye should be cast over any assertion of legal or moral authority by non-Indigenous people to adjudicate disputes between traditional and non-traditional artists'.[69]

NOTES

1. See [1963] *Le Droit d'Auteur* 250.
2. Cameroon, Congo, Dahomey, Gabon, Ivory Coast, Madagascar, Mali, Niger, Senegal, Upper Volta [1967] *Le Droit d'Auteur*, 132–3.
3. See for example S. Ricketson, *The Berne Convention for the Protection of Literary and Artistic Works; 1886–1986*, London, CCLS, 1987, at 607–20.
4. *Study on the International Regulations of Intellectual Property*, UNESCO/WIPO/WG.1/FOLK/3, Tunis, 11–13 July 1977.
5. 'Report', [1985] *Copyright: Monthly Review of the World Intellectual Property Organization*, 40 at 41.
6. '1967, 1982, 1984: Attempts to Provide International Protection for Folklore by Intellectual Property Rights', WIPO doc., UNESCO-WIPO/FOLK/PKT/97/19 (21 March 1997), 15.
7. WIPO doc, UNESCO-WIPO/FOLK/PKT/97/1 (17 March 1997).
8. Ibid., 3.
9. Ibid.
10. For example see Janke, 'UNESCO-WIPO World Forum on the Protection of Folklore: Lessons for Protecting Indigenous Australian Cultural and Intellectual Property' (1997) 15 *Copyright Reporter* 104 at 109.
11. Ibid., at 110.
12. Working Group on Indigenous Populations, *Study on the Protection of the Cultural and Intellectual Property of Indigenous Peoples*, E/CN.4/Sub.2/1993/28, 28 July 1993.
13. For example Puri, 'Copyright Protection of Folklore; a New Zealand Perspective' (1988) 22 (3) *Copyright Bulletin* 18; Blain and De Silva, 'Aboriginal Art and Copyright' (1991) 75 *Copyright Bulletin* 1; Blakeney, 'Protecting Expressions of Australian Aboriginal Folklore under Copyright Law', [1995] 9 *EIPR* 442; Chengsi, 'On the Copyright Protection of Folklore and Other Legislation in China' (1996) 3 *China Patents and Trade Marks* 91; Puri, 'Preservation and Conservation of Expressions of Folklore' (1998) 32 (4) *Copyright Bulletin* 5; Brown, 'Can Culture be Copyrighted?' (1998) 39 *Current Anthropology* 193.
14. For example see Blakeney, 'Bioprospecting and the Protection of Traditional Medical Knowledge of Indigenous Peoples: An Australian Perspective' [1997] 6 *EIPR* 298.
15. See Blakeney, 'Biodiversity Rights and Traditional Resource Rights of Indigenous Peoples' [1998] 2 *Bio-Science Law Review* 52.
16. T. Simpson, *Indigenous Heritage and Self-Determination*, IWGIA Document 86 (Copenhagen, 1997), 55.
17. On the biodiversity rights of indigenous peoples see Blakeney, 'Access to Genetic Resources: the View from the South' [1997] 3 *Bio-Science Law Review* 94.
18. See Blakeney, 'Bioprospecting and the Protection of Traditional Medical Knowledge of Indigenous Peoples: an Australian Perspective' [1997] 6 EIPR 298.
19. See Appendix 1 for a full list of Indigenous Peoples' Declarations.
20. *Study of the Problem of Discrimination Against Indigenous Populations*, E/CN.4/Sub.2/1986/7 and Add.1–4.
21. Daes, 'Rights of Indigenous Peoples', paper presented at Pacific Workshop on the United Nations Draft Declaration on the Rights of Indigenous Peoples, Suva, Fiji, September, 1996, 28.
22. Jabbour, 'Folklore Protection and National Patrimony: Developments and Dilemmas in the Legal Protection of Folklore' (1982) 17 (1) *Copyright Bulletin* 10 at 11–12.

23. *Bulun Bulun v Nejlam Pty Ltd*, Federal Court of Australia, Darwin, 1989 (unreported), referred to in Golvan, 'Aboriginal Art and copyright. The Case for Johnny Bulun Bulun', [1989] 10 *European Intellectual Property Reporter* 346; C. Golvan, *An Introduction to Intellectual Property Law* (Sydney: Federation Press, 1992), 51.
24. Ibid.
25. (1995) 91-116 *CCH Australian Intellectual Property Cases* 39,051.
26. See also the discussion of this case in Miller, 'Collective Ownership of the Copyright in Spiritually-Sensitive Works: Milpurrorru v Indofurn Pty Ltd', (1995) 6 *UNSW Law Jnl*. 185.
27. (1991) 2 *Intellectual Property Reports* 481.
28. (1991) 2 *Intellectual Property Reports* at 490.
29. Ibid., at 492.
30. See Blakeney, 'Communal Intellectual Property Rights of Indigenous People in Cultural Expressions', (1998) 1 *Jnl of World Intellectual Property* 985.
31. (1995) 91-116 *CCH Australian Intellectual Property Cases* at 39,077.
32. E.I. Daes, *Discrimination Against Indigenous Peoples: Study on the Protection of the Cultural and Intellectual Property of Indigenous Peoples* (1993), para.26 quoted in Puri, 'Cultural Ownership and Intellectual Property Rights Post-Mabo: Putting Ideas into Action', (1995) 9 *Intellectual Property Journal* 293 at 308.
33. [1998] 1082 FCA (3 September 1998), reported at <http://www.austlii.edu.au/au/cases/cth/federal_ct/1998/1082.html>.
34. Citing, Asante, 'Fiduciary Principles in Anglo-American Law and The Customary Law of Ghana' (1965) 14 *International and Comparative Law Qtly* 1144 at 1145.
35. See P. Finn, *Fiduciary Obligations* (Sydney; Law Book Co, 1977), 1; Weinrib, 'The Fiduciary Obligation' (1975) 25 *University of Toronto Law Jnl*.1 at 4; Sealy, 'Fiduciary Obligations, Forty Years On' (1995) 9 *Journal of Contract Law* 37.
36. For example see van der Berg, 'Intellectual Property Rights for Aboriginal People', *Oceania Newsletter*, 20 March, 1998, [Internet] http://www.kun.nl/cps/20/nb20c.html.
37. NIAAA, *Stopping the Ripoffs*, Sydney, May, 1995, 5.
38. See J. Isaacs, *Australian Dreaming: 40,000 Years of Aboriginal History*, Sydney: Ure Smith, 1980, 73.
39. Ibid., 74.
40. See also Golvan, 'Aboriginal Art and the Protection of Indigenous Cultural Rights', (1995) 2 *Aboriginal Law Bulletin*, 5.
41. (1976) 14 *Australian Law Reports* 71
42. Applied also in *Pitjantjatjara Council Inc. v. Lowe* (Unreported, Vic. Sup Ct, 26 March 1982) noted in (1982) 4 *Aboriginal Law Bulletin* 11.
43. NIAAA, n.4, *supra*, 7.
44. Oman, 'Folkloric Treasures: The Next Copyright Frontier' (1996) 15(4) *Newsletter* (ABA Section of Intellectual Property Law), 3.
45. See Wiener, 'Protection of Folklore: A Political and Legal Challenge' (1987) 18 *IIC* 59 at 67.
46. Chengsi, 'On the Copyright Protection of Folklore and Other Legislation in China' (1996) 3 *China Patents and Trade Marks* 91 at 93.
47. For example see R. Coombe, *The Cultural Life of Intellectual Properties: Authorship, Appropriation and the Law* (Duke University Press, 1998) and Coombe, 'Critical Cultural Legal Studies', (1998) 10 *Yale Jnl of Law and the Humanities* 463.
48. Puri, 'Cultural Ownership and Intellectual Property Rights Post Mabo: Putting Ideas into Action' (1995) 9 *IPJ* 293.
49. Daes, n.xvii, *supra*, para.26.
50. Golvan, 'Aboriginal Art and the Protection of Indigenous Cultural Rights' [1992] 7 *EIPR* 227 at 230.
51. See Australian Copyright Council, n.xiii, at 43–4.
52. For a recent survey, see Berryman, 'Towards a More Universal Protection of Intangible Cultural Property', (1999) <www.lasch.uga.edu/~jipl/vol.1/berryman.html>.
53. See 'Study of Comparative Copyright Law: Protection of Works in the Public Domain' (1981) 15(2) *Copyright Bulletin* 33.

54. Tunis Model Law on Copyright for Developing Countries, s.17.
55. For example Jabbour, n.xvi, *supra*, at 14; Niedzielska,'The Intellectual Property Aspects of Folklore Protection' (1980) 16 *Copyright* 339 at 344.
56. See Annas, 'The Label Authenticity: A Certification Trade Mark for Goods and Services of Indigenous Origin' (1997) 3 *Aboriginal Law Bulletin* 4.
57. UNESCO/PRS/CLT/TPC/II/3, 30 November 1984.
58. See Shyllon, 'Conservation, Preservation and the Legal Protection of Folklore in Africa: a General Survey' (1998) 32 (4) *Copyright Bulletin* 37 at 42.
59. See Niec, 'Legislative Models of Protection of Cultural Property' (1976) 27 *Hastings Law Jnl* 1089.
60. For example the Copyright Acts of Angola, Gabon, Democratic Republic of Congo, Malawi, and Tunisia, discussed in Shyllon, 'Conservation, Preservation and the Legal Protection of Folklore in Africa: a General Survey' (1998) 32 (4) *Copyright Bulletin* 37.
61. Pask, 'Cultural Appropriation and the Law: An Analysis of the Legal Regimes Concerning Culture' (1993) 8 *IPJ* 57 at 61.
62. Daes, 'Study on the Protection of the Cultural and Intellectual Property of Indigenous Peoples', paper presented to the 45th session of the UN Sub-Commission on Prevention of Discrimination and Protection of Minorities, Geneva, 1993, quoted in Australian Copyright Council, n.xiii, 56.
63. Committee of Inquiry into Folklife, *Folklife: Our Living Heritage*, Canberra: AGPS, 1987.
64. Department of Aboriginal Affairs Review Committee, *The Aboriginal Arts and Crafts Industry*, Canberra: AGPS, 1989.
65. Ministers for Justice, Aboriginal and Torres Strait Islander Affairs, Communications and the Arts, *Stopping the Rip-Offs – Intellectual Property Protection for Aboriginal and Torres Strait Islanders*, Canberra: AGPS, 1994.
66. Available at http://www.icip.com.au
67. For example see Fourmile, 'Aboriginal Heritage Legislation and Self Determination' (1989) 7 *Australian-Canadian Studies, Special Issue*, 45.
68. For example see Maddocks, 'Copyright and Traditional Design: An Aboriginal Dilemma' (1988) 2(34) *Aboriginal Law Bulletin* 6.
69. Gray, 'Black Enough? Urban and Non-traditional Aboriginal Art and Proposed Legislative Protection for Aboriginal Art' (1996) 7 (3) *Culture and Policy* 29.

7. Should the logic of 'open source' be applied to digital cultural goods? An exploratory essay

Lee Davis

INTRODUCTION

While digitization has affected all forms of intellectual property rights (IPRs) – patents, trademarks, copyrights, and the like – its strongest impact has been felt in the copyright industries. For example while patent protection has been extended to cover many inventions in software and software-implemented business methods, most patented products (such as drugs, chemicals, electronic circuits and machines) have retained their physical form. Similarly, while the trademark system has been the focus of bitter conflicts over the rights to use particular marks as Internet domain names without confusing and misleading customers, most trademarked products (such as automobiles, soft drinks, cereals and perfumes) have remained physical as well.[1]

In industries where copyrights are important, digitization has affected every form of innovation, in terms of both the underlying technology used to produce them, and the inventions themselves. Software programs are the most obvious example. But almost all cultural works, including paintings, literature, recorded music, TV broadcasts, films and video games, can now be expressed in virtual form. These works can be transmitted over the Internet, easily accessible to anyone, anywhere, around the world, readily altered by the click of the mouse. Not only have the copyright industries grown extremely rapidly in recent years, but pervasive digitization has also challenged the foundations of copyright law.

One result has been an increased interest in the economic role of copyrights, either specifically (Landes and Posner 1989), or in the context of a comparative analysis of the different forms of IPRs (for example Besen and Raskind 1991; Landes and Posner 2003; Maskus 2000). But most studies still focus on patents (for example Andersen 2004; Davis 2004; Gallini and Scotchmer 2002; Mazzoleni and Nelson 1998). While a number of empirical studies have examined the effectiveness of different strategies of appropriability (for example

Cohen et al. 2000; Levin et al. 1987), none has looked at copyrights in this connection. This chapter seeks to contribute to the growing literature on the changing role of copyrights in light of the increasingly pervasive digitization of cultural and artistic creations (for example Andersen et al. 2004; Arkenbout et al. 2004; Band 2001; Beal and Marin 2003; Cheverie 2002; Landes and Lichtman 2003; Langenderfer and Kopp 2004; Strickland 2003, 2003–2004; Towse 2001). Much of what is discussed in this exploratory chapter however has not yet been described in the scholarly literature, but is based on searches of the Internet and articles in the trade press.

We will focus on the implications of one of the most compelling developments in recent years: that the copyright has inspired its own antithesis, with the growth of the 'open source software' (OSS) movement (for example Bonaccorsi and Rossi 2003; Gallaway and Kinnear 2004; Kogut and Metiu 2001; Merges 2004; Mustonen 2004; O'Mahony 2003; Varner 2000; Weber 2004; West 2003). Here the copyright serves not to exclude others, but as the legal basis for a novel licensing scheme, the General Public Licence (GPL), popularly known as 'copyleft'. This licence stipulates that anyone has the right to use, modify and distribute the program covered by the licence, on the condition that any changes or additions those users make to the program will themselves be licensed out under the same liberal terms. In the open source approach, technological development is driven by the mutual and open exchange of technical know-how, ideas and source codes within a virtual community of software innovators, whose contributions are coordinated and integrated over the Internet.

Against the background of these changes, and the all-encompassing digitization of the copyright industries, this chapter seeks to explore in a preliminary manner the implications of the application of the open source approach to digital cultural creations in literature, music, film and art. Here, the copyright would establish the legal basis by which artists could cooperate in the continuous development of creative works by facilitating free access to these changes. To what extent, and in what ways, would this approach be beneficial – or destructive? Should art be seen as static, or dynamic – or both? To what degree should works of art of previous centuries be allowed to preserve their cultural integrity? Against this background, we discuss the relevance of our arguments for the contemporary use of the stories of Hans Christian Andersen.

The technology to accomplish changes of this type in fact already exists. A number of Internet sites can now be accessed that contain the full text in English of Andersen's major fairy tales. This is true for example of 'The Ugly Duckling', available at: http://en.wikipedia.org/wiki/The_Ugly_Duckling. Two English translations of 'The Emperor's New Clothes' may be accessed at http://en.wikipedia.org/wiki/The_Emperor's_New_Clothes. At the time of writing (March 2005), 21 fairy tales have been published in this manner. The stories are extensively linked to other home pages. Thus after accessing the Internet text of 'The Emperor's New Clothes', readers can link into other sites through words in the text like 'clothing', 'invisible' and 'nothing on at all', to learn what these words mean. Or they can link into a description of how Andersen himself might have received his inspiration. Such texts might well provide a child's first knowledge of Andersen's fairy tales, and can increasingly be expected to do so in the future.

And this is not all that readers, technically, can do. They can copy the text of the fairy tale, paste it into a word document, and then freely play with, and manipulate, Andersen's words. If they wish, they can combine these textual modifications with contributions from other digital media. For example a person could download the text of 'The Emperor's New Clothes', add some new characters, replace the Emperor with an Empress, delete some events, modernize the dialogue, illustrate the revised text with pictures accessed on the Internet, insert a medley of themes from pop and classical music to set the mood, and upload the new file onto the Internet for others to enjoy. More ambitious readers could turn the story into an interactive game. Everyone who accessed the revised file would be free to add their own modifications, resulting in a continuous stream of changes.

The results might be highly creative. But they might just as easily be 'mush'. Whatever the case, the stories created would be far from Andersen's original work.

This chapter starts with a discussion of how increasing digitization has challenged the economic role of the copyright. The next section traces the genesis and development of the open source movement. The following section explores how the logic of open source might be applied to cultural and artistic works, and some of the advantages and disadvantages. The chapter concludes with a discussion of some of the wider implications of our analysis.

THE DIGITAL CHALLENGE TO COPYRIGHTED GOODS

The purpose of intellectual property rights is both to provide incentives for innovators to invest in creating or improving new products and processes, and to promote the diffusion of these inventions throughout society. Like a patent, a copyright gives the innovator the legal right to exclude others from making, selling or using the good, and thereby to appropriate the associated profits, which might otherwise be captured by imitators or other market participants. Other market players can learn from and build on the protected work, using this knowledge as an inspiration for their own activities. Patents and copyrights can be seen as a means of coordinating innovative activity and distributing the associated costs and benefits.

But the two differ in important respects. A copyright protects the form or configuration by which an idea is expressed. A patent protects the underlying idea of the invention. A copyright arises spontaneously upon the publication of a work; the only requirement is that the work be original. To be patented, an invention must fulfil specific criteria (novelty, non-obviousness, industrial utility). Application must be made to a government agency, the Patent and Trademark Office. After several years, this agency may, or may not, decide to issue the patent. But the thoroughness of the application process means that the patent is a much stronger form of IPR than a copyright. A copyright holder, like a patent holder, has the right to prevent unauthorized use. But important exceptions for copyrights exist. For example satires of existing works are normally not felt to infringe the copyright. The more limited scope of copyright protection means that it is relatively easy to obtain a new copyright on a slightly different version of a work.

Pervasive digitization has exacerbated the problems faced by copyright holders in capturing value from their investments in creative work, since all works of art and music, and most works of art (sculpture and architecture are exceptions), can be digitized. Digital information goods differ from other types of economic goods in that they can be encoded as streams of bits, drastically lowering both reproduction and distribution costs (Beal and Marin 2003; Davis 2002; Shapiro and Varian 1999). Digital copies are also indistinguishable from the originals, and can easily be manipulated. Alterations to a typed page of paper (facilitated by 'white out', for example) will always be visible, while alterations to a digital copy will not, since the altered copy can be printed to look like an original. In addition, digital information goods consist of information, which has certain of the characteristics of a public good. Once provided, its use by one party does not diminish its availability to others. The creators of information can also find it difficult to exclude others from using the information, even though intellectual property rights, if effectively implemented, can raise the costs of doing so. Information also represents an extreme form of 'experience good'. For consumers to fully understand its value, they must experience it.

Generally speaking, firms can choose to enforce their copyrights rigidly, or leverage them to create value in other ways. A case in point concerns the contrasting approaches of the creators of Disney films and of Barney the Dinosaur, as described by Shapiro and Varian (1999). Disney strongly enforced its copyrights and demanded that any kindergarten that showed videos of its films pay licence royalties. Sheryl Leach, the creator of Barney the Dinosaur, made the video available free to kindergartens. Disney's policy insured a continuous income stream. But Leach's tactic generated considerable momentum for Barney, since many children who had seen the video demanded that their parents buy a copy of it in stores. This enabled Barney to acquire an expanding market niche. Leach's success underlines that innovators, by not enforcing their copyrights, may be able to gain an even larger market share than they would obtain through a more exclusive approach.

The new digital technologies carry some advantages for copyright holders. Since information is an experience good, even if consumers know what a book is, they cannot fully appreciate the value of a particular book until they read it themselves. To whet their appetites, a publisher can make portions of the text available online, giving potential readers a sense of what the book is all about. Given that most people prefer to read a paper copy than an electronic version of a book, this may increase the sales of the physical copies. This advantage is less pronounced for physical inventions that are protected by patents. While consumers might be persuaded to buy the product after seeing a picture of it on the Internet, they cannot actually experience the good in cyberspace.

For the most part however, digital technologies make copyrighted works more vulnerable to abuse. Once a consumer buys a book, he or she can scan it digitally, and make copies available over the Internet. CDs, films and video games can be uploaded directly onto the Internet, and distributed widely, without the authors even becoming aware of this. Digitization makes it easier for other market agents to make small changes in an original work, in order to take out their own copyrights. And while it is never legal to imitate a patented invention without the permission of the owner, according to copyright law, private individuals may make individual copies of copyrighted goods for their own perusal. Copyright law thus seeks to differentiate between private and commercial use.

But again this creates a dilemma for the copyright industries. There can be little doubt that the publishers of academic journals benefit if potential readers learn about their articles via online access over the Internet. But if users simply download and print the articles of interest to them, and university libraries do not buy hard copies, these publishers may well lose revenues (depending on the nature of the copyright agreement between the publishers and the university). A complicating factor is that users are regulated according to their national jurisdictions. How, then, can a firm effectively pursue infringers when its website is accessed by users outside the firm's own national jurisdiction?

Widespread Internet access among music lovers, and the advent of decentralized file-sharing services, have exacerbated infringement problems. One response, as recently exercised by the music and film industries in the United States, is to initiate legal action. In the autumn of 2003, the Recording Industry Association of America, which represents the five major music companies, filed 261 lawsuits against people who share music files online. They justified this action by arguing that they cannot simply sit back and do nothing, as their revenues decline in the wake of the torrent of illegal downloads. But infringement suits punish the very people these firms depend upon for their business.

The lawsuits resulted in a stream of negative publicity, leaving a residue of bad will among their customers, who objected to the idea of people being sued just because they enjoyed the companies' own products!

These trends have led to considerable soul-searching among the copyright industries. One result has been the movement to make the existing copyright framework more flexible, with the establishment of more varied and more liberal licensing schemes. For example Lawrence Lessig's Creative Commons (http://creativecommons.org) helps artists, writers, programmers and others obtain flexible, customizable IP licences free of charge, so that they can define legally which uses of their work are acceptable, and which are not. Some licences allow others to copy, distribute, display or perform a work, or works derived from it, as long as they give the author credit and/or use it solely for non-commercial purposes. The licence can also exclude derivative works. Another choice is to allow others to distribute derivative works, but only under the conditions of the licence governing the distribution of the author's original work. In this chapter, we investigate the applicability of one such scheme: extending the logic of the open source approach to software development to digital cultural goods.

THE GENESIS AND DEVELOPMENT OF THE OPEN SOURCE APPROACH TO SOFTWARE DEVELOPMENT

The open source software (OSS) movement was spawned in the 1970s by academics and hackers, driven by a vision to ensure that innovations in computer programs should remain publicly available to a community of users. Working together and communicating with each other across cyberspace, OSS users contributed to the continued development and improvement of existing software. All modifications were made freely available via the General Public Licence (GPL). This was legally based on copyright law, but formulated in such a way as to ensure that no user could earn profits from privatizing the software (O'Mahony 2003). The GPL, in other words, was 'viral' in nature, forcing any programs derived from the original program to be governed by the GPL terms. Software innovations such as Linux and Freenet were specifically designed as non-proprietary, and at least in part motivated by the desire to erode the proprietary positions of companies like Microsoft.

The open source approach to software development differs from the more liberal approach to copyrights described above with regard to Barney the Dinosaur. Sheryl Leach made copies of the video freely available to kindergartens, but did not encourage children to become involved in the innovation process. Under the OSS framework, users would be encouraged to contribute actively to the further development of the product. The tangible nature of the videotape also limited the amount of copying that could occur.

During recent years, the concept of 'open source software' has become blurred. Today, the term is more generic, referring to projects characterized by open access and ongoing community participation and development. Novel licensing schemes have been introduced that differ from the GPL, in that they allow some restrictions in the availability of the software (see http://opensource.org). This somewhat looser definition forms the basis of the arguments below. It is also necessary to adopt this concept of open source in a chapter exploring its potential applicability to the stories of Hans Christian Andersen, since the author is no longer alive to control the terms of possible use of his work. Thus it could not be part of a typical contemporary GPL arrangement.

One of the most baffling questions, since the introduction of OSS, is what motivates people to participate in its development, given that they cannot exercise exclusive rights to their inventions through copyrights. Scholars who have addressed this problem (for example Bonaccorsi and Rossi 2003; Kogut and Metiu 2001; Mustonen 2003; Von Krogh and Von Hippel 2003) agree that the answer is that OSS creates a special type of incentive structure based on recognition and reputation benefits. These are briefly summarized below:

- First, contributors say they find the process enjoyable and rewarding. Being part of a larger OSS endeavour provides intrinsic utility in the form of intellectual gratification and satisfaction.
- Second, contributing to an OSS project also enables people to continue to update their own knowledge. And because the system is available to all, the programmers knew that not only would others gain access to their own contributions, but also that they would be able to access work done by others, both at present and in terms of future modifications.
- Third, the fact that the source code is available to all creates a powerful incentive for all to contribute well-written code. When programmers can collaborate freely on source code, this enables them to correct errors and ease adaptation to different needs and hardware platforms, leading to improvements. Thus OSS is said have a high degree of reliability.
- Fourth, contributing to an OSS project is a way to signal one's competence to others, and to strengthen one's reputation, possibly opening up new career opportunities.
- Fifth, there may be practical reasons. Programmers who have looked in vain for a program to solve their problem may find that OSS provides the answer. By helping others, they can also get help in developing code to satisfy their own needs. An additional benefit is that contributors know that they will never have to pay for code created in this manner.

- Finally, OSS providers can enhance the rapid diffusion of technology (spillovers to other products that are protected by IPRs), possibly contributing to the creation of a standard. Thus while the Linux operating system is freely available to all, its creator can earn money by giving lectures about the system – and thereby also spread word of the system to people who otherwise might not have known about it.

The benefits of OSS have even convinced for-profit companies like Red Hat to use it as the basis of their business model, and others, like IBM, to incorporate OSS into some of their operations (for further details see Davis 2005; Weber 2004; West 2003).

As can be seen, the motivations to use copyright as the legal basis to exclude others, and as the legal basis for an open source approach, differ. In the first case, the incentive effect derives from the copyright holder's ability to prevent imitation. In the second case, the incentive effect derives from the advantages enjoyed by a community of contributors to a larger creative effort. Thus developments in OSS have challenged the traditional argument that intellectual property rights are essential as incentives to R&D.

In recent years it has been argued that the concept of open source could be applied to other industries. It has been suggested for example (*The Economist*, 12 June 2004) that the same kind of collaborative approach that infuses OSS might also help to revitalize other science-based fields such as medical research, enabling scientists to contribute to each other's knowledge development, to the benefit of both their own research and society more generally. Open source research might be particularly useful in two areas: to enable the further development of non-patentable drugs whose patents have expired, and to encourage the invention of new treatments for diseases that afflict small numbers of people, like Parkinson's, or that have their main markets in the developing countries, like malaria.

For example a proposal was made by Stephen Maurer, Arti Rai and Andrej Sali at the Biotechnology Industry Organisation's annual 2004 conference to create a website by which researchers could explore and perform experiments on shared data, and discuss their results in chat rooms. In this approach the final development of promising drugs would be awarded to a pharmaceutical laboratory, on the basis of competitive bids, to raise the chances that the drug would be developed and delivered. While this differs from the logic of OSS it demonstrates that the 'spirit' of open source might be applicable to other kinds of products.

Furthermore, according to Merges (2004), biotechnology firms have invested millions of dollars in making information about new genes available in the public domain, thereby preventing other firms from protecting the information through intellectual property rights. This was due to concerns that the proliferation of patents in the field of biomedical research and development would lead to a fragmentation of research activities, and that patents would end up deterring innovation rather than encouraging it. The greater the number of patents on different gene sequences, the greater the chances that firms seeking to develop effective diagnostics for the presence of a particular gene or therapeutic drug would have to licence the rights to a large number of discrete, independently held patents.

In February 1995, Merck Pharmaceuticals, in cooperation with Washington University in St Louis, announced the creation of the Merck Gene Index, a public database of gene sequences corresponding to expressed human genes (that is, those genes that code for a protein product in the human body). Merck stated that it would characterize as many gene sequences as soon as possible and make them freely available. By 1998, the Index had published over 800 000 gene sequences. Merges notes that genes are different from software. When genes are revealed, they are freely available to all, leaving no opportunity to establish property rights.

Open source software is different, in that the act of writing a complex program is collaborative. Each piece of code must work with pre-existing code. But in both cases there is an effort to preclude property rights entanglements on a key input.

These examples also do not involve digitization *per se*, but are based on the logic of open source. To what degree then might the logic of the open source approach be applicable to digital cultural and artistic works?

APPLYING THE OPEN SOURCE APPROACH TO DIGITAL CULTURAL GOODS

Throughout the history of mankind, stories have been orally passed on from generation to generation. The tale was never told in quite the same way. Over the years, specific events were embellished, played down, eliminated. New features were added. Today the same dynamic applies to rumours and night-club jokes. Someone repeats it to someone else, and the story evolves.

Consider as well the children's game called 'Chinese Whispers' or 'Telephone'. One child whispers a sentence to the child sitting next to him or her, who whispers it to the next, and so forth. The last child in the chain repeats the (battered and unrecognizable) sentence out loud to the whole group, amidst peals of laughter. Had these children, instead of whispering to each other, chosen to collaborate on trying to improve the sentence, to enrich it, develop it and add new dimensions until the sentence became a paragraph, and then two paragraphs, and then a whole story, they would approximate, if crudely, the open source ideal as applied to cultural creations.

But how generalizable is the concept of open source to the music, TV broadcasting and film industries? At first glance, this would seem to be difficult. A work of art or music, once created, would not seem to require further community development. In fact the idea of subjecting such a work to further change might appear distasteful. But consider the difference between a classical symphony and jazz. A work of Bach or Beethoven is carefully specified in terms of musical notes and notations. Conductors have some room to interpret these works, but the music itself may not be altered. Jazz is quite different. Musicians start with a basic tune and then improvise, combining the sequence of the notes in new ways, taking the tune in new directions, imposing new rhythms. If their improvements were openly shared with other jazz musicians, and these musicians systematically cooperated in changing the basic melody, which they then made publicly available, they too would be following the logic of open source.

People who download a new CD typically do not intend to add to its further development, but simply to enjoy it. Yet this practice too is changing. A case in point concerns a DJ known as Danger Mouse, who created the *Grey Album* by mixing the Beatles' *White Album* with rap artist Jay-Z's *Black Album*. Both EMI, owner of the master recording to the Beatles album, and Sony, co-owner of the rights to the songs on the album, took legal action to block distribution of the new hybrid. In reaction to this, hundreds of websites were set up to make copies of the *Grey Album* available for downloading. To take another example, a software program from Apple called GarageBand reportedly provides loops of pre-recorded music and a set of software tools that enable users legally to mix and create their own songs (Cheng and Waters 2004). Given the attitudes of music lovers to copyright protection, and the general trend in society towards more individualized solutions for people, such products and technologies may well increase in popularity.

A number of open source computer games have been released on the Internet as well. Not only are the games freely redistributable, but their source code is also made publicly available, so that anyone who wishes can access, modify or recompile it (see http://www.the-underdogs.org/collect.php?name= Open+Source+Games). Open source games are also available through the JavaScript Forum, though the site features a warning to potential users that since many of the scripts are long and complicated, users should not try to modify them unless they are sure they know what they are doing! (See http://javascript.internet.com/games/.)

The logic of open source software, if applied to digital cultural goods, would have important implications. First and foremost, the concept of a final product would be eviscerated. Digital photographs can nowadays be so easily manipulated that it is no longer possible to vouch for their originality and identity. The same applies to any painting reproduced on the Internet. A case in point is Leonardo da Vinci's *Mona Lisa*, revered as a masterpiece for five centuries. Countless art students have spent countless hours honing their skills by reproducing their own copy of the painting while standing in front of it at the Louvre. But such copies still existed in physical form. Once created, they could not be changed, unless repainted. In cyberspace, the virtual image of this painting can be altered in the blink of an eye. One result has been a plethora of digital *Mona Lisa* images. In some, her smile has been replaced by a grimace. In others, her eyes have been widened in astonishment. Her face can easily be superimposed on cartoon characters, perhaps in animated form. While most of us living today can differentiate these images from the genuine *Mona Lisa*, this will no doubt be less true in the future.

Another example of the adoption of open source, in the publishing industry, concerns the *Wikipedia*. This dictionary is available only over the Internet. Definitions change as new users log on to the system.[2] Who is to say which definition is best? The ideal is to encourage users to challenge each other and alter each other's definitions until, perhaps, a consensus is reached. But is this consensus necessarily correct? In the past, experts were responsible for setting standards and specifying definitions, backed by their scholarly reputations. The open source ideal is based on self-monitoring by contributors, who can thereby signal their expertise. But its credibility depends on the degree to which people are serious in their contributions – and the degree to which knowledgeable experts monitor the 'self-monitors'.

What consequences might the application of the open source approach have for the work of Hans Christian Andersen? Should older works of literature and art receive special attention? Who should decide what is permissible, and what is not? On what grounds?

First of all, Andersen's works *have* been changed. Even before digitization, as Lawrence Lessig (Chapter 1, this volume) and others have described, Andersen's stories were cleverly manipulated, not least by Walt Disney in his films, where stories with tragic endings end well. The main impact of digitization has been to make such alterations easier, and facilitate changes in the texts themselves, not just in derivative works such as films.

Andersen's tales have been extensively translated. Every translation does some violence to the original. It is the job of the translator not only to express the author's meaning so that it is understandable to readers from a different culture, but also to capture the rhythm and poetry of the original language. A good translator will not attempt to reproduce the work literally, but also spiritually. Sometimes these two goals conflict. Authors who understand the language into which they are translated are not always pleased with the result.

Other aspects of Andersen's work have been altered. In December 2004 for example, the Copenhagen department store Magasin displayed one of Andersen's paper cuttings in its windows as part of its Christmas decorations.

The cutting showed a man and a woman holding hands. However the original Andersen cutting showed two men. The department store had altered the cutting, apparently fearing the image of two males holding hands would offend some customers.

Even so, there are still limits to which a translator, a department store, or even a film-maker like Disney, can change an existing physical work. The novelty of an open source approach would be to permit, and in fact encourage, other artists – or readers – to use digital tools to develop these stories further, changing them perhaps even beyond recognition. While this might seem distasteful, would it be more wrong than downloading a piece of popular music from the Internet and digitally altering it?

Generally speaking, the main benefit of applying the logic of the open source approach to digital cultural goods would be to harness the creative potential of a community of artists to improve existing works, instead of passively accepting that the original is the best expression of the idea. The main disadvantage would be to destroy the integrity of the original. Ultimately it would also become much more difficult to verify the authenticity of original works. But how applicable is the concept of open source, developed for the software industry, to digital works of art, music, and literature?

To answer this question, let us return to the discussion of why people contribute to open source software projects. In certain respects, the motivations to engage in common software innovation and cultural creation would be the same. Participants would find the process intrinsically enjoyable and rewarding, and could use it as a platform to signal their competence to others. Both groups would find it beneficial to disseminate their work, creating greater awareness of it. But important differences exist as well. Contributing to an open source art project would not bring the same level of learning benefits. Quality and reliability for open source software are assured because the computer programmers involved realize that their reputations are at stake, and carefully check their own contributions. The same kind of reputational effects would not necessarily apply to the users of cultural and artistic works – unless an expert community could be defined and mobilized with the necessary qualifications (and entry barriers).

With open source software, it is more straightforward to define what an improvement is. When computer engineers root out the bugs in a program, this makes the software better. What is the equivalent of a 'bug' in the work of Hans Christian Andersen? Community involvement might improve the story of 'The Princess on the Pea'. But it is also quite possible that no common effort could surpass Andersen's genius. If so, is it justified to extend the logic of OSS to such innovations? Where should we draw the line?

An important benefit of open source software development is that programmers can learn from other programmers, including receiving help to solve particular problems. In other words, it is not ordinary consumers who contribute to an OSS project, but experts. Should the same distinction be made for digital cultural goods, restricting access and further development to people who themselves are artists? In software, the difficulty and complexity of the technology provides a natural barrier to the number of participants in the OSS community. But for paintings and music and stories, that barrier disappears. Anyone who considers themself an artist can contribute. In an OSS project, the need for the cooperation of large numbers of programmers can be justified in terms of the sheer size of the effort. The same cannot be said for a work of art.

There is a clear societal need for the development of new software programs, and the competition between the purveyors of the open source approach and of the proprietary approach is healthy, contributing to innovation and dynamic growth. Moreover while the emergence of open source software can be justified as a reaction to the proprietary approach adopted by Microsoft and other large software producers (with the resultant monopoly costs to society), no such justification exists with regard to art. Technological progress is dependent on the continuous improvement of software programs. The same logic does not apply to cultural and artistic works, which are not only limited in technical complexity, but which do not 'need' to be further developed.

An effective coordination system has been designed for open source software projects based on the principles of modular development, where individuals can contribute to specified portions of the source code. The success of this coordination scheme is supported by the presence of widely accepted behavioural norms emphasizing reliability and integrity. For software, a community effort may make sense in that it encourages the more efficient development of new software, not least because users themselves facilitate the debugging process (Kogut and Metiu 2001). Yet these shared values are not necessarily characteristic of users of art, music and literature.

The nature of innovation is different as well. Software technologies are characterized by strong network externalities, where the value of the good to the individual user increases with the number of users. A case in point is Microsoft's program Word, which has become the standard for word processing. The more Word users there are for example, the more the opportunities for people to cooperate in creating shared documents. Again, the same logic does not apply to cultural and artistic works that are valuable simply because they are unique. If they are changed their uniqueness will change, and their value may not increase, but decrease. With open source software, the chances are greater that the value of the software will increase, not least due to the reputational gains that can be realized by programmers that contribute viable improvements.

An open source program is also bounded by its own technology. But a substantial risk of permitting continuous and unrestricted changes in works of art would be that everything would blend into everything else. It is more straightforward to define what open source software is, where it is going and where it cannot go. Cultural works are different.

For example for centuries musicians have composed music by writing down a few notes, playing it, adjusting it and improving it. Subsequently the music was adapted to various ends. Mozart's music for example has been used in many films, not least for the theme of the movie *Elvira Madigan*. But in all of these cases, the musical notes had to be written down. When the Boston Pops played orchestral music, their point of departure was the original written work. Today, by contrast, digital mixing technology permits notes to be combined without writing anything down. Not only does this save time, but it also enables the mixture of genres. Themes from classical music have not infrequently been inserted into popular music tracks. The original classical themes can quickly be altered, perhaps beyond recognition. As mentioned earlier, it is now technically possible to make changes in several media at the same time, creating new combinations of text, music and art. These can be made digitally available to others to develop further.

A final factor of import is to protect against malicious community development. For example techniques for hacking into websites have reportedly become so refined that knowledgeable individuals or firms can now reproduce the site of a known company, give it a slightly different Internet domain name, and encourage consumers to do business from the false site.[3] Such techniques could also be used to falsify cultural works.

Would Hans Christian Andersen have approved of the digitization and widespread availability of his works over the Internet, with the potential for manipulation? There is of course no way for us to know. But it is worth remembering that Andersen himself sought inspiration from earlier tales. He was also ahead of his time in many respects, not only in his literary specialization, but also in his interest in travelling widely and his enjoyment of meeting people from different cultures. Had he been born today, he might well have been eager to embrace the new trends of the times.

Many people are critical of the Disney adaptations of Andersen's stories. But where would his stories be, in people's consciousness, without Disney? Might Andersen perhaps have recognized the potential of the new technology for spreading the availability of his work? Might he not have believed that seeing the film might induce a child to read the actual story?

Consider the fate of Whistler's painting of his mother, which has been portrayed in innumerable ways, not all of them flattering. But perhaps for this very reason, knowledge of this particular painting is universal. Is this so bad? Would Whistler have approved?

Similarly, one can ask: Would Andersen have preferred a more restricted audience for his own works, who read texts that were true to the original? Or would he have been pleased that so many children, in so many countries, thanks in no small measure to Disney, had heard of his work? Taking this logic one step further, in an open source direction, might Andersen himself not have seen it as a fascinating experiment to watch to see if children could have improved upon his original story?

CONCLUDING REMARKS

This exploratory chapter has touched on some of the recent changes in the institutional framework for copyrights, including the emergence of open source software. We found that the increasing digitization of copyrighted goods raises new questions as regards the economic role of the copyright. We described the appearance of copyright's antithesis, open source software, and asked whether or not the logic of open source might not be extended to works of art, music and literature.

The wider applicability of the open source approach to cultural creations is by no means without problems, particularly when applied to products and technologies where continuous development may not be desirable. There is a trade-off between stimulating the further development and improvement of these works, weighed against the risk that they might somehow become degraded or lost.

Who is to say for example that the *Mona Lisa* could not be improved? Or to return to Hans Christian Andersen, is his story of 'The Little Mermaid' necessarily the best one? Why couldn't the story have several different endings, depending on the preferences of particular readers? Why shouldn't it? At what point would the story be so changed that it would have to be called something different?

The simple answer to such questions is: It does matter. Something valuable would be lost if the works of Hans Christian Andersen were subjected to destructive manipulation, or reduced to 'mush'. And yet the technology is here to stay, and it will inevitably be used.

Solutions therefore need to be found that both enable artists to maintain the integrity of their works, and enable other interested parties to experiment with these works in new ways. Possibly a dual system could be envisaged, one that guaranteed the identity of original works while also permitting community modification. In such a system, the symbol for copyright, ©, could be used to mark the original, and another applied to derivative works based on the logic of open source. A distinction could be made between projects involving the participation of experts, and of non-experts, again perhaps denoted by a distinct symbol.

Such an approach would underline the distinction that exists between the positive dynamics of the jazz concert, where further development is meant to enhance the existing work, and the negative dynamics of the Telephone Game, or 'Chinese Whispers', for which the purpose is deliberately to damage the integrity of the original work. The challenge for the modern institutional framework for copyrights would be to find a new balance, maximizing the benefits of the remarkable opportunities embodied in the new digital technologies, while minimizing the potential for abuse.

NOTES

*   Preliminary research for this chapter was funded by the Danish Social Sciences Research Council, as part of the international research project, Mobilising Knowledge in Management of Technology, under the Centre for Interdisciplinary Studies in Technology Management program (CISTEMA), at the Copenhagen Business School. A previous draft was presented at the conference, Hans Christian Andersen and Copyright, University of Southern Denmark, Odense, Denmark, 5 November 2004. I would also like to thank Jerome Davis for valuable comments on earlier versions of this chapter.
1. Trademarks, which protect the word or symbol that identifies the origin of a good, will not be further discussed here, since the economic function of the trademark is to serve as a guarantee of quality, enabling firms to capture value from product differentiation. Patents and copyrights, by contrast, protect the invention itself.
2. The *Wikipedia* is also the source of the digital versions of Hans Christian Andersen's tales, as described in the Introduction.
3. Internet domain names are web addresses. The most common top-level domain names include .com and .org. Many companies have had problems with parties who have purchased the rights to domain names that are only slightly different from their own, with the result that if the consumer types in a slightly different address, they are directed to a totally different site. The problem referred to here takes this behaviour one step further, since consumers who land on the wrong home page may not even know it, since it resembles (or is nearly identical to) the legitimate one. The potential for abuse is staggering. An example would be a company that enables customers to pay online for the purchase of products or services by credit card. Any consumer who did this in relation to the illegitimate site would leave themselves wide open.

REFERENCES

Andersen, B. (2004), 'If "Intellectual Property Rights" is the Answer, What is the Question? Revising the Patent Controversies', *Economics of Innovation and New Technology*, **13** (5), 417–42.

Andersen, B., R. Kozul-Wright and Z. Kozul-Wright (2004), 'Rents, Rights n'Rhythm: Conflict and Cooperation in the Music Industry', unpublished paper.

Arkenbout, E., F. Van Duk and P. Van Wijck (2004), 'Copyright in the Information Society: Scenarios and Strategies', *European Journal of Law and Economics*, **17**, 237–49.

Band, J. (2001). 'The Copyright Paradox: Fighting Content Piracy in the Digital Era', *Brookings Review*, Winter, 33–4.

Beal, B. and D. Marin (2003), 'Confronting the Information Age: Strategy, Copyright, and Digital Intellectual Goods', *Business Horizons*, July–August, 21–31.

Besen, S. and L. Raskind, (1991), 'An Introduction to the Law and Economics of Intellectual Property', *Journal of Economic Perspectives*, **5** (1), 3–27.

Bonaccorsi, A. and C. Rossi (2003), 'Why Open Source Software Can Succeed', *Research Policy*, **32**, 1243–58.

Cheng, I. and R. Waters (2004), 'Piracy: Overkill gives way to Pragmatism Part II: Digital Rights, Digital Wrongs', *Financial Times*, 14 April, p. 14.

Cheverie, J.F. (2002), 'The Changing Economics of Information, Technological Development, and Copyright Protection: What are the Consequences for the Public Domain?' *Journal of Academic Librarianship*, **28** (5), pp. 325–31.

Cohen, Wesley M., Richard R. Nelson and John P. Walsh (2000), 'Protecting their Intellectual Assets: Appropriability Conditions and why US Manufacturing Firms Patent (or Not)', National Bureau of Economic Research Working Paper (Cambridge, MA).

Davis, L. (2002), 'Is Appropriability a "Problem" for Innovations in Digital Information Goods?' LEFIC (Center for Law, Economics and Financial Institutions, Copenhagen Business School) Working Paper 2002–2.

Davis, L. (2004), 'Intellectual Property Rights, Strategy and Policy', *Economics of Innovation and New Technology*, **13** (5), pp. 399–415.

Davis, L. (2005), 'Can Open Source Software become Commercially Feasible on a Wide Scale?' paper to be presented to the PICMET Conference, Portland, Oregon, 31 July–4 August.

The Economist (2004), 12 June.

Gallaway, T. and D. Kinnear (2004), 'Open Source Software, the Wrongs of Copyright, and the Rise of Technology', *Journal of Economic Issues*, **38** (2), pp. 467–74.

Gallini, N. and S. Scotchmer (2002), 'Intellectual Property: When is it the Best Incentive System?' *NBER/Innovation Policy and the Economy*, **2** (1), 51–77.

Kogut, B. and A. Metiu (2001), 'Open-Source Software Development and Distributed Innovation', *Oxford Review of Economic Policy*, **17** (2), 248–64.

Landes, W. and D. Lichtman (2003), 'Indirect Liability for Copyright Infringement: Napster and Beyond', *Journal of Economic Perspectives*, **17** (2), 113–24.

Landes, W.M. and R. Posner (1989), 'An Economic Analysis of Copyright Law', *Journal of Legal Studies*, **18**, (June) 325–63.

Landes, W. and R. Posner (2003), *The Economic Structure of Intellectual Property Law*, Cambridge, MA and London: Belknap Press of Harvard University Press.

Langenderfer, J. and S. Kopp (2004), 'The Digital Technology Revolution and its Effect on the Market for Copyrighted Works: Is History Repeating Itself?' *Journal of Macromarketing*, **24** (1), 17–30.

Levin, T.C, A.K. Klevorick, R.R. Nelson and S.G. Winter (1987). 'Appropriating the Returns from Industrial Research and Development', *Brookings Papers on Economic Activity*, 3, 783–820.

Maskus, K.E. (2000), *Intellectual Property Rights in the Global Economy*, Washington, DC: Institute for International Economics.

Mazzoleni, R. and R.R. Nelson (1998), 'Economic Theories about the Benefits and Costs of Patents', *Journal of Economic Issues*, **32** (4), 1031–52.

Merges, R.P. (2004), 'A New Dynamism in the Public Domain', *University of Chicago Law Review*, **71** (1), 183–203.

Mustonen, M. (2003), 'Copyleft – the Economics of Linux and other Open Source Software', *Information Economics and Policy*, **15**, 99–121.

O'Mahony, S.O. (2003), 'Guarding the Commons: how Community Managed Software Projects Protect their Work', *Research Policy*, **32**, 1179–98.

Shapiro, C. and H.R. Varian (1999), *Information Rules*, Cambridge, MA: Harvard Business School Press.

Strickland, L.S. (2003), 'Copyright's Digital Dilemma Today: Fair Use of Unfair Constraints? Part 1', *Bulletin of the American Society for Information Science and Technology*, **30** (1), 7–11.

Strickland, L.S. (2003–2004), 'Copyright's Digital Dilemma Today: Fair Use of Unfair Constraints? Part 2', *Bulletin of the American Society for Information Science and Technology*, 30 (2), 18–23.

Towse, R. (2001), *Creativity, Incentive and Reward. An Economic Analysis of Copyright and Culture in the Information Age*, Cheltenham, UK and Northampton, MA: Edward Elgar.

Varner, P. (2000), *The Economics of Open Source Software. Open Software Economic Models*, Charlottesville, VA: University of Virginia.

Von Krogh, G. and E. Von Hippel (2003), 'Editorial: Special Issue on Open Source Software Development', *Research Policy*, **32**, 1149–57.

Weber, Steven (2004), *The Success of Open Source*, Cambridge, MA: Harvard University Press.

West, Joel (2003), 'How Open is Open Enough? Melding Proprietary and Open Source Platform Strategies', *Research Policy*, **32**, 1259–85.

http://en.wikipedia.org/wiki/The_Ugly_Duckling
http://en.wikipedia.org/wiki/The_Emperor's_New_Clothes
http://opensource.org
http://www.the-underdogs.org/collect.php?name=Open+Source+Games
http://javascript.internet.com/games/

8. Imagining a world without copyright: the market and temporary protection, a better alternative for artists and the public domain

Marieke van Schijndel and Joost Smiers

HARD TO IMAGINE

Some serious cracks are surfacing in the system of copyright as we have known it in the Western world for a couple of centuries. The system is substantially more beneficial for cultural conglomerates than for the average artist; a situation that cannot last. Furthermore it seems inescapable that digitization is undermining the foundations of the copyright system. It must be acknowledged that several authors have recently presented analyses of the untenability of the contemporary system of copyright. Yet most of their observations only allude to – but do not address – what we deem the most fundamental question of all: If copyright is inherently unjust, what could come in its place to guarantee artists – creative and performing – a fair compensation for their labours, and how can we prevent knowledge and creativity from being privatized (Bettig 1996; Bollier 2003, 119–34; Boyle 1996; Coombe 1998; Drahos and Braithwaite 2002; Drahos and Mayne 2002; Frith and Marshall 2004; Lessig 2002, 2004; Litman 2001; Perelman 2002; Vaidhyanathan 2003)? It is time to move beyond merely criticizing copyright. The pressing question is: What alternative can we offer artists and other cultural entrepreneurs in rich as well as poor countries that benefits them, and that brings the increasing privatization of creativity and expertise to a halt? Our goal in this chapter is to develop such an alternative, and to move beyond any notion centred on private intellectual property rights.

This text is an essay. We cannot erase the product of centuries of Western thought on intellectual property rights with a single stroke of the pen. It is hard to imagine for Western man that a world without copyright could still yield films, theatre productions, novels, music pieces, paintings and multimedia spectacles; even though people born and living in non-Western cultures find this a lot less hard to believe (Boyle 1996, xiv). In this chapter we therefore present a thought-experiment. We begin by making a few observations, followed by a proposition, an alternative. It must be clear that we aspire only to sketch the contours of an approach that will require further development and study. Without any doubt, the analysis we present for copyright is transferable to other systems of intellectual property rights, such as patents and trademarks. These systems influence, as well, the creation, production, distribution and promotion of works of art of different ilk.

SOME OBSERVATIONS

A first observation must be that the present Western copyright system pays little attention to the average artist, especially those in non-Western societies. The system disproportionately benefits a few famous artists and especially a few major enterprises, but it has little to offer for most creators and performers (Boyle 1996, xiii; Drahos and Braithwaite 2002, 15; Kretschmer 1999; Kretschmer and Kawohl 2004, 44; Vaidhyanathan 2003, 5). The copyright system does enable a handful of cultural enterprises to dominate the market, and to withdraw substantive diversity from the public eye (Bettig 1996, 34–42, 103; Boyle 1996, 121–5; Coombe 1998, 144; Drahos and Braithwaite 2002, ix–x, 74–84; Litman 2001, 14; McChesney 1999). Copyright has thus become a mechanism for a few cultural conglomerates to control the broad terrain of cultural communication. Something that has been derailed to such a large extent, and that hurts the interests of most artists and the public domain, can no longer be cut back to normal proportions.

For most artists, the profits deriving from copyright do not form much of an incentive to create and perform artistic work, simply because they hardly receive the proceeds. This has been the case in the past, it still is the case in the present, and it holds for almost every culture. From an historical perspective, we may note that the concept of private intellectual property rights has traditionally been absent from most cultures. Yet there have always been artists who created and performed works (Bettig 1996, 25, 44, 171; Boyle 1996, 38–9). The incentive argument – artists stop their labours if they stop receiving copyright payments – therefore does not hold: 'Copyright today is less about incentives or compensation than it is about control' (Litman 2001, 80). 'Firms in the creative industries are able to "free-ride" on the willingness of artists to create and the structure of the artists' labour markets, characterised by short term working practices and oversupply, make it hard for artists to appropriate awards' (Towse 2003, p. 10). One may add to this observation that value of copyright royalty rates is decided in the market place and it is therefore artists' bargaining power with firms in the creative industries that determines copyright earnings. Artists' bargaining power is, however, considerably weakened by the persistence of excess supply of creative workers to the creative industries . . . As with artists' earnings from other art sources, the individual's distribution of copyright earnings is highly skewed with a few top stars earning considerable sums but the medium or 'typical' author earning only small amounts from their various rights. (Towse 2003, 11)

For non-Western countries, the Western intellectual property rights system is nothing but a disaster. Their knowledge and creativity is obfuscated from them, and they have to pay dearly to receive the fruits of these sacrifices in return. This even explains the unfavourable debt position of these countries to some extent (Boyle 1996, 34, 125–30, 141–2; Chomsky in Smiers 2003, 77; Coombe 1998, 208–47; Correa 2000; Grosheide and Brinkhof 2002; von Lewinski 2004; Mitsui 1993; Perelman 2002, 5–7; Rifkin 2000, 229–32, 248–53; Shiva 1997, 2001).

Let's face the reality that digitization is axing the roots of the copyright system (Alderman 2001; Lessig 2002; Litman 2001, 89–100, 112–16, 151–70; Motavalli 2002; Rifkin 2000, 218–29; Schiller 2000; Vaidyanathan 2003, 149–84). By abolishing copyright, the process of creative adaptation will once again enjoy every imaginable opportunity. This is all the more interesting in the digital age. After all, digital sampling enables the production of creative works, much as those have always been produced. How? Indeed, by finding inspiration, themes or certain forms of expression in works previously produced, long ago or yesterday. Digitization enables this lending and borrowing of inspiration, and is helpful as well from another perspective. In the world of copyright there has always existed a bizarre distinction between an idea and the expression: however in the digital age a work is no longer fixed, and separating idea from expression is no longer possible. The artificial distinction and the endless discussions about it have become superfluous.

Another observation, linked to what creative sampling makes possible, is that the philosophical basis of the present system of copyright is founded on a misunderstanding: notably that of the sheer boundless originality of the artist, regardless of whether he or she is a creator or a performer. But let us keep a keen eye on reality. One always builds on the labours of predecessors and contemporaries. Subsequent artists add something to the existing corpus of work, nothing more and nothing less. We may highly respect and admire those additions, but it would be incorrect to provide a creative or performing artist, or his or her producers, with an exclusive, monopolistic claim to something that has largely sprung from knowledge and creativity in the public domain, and that is indebted in important respects to the labours of predecessors (Barthes 1968; Boyle 1996, 42, 53–9).

Of course we are well aware that an artist receives a copyright for the addition he or she makes to what can be found in the public domain of knowledge and creativity. Again, this addition can be very impressive (or banal). But it is quite a stretch to extend to him or her an exclusive, monopolistic property right for that addition, guaranteed until 70 years after his or her death, and which can on top of that be transferred to an individual or corporation that had nothing to do with the creative process in the first place. The credibility of the system really starts to fall apart when we realize that the author and his or her rightful claimants can forbid almost anything that resembles the copying of 'their' work (Coombe 1998, 92–8).

The development of the public domain of creativity and knowledge deserves a reappraisal. Besides, subsequent artists must be enabled to delve into that domain in order to find a supply of artistic materials that they can build on. That road will be closed when artistic materials from the present and past fall into private hands, something that is occurring to an increasing extent under the present system of copyright. This privatization of our past and present cultural heritage is devastating for the further development of our cultural life (Locke in Boyle 1996, 9). In fact an 'author-centred regime can actually *slow down* scientific progress, *diminish* the opportunities for creativity, and *curtail* the availability of new products' (Boyle 1996, 119; also see Perelman 2002, 7–9).

For cultural conglomerates which control the bulk of the property rights worldwide, the possibility to forbid reproduction is exceptionally interesting: it enables them to dominate broad areas of artistic expression in which no contradiction, no counter-melody, no counter-image, in short no dialogic practice is tolerated (Coombe 1998, 42, 46). Yet, we have to realize that

> culture is not embedded in abstract concepts that we internalise, but in the materiality of signs and texts over which we struggle and the imprint of those struggles in consciousness. This ongoing negotiation and struggle over meaning is the essence of dialogic practice. Many interpretations of intellectual property laws squash dialogue by affirming the power of corporate actors to monologically control meaning by appealing to an abstract concept of property. Laws of intellectual property privilege monologic forms against dialogic practice and create significant power differentials between social actors engaged in hegemonic struggle. (Coombe 1998, 86)

It is prerequisite for any democratic society that a surplus of opinionating and emotion-evoking claims can be contradicted (Bettig 1996, 103–6). The broad copyright as we know and have it virtually renders that difficult and sometimes impossible.

ALTERNATIVES?

After this summation of the fundamental shortcomings of the copyright system, it may not come as a surprise that we feel the need to investigate alternative ways to protect the public domain of knowledge and creativity, and to assure many artists and other cultural entrepreneurs a fair income for their labours. As stated, this type of investigation happens too sporadically. Recently a few scholars and policymakers have presented alternatives to the system. But their proposals have many disadvantages and they therefore do not constitute a real alternative to the copyright regime.

The most far-reaching reorientations have been systems like the General Public Licence and the Creative Commons (Bollier 2003, 27–30, 99–118; Boyle 1996, 132–3; Lessig 2002 and 2004, 282–6). The idea behind this approach is that A's work must be available for use by others, without them being obstructed by prevailing copyright. In turn, the others cannot appropriate the work. Why not? The Creative Commons entails that A supplies some kind of public licence for his or her work: go ahead, do with the work as you please, as long as you do not bring the work under a regime of private ownership. The work is thus subjected to a form of 'empty' copyright. This 'hollow' copyright constitutes the most extreme option the author has under the Creative Commons regime. More often however, the author opts for the choice 'some rights reserved', for example that the usage of a work is restricted to not-for-profit activities. It is an uncertain form of contract law that will keep lawyers busy. The sympathetic aspect of Creative Commons-like constructions is that it becomes possible, to a certain extent, to withdraw oneself from the copyright jungle. It is of course always laudable to start a new world order on an island, and there is no scepticism in this statement. We hope that more and more artists will renounce the system of copyright that disadvantages them so badly, and begin hollowing it out by embracing the idea of a Creative Commons. Without any doubt this system is helpful for museums and archives that wish to spread their stocks of cultural heritage to the public, but also like to avoid it becoming copyrighted or used inappropriately by others.

As long as the system of copyright is still in place, the Creative Commons appears to be a useful solution that may even serve as an exemplar. But there are some strings attached. The Creative Commons does not paint a clear picture of how a diverse set of artists from all over the world, as well as their producers and patrons, might generate an income. But we have to prepare an answer to that question. Most artists will not dare to put the existing copyright regime to rest until they have been offered a clear view of a better alternative – even though the present regime only has smoke and mirrors to offer. That is easily understandable. A second drawback of Creative Commons-like approaches is that they do not fundamentally question and challenge the copyright system.

The Creative Commons licence suggests that the author wants to exercise some form of control nonetheless. Another quite essential objection to the Creative Commons-like approaches is that they involve only those artists who are willing to adhere to this philosophy. Cultural conglomerates however, which have the ownership of big chunks of our cultural heritage from past and present, will not. This downgrades and limits the sympathetic idea of the Creative Commons. Not free of contradictions is the fact that one of the most outspoken advocates of Creative Commons, Lawrence Lessig, is a strong adherent of the idea that knowledge and creativity can be owned as individual property (Lessig 2004, xiv, xvi, 10, 28, 83). Isn't the title of his 2004 book *Free Culture* a bit misleading? Below we will argue that there is much to say against this private property claim on knowledge and creativity.

A second alternative for copyright is connected to different forms of art created and produced in a collective manner (regardless whether it concerns more traditional or contemporary works), as is the case in most non-Western countries. In those societies the individual approach of the Western copyright system does not fit the more collective character of creation and performance. If one stays within the paradigm of the private ownership of knowledge and creativity, it is obvious that a concept like collective ownership comes to mind. Is it not possible to grant so-called 'traditional' societies a tool that resembles copyright, but is in fact collectively owned? Would this not enable them to protect their artistic expressions from inappropriate use and/or guarantee their artists an income?

The problems for effectively introducing a system of collective intellectual ownership rights are abundant. For instance one may wonder who represents the community and is able to speak on behalf of the community. It is not by definition the case that everybody agrees on how to deal with artistic creations of the past and present. Copyright is about the exploitation of works, but many people in those societies may consider this a blasphemy, or would not like to see their works being used in specific contexts. The appropriation of knowledge and creativity is something that pinches even in the Western world, and it does so all the more in countries where this strange system has never existed, and where artists use each other's works, and so on and so forth, as was the case in the Western world before the introduction of the copyright system. There is thus, even without considering the position of Western cultural conglomerates, reason to understand why the polite, weak and bleak trials of elaborating a collective intellectual property system have failed thus far.

Is the tweaking of the current system a solution to the problems as we have described them? Several scholars, critical of the present copyright system, propose optimizing it. Their contributions vary. Some argue for the re-establishment of the fair use principle, which has suffered enormously, or making copyright solely applicable to real authors, creators and performers.

Others favour a much shorter period of protection, for instance 14 years. Again, others believe there is no real problem in the European context, because in those countries the collecting societies put aside a portion of the copyright earnings for cultural projects, and their distribution scheme favours individual artists in comparison to the Anglo-Saxon copyright system. Unfortunately it is unthinkable to bring the current system back to normal proportions, because it is not in the interest of the main partners of the system, the cultural conglomerates, to assist in this quest. On the contrary, they have been very eager and highly successful in extending and broadening the copyright system. Moreover digitization is greatly impacting upon the functioning of the system. At what point must a society decide that when almost everybody is participating in an 'illegal' practice – like P2P music or film exchange – it can no longer be considered illegal (Litman 2001)? And even if the European collecting societies have a higher moral ground than those in the Anglo-Saxon world, even then the problem of the individual appropriation of knowledge and creativity, which is the basis of our critique of the system, continues to exist. In the following sections we address this issue more thoroughly.

ARTISTS, PRODUCERS AND PATRONS: ENTREPRENEURS

Before presenting our proposal we must observe that artists are inclined to sell their work on the market and – if it all works out – make a living for themselves. Artists have always been merchants and small shopkeepers. They live off an acquisitive audience that wants to admire, enjoy and buy their produce. To that audience also belong institutional buyers like kings, churches, Maecenases, labour unions, banks, hospitals and other societal institutions (Hauser 1972). This conclusion, as will be demonstrated further on in this chapter, will provide us with something to go by while developing an alternative for copyright.

Artists, as well as their producers and patrons, thus apparently are entrepreneurs. This requires a risk-prone mentality, and it involves competition as much as possible for many artistic expressions and their artists. The observation that artists, and their producers and patrons, are entrepreneurs makes one wonder what the decisive reason is for reducing the entrepreneurial risks of cultural producers, because this is precisely what copyright does. Copyright renders a product exclusive, and provides the entrepreneur with a *de facto* monopoly. This system of institutionally protected gifts is seemingly bizarre in an era in which even cultural conglomerates themselves herald the blessings of free market competition. Major entrepreneurs in cultural sectors bargain for ever-stricter intellectual property rights in the form of extensions and expansions of existing copyright legislation, but this is completely at odds with the so-called rule of the free market. We also observe the exact same phenomenon in the area of patent law and other intellectual property laws such as trademarks, database rights, plant breeder rights and design rights (Drahos and Braithwaite 2002; Perelman 2002; Rifkin 1998, 2000; Shiva 1997, 2001; Shulman, 1999).

Before we try our luck by presenting a new system, we must first identify the locus of the impulse to create. That brings us to the following summation, a three-pronged road. One possibility is that a work is being commissioned. The second option is that the artist himself or herself takes the initiative to make an artistic work, possibly in collaboration with multiple, differentially endowed creators and performers. Thirdly, a producer can be a binding factor and bear the responsibility and risk involved in an artistic venture.

In all three cases – the initiative coming from a patron, someone who commissions; from one or several artists themselves; or from a producer – there is a person or an institution that intentionally makes itself responsible and accountable for creating or performing a certain artistic work. To be responsible and accountable not only implies undertaking a broad range of activities to give the artistic project momentum, but also to bear, amongst other things, the financial risks involved. The initiator then becomes an entrepreneur and bears the risk that unavoidably comes with entrepreneurship. In our alternative for copyright it is not the artist who takes centre stage, but the entrepreneur, regardless of whether he or she is an artist, a patron or a producer.

THE SOLUTION: THE MARKET AND TEMPORARY PROTECTED USUFRUCT

While recognizing the fact that artists, patrons and producers are cultural entrepreneurs, we find that they can be confronted with three types of situation, each of which grants a specific reaction or option. What are those three options in our proposed solution? Firstly, cultural entrepreneurs experience a competitive advantage, for example by being the first to market a product. Ancillary forms of protection are then rendered unnecessary. Secondly, in some cases high risk and high investment are involved in the realization of certain creative works. Temporary protected usufruct is granted to offset market failure. Thirdly, the market as yet lacks the resilience to finance a product and there are many reasons making it desirable for it to flourish. Subsidies are then distributed. In all three cases or options the works fall immediately in the public domain. This is the key principle of our proposed solution.

Let's take a closer look at those three options. What are the contours of the system that we find worth exploring? The core of the matter is that we distance ourselves from the present system of copyright, as is probably clear by now. What does that yield? As stated, the protective corral of property rights that is artificially erected around a creative work will disappear. The consequence thus is that the work – regardless of whether it involves a (new) creation or a performance – will have to be marketed from the moment of its announcement onwards. We will nuance this position further on in the chapter when we discuss the second option. What is essential is that the entrepreneurial patron, artist or producer obtains a competitive advantage by creating or performing a work (Picciotto 2002, 225). This renders additional protection unnecessary. This is the first option.

What we have in this first option is a first-mover advantage. The first person to bring a work to market can use the advantage to reap revenues. The entrepreneur thus has 'lead-time'. What we propose is not completely new. In 1934 Plant stated 'that copyright encourages moral hazard in publishers (firms in the creative industries) without sufficiently rewarding authors (creators) who supply the creative input. He believed that publishers should rely on the temporary monopoly of lead time to establish new products in the market' (in Towse 2003, 19). This time gives the first mover a lead over possible competitors, the opportunity to skim the market for the new cultural product, ask a good price for it and thus earn a return on investment. After all, it will take several months before, say, the same play or music piece will see its opening night elsewhere, or the same chair is eligible for production in another location. It should be understood that the work falls immediately in the public domain; thus it can be used by others as well, and everybody is free to adapt this work creatively. The competitive advantage that most artists possess in one form or other is put at the very core of our new system. If such advantages are allowed and able to do their work, ancillary forms of protection, like copyright, will be unnecessary.

The counter-argument however might be that, with an eye on digitization, the reality is that lead-time is only a couple of minutes or perhaps hours (Towse 2003, 19). Does this mean that there are almost no works that can benefit from a competitive advantage? We do not believe so. Apart from the first-mover advantage, many artists are able to add value or create advantages in other ways. In order to understand this, we should keep in mind that cultural production and distribution will reshuffle considerably after the abolishment of copyright. For instance in the field of music, concerts and performances will become much more important, also as a source of income for the artists. Live, direct contact with an audience generates inimitable value. Performing qualities are even now, in the present era, of decisive importance for long and lasting careers of musicians. This is what gives them a good reputation. Reputation creates value. Reputation has a signalling effect. It indicates guaranteed quality.

Customers are more loyal and are willing to pay higher prices for cultural products from artists with a good reputation and it makes them aficionados (Fombrun 1996). Cultural production and distribution will change in a world without copyright. But let us at this point stress that service qualities of artistic works will become much more important than the individual product.

From what we have stated before about the philosophically doubtful concept of the originality of the author, it is clear that we claim that any artistic creation or performance belongs to the public domain. It is derived from the commons, based on the works of predecessors and contemporaries, and therefore from its moment of conception onwards it takes its place in the public domain. We use the concepts 'public domain' and 'commons' without distinction. However we know that in legal traditions there may be differences between the two concepts. We define the public domain or the commons as the space in any society that belongs to all of us and can be used by all of us. It is a misunderstanding to think that the commons, or the public domain, is an unregulated space. Of course not: always in history and in all societies those common spaces have been regulated one way or another, for example on the conditions of its usage. In our alternative we return to the commons what has always belonged to it – no more and no less. We give back to all of us what has been privatized in the fields of creativity and knowledge in the Western world over the last centuries (Hemmungs Wirtén 2004, 133–4).

The second option takes into consideration that sometimes the realization of a certain work requires a rather substantial up-front investment. Think of movie productions for example, which can easily rake in several million euros in costs. Another example is writing a book; an author has to work on such a large project for a considerable period of time, but the revenues will not begin flowing until (much) later. It could also be that the risk of an undertaking is too great to be borne privately. Often high investments, high risks and uncertainty go hand in hand. This can lead to what economists call 'market failure' (Towse 2004, 56). This is an economic condition under which competitive markets have difficulty developing. State intervention is then granted. In these special cases, in which the process of selling is time-consuming, or must consist of multiple transactions before an agreeable income has been reached, one can think of a temporary protected usufruct for the person taking the entrepreneurial risk. The cultural entrepreneur is offered temporal protection to harvest the fruits of his or her work. However no private property emerges, as was the case under a copyright regime.

The concept of usufruct is better known in societies under civil law than in those that are governed by common law, like the Anglo-Saxon parts of the world. Characteristic of usufruct is that one does not have the ownership of an item; however one is entitled to the usage of the fruits of the item. If the item is say a house, the entitlement could be for instance the usage of the house without owning it. The person that holds usufruct is for example allowed to live there for free or to receive the proceeds of any rental activity. In our case, the item might be a book; from the moment of its publication it belongs to the public domain and the holder of the usufruct is entitled to the takings and receipts of the book. Under the present system of law, usufruct can only emerge when it is derived from an ownership title. What we envision is that the creative work, as we will argue below, exists only in the public domain, its ownership is shared amongst all, and thus belongs to the commons. Whoever enjoys the temporary usufruct of a certain artistic work has thus received it from the public domain. The usufruct keeps unimpeded the freedom of everybody to adapt works of art – creations and performances – in a creative manner. The technical details concerning the implementation of this matter will still have to be worked out.

De facto, the temporary usufruct implies that the costs of preparing the work, including the artist's wage, are spread out over a number of customers. But we will have to apply strict boundaries to the timeframe over which this applies. Hence we speak of a temporary usufruct. In terms of its scope and duration, protection will be less than under present copyright regimes. In our approach an artistic work, whether creation or performance, immediately enters the public domain from its moment of conception onwards, as has been stated before; or better still remains in it, because it derives from it to a large extent. Only, it may happen that the usufruct is protected for a certain period of time, to make the work profitable for the creator, performer, producer or patron. At present we are thinking of a period not extending beyond a year. A lot of economic research is required possibly to refine this period of temporarily protected usufruct, depending on the specific artistic discipline. However this term of one year is not picked randomly. 'Of all the creative work produced by humans anywhere, a tiny fraction has continuing commercial value'; for instance, 'most books go out of print within one year' (Lessig 2004, 134, 225). This market reality supports our proposal of a strict timeframe for protection.

Of course it might happen that even this temporary usufruct does not provide enough perspective on the ability to break even on certain artistic creations and performances. And with this we arrive at our final and third option: subsidies. It may happen that the market as yet lacks the resilience to finance a certain type of artistic work, but that there are various reasons making it socially desirable for this work to bloom and become available (for the sake of cultural diversity, or because the public is still developing a taste for certain forms of expression, for example). In that case it is important that governments use subsidies and other facilities to enable the creation, performance and diffusion of such works, for shorter or longer periods of time. In the case of financing by the government, the work immediately becomes part of the public domain.

After all it appears absurd that publicly financed productions can become the exclusive property of a person or organization, as is presently the case in many countries with programmes developed by their public broadcasting corporations.

COMMENTING UPON OUR ALTERNATIVE

Is what we propose not some kind of dressed-down version of the present copyright system? One could say that. But there are remarkable differences between the copyright approach and our alternative, in which we first let market processes take their course, perhaps followed by a form of limited protection. Firstly, under the regime of intellectual property rights, a protective shield of copyright becomes affixed to an artistic work by definition, from its moment of inception onwards. This does not hold true for our alternative, on the contrary. The maker, producer or patron has a competitive advantage in the market by being the first to offer a certain kind of product: let markets be markets! Secondly, if it is somehow necessary to offer a certain kind of protection, as when a work could not be made profitable by any other means, then that protection will remain incomparably less elaborate in terms of its scope and duration than the sheer boundless system of institutionalized gifts with which the copyright system presently spoils the 'holder of an intellectual property right'. A period of about a year of usufruct is something quite different than 70 years after the death of the author, and also in the case of neighbouring rights the duration of the protection may be called generous. Under the present system of copyright, creative adaptation is at risk of being interpreted as a wrong and of being fined by the courts, so the scope and duration of the protection are immensely important. In our approach, creative adaptation is instead applauded and encouraged.

There is also a third reason as to why what we propose is completely different from copyright. Our alternative redefines ownership and property of creativity and knowledge. Creative works are not owned in the same way as, for instance, a table. A table is the property of person A, but not at the same time also of person B, unless they are married. But this is not the case with artistic creativity and knowledge. After its usage by someone it has not been exhausted. It is a public good. That is, as we have argued before, why those works of the intellect and of the creative mind belong to the public domain. Strategically it is important to underpin this public character of knowledge and creativity time and time again. Jack Valenti, the former president of the Motion Picture Association of America, once unhesitatingly said: 'Creative property owners must be accorded the same rights and protection resident in all other property owners in the nation' (in Lessig 2004, 117). This quote makes clear why it is necessary to make a distinction between knowledge and creativity on one hand and the ownership of, for instance, a house on the other. They are not the same and should not be treated the same.

RESULT: A NEW CULTURAL MARKET AND A LEVEL PLAYING FIELD

With our new system a new cultural market will emerge. The first observation is that with the abolition of copyright, cultural conglomerates will lose their grip on the agglomeration of cultural products, with which they determine the outlook of our cultural lives to an ever-increasing extent. Because what will they lose? They have to give up control over huge chunks of the cultural markets. They lose the monopolistic exclusivity over broad cultural areas because everyone is allowed to exploit artistic materials that are not protected by temporary usufruct, and absolutely no limitations are put on creatively adapting works of art. With these new conditions, the rationale is then lost for cultural conglomerates to make substantial investments in blockbusters, bestsellers and stars. After all, by making creative adaptation respectable again and by undoing the present system of copyright, the economic incentives to produce at the present scale will diminish. However it will not be forbidden for a cultural entrepreneur to invest millions of dollars or euros in, for instance, a film, game, CD or DVD. Of course not, but the investment will no longer be made under an endless wall of protection.

There will once again be room to manoeuvre in cultural markets for a variety of entrepreneurs, who are then no longer pushed out of the public's attention by blockbusters, bestsellers and stars. Those plentiful artists are more likely to find audiences for their creations and performances in a normal market that is not dominated by a few large players. There is not a single reason to believe that there would be no demand for such an enormous variety of artistic expressions. In a normalized market, with equal opportunities for everyone, this demand can be fulfilled. This increases the possibility that a varied flock of artists would be capable of extracting a decent living from their endeavours.

A second observation is about cultural adaptation and how the market should be regulated with respect to fraud and plagiarism. We stress the fact that we do not like theft. We of course do not propose that X can attach his or her name to Y's book or film, claiming to be the author of that work. That is plain misrepresentation or fraud. If that is found out, and that is bound to happen sooner or later, then the lazy fraudster will receive his or her fair penalty in the court of public opinion; we do not need a copyright system to accomplish that. It is up to all of us not to be afraid publicly of accusing artists of misrepresentation or fraud. This will only happen if we are culturally alert, and we have to be if we want to do without judgments of the courts, which have made us culturally lazy in the past. We should critically discuss what we consider culturally inappropriate use.

What we have suggested thus far is that it is quite feasible to have a flourishing cultural domain without the existence of a copyright system, while at the same time many artists in the Western and non-Western countries alike can make a reasonable income from their labours. However it is evident that the completely new approach that we propose does not immediately eradicate all conceivable problems. With this we come to our third observation. If cultural enterprises can no longer control the market with copyright in hand, they must resort to a second protective mechanism, which they will then attempt to apply with even greater force than is presently the case. That is the far-reaching control over distribution and promotion of cultural expression that they possess and wield.

This too must be limited with metes and bounds. After all, from a democratic perspective it is impermissible that a limited number of cultural giants are able to determine the contents of artistic and cultural communications, using traditional as well as new media (Smiers 2003). Democracy is not the privilege of a few cultural conglomerates. It is a necessity to use ownership and content regulations to organize the cultural market in such a way that cultural diversity gets the best possible chance. First of all, there should not be dominant modes of distribution. It cannot be the case that a single owner dominates, controls or concerts the market for music, films or books. Vertical integration and other forms of cross-ownership must be condemned. Content regulations may take the form of diversity prescriptions. That is to say, diversity in terms of genre, musicians' backgrounds and geographical diversity, and the latter representing diversity from the home country, neighbouring countries and many other parts of the world. Of course there will be outlets specializing in a certain genre that want to be known for it. These too will be subject to diversity prescription, albeit within that genre (Smiers 2004). This type of regulation does not take anything away from a free market economy. To the contrary, these rules, while in need of further elaboration, serve to create a free market, or differently put, to 'normalize' the market and to bring about a level playing field. No one should be able to dominate the cultural market or to have such a strong position that cultural diversity will be suppressed, pushed aside or taken away from the public attention. This demands some regulations: on the one hand the elimination of the control mechanism copyright and on the other the instalment of some regulations concerning ownership and content that protect and promote the flourishing of artistic diversity.

DISCUSSION AND CONCLUSION: THE MUSE OF THIS CENTURY

In this chapter we have presented a thought-experiment. We urge everybody to participate in our quest. Who for instance should our strategic partners be in our journey into a world without copyright? What is at stake is once again to begin respecting the public domain of creativity and knowledge. Our main concern is providing artists, producers and entrepreneurs with a decent income and sufficient possibilities to bring their work, in all its diversity, to the attention of many audiences. The system of copyright has existed for well over a century in Western societies. It has been long enough. It is not equipped to withstand the digitization that has once again supplied artists with a magnitude of entrepreneurial freedom.

Admittedly it may take a while to get used to letting go of the system of copyright. It urges us to make a mental and economic transition, but this is worth the trouble in every conceivable way. Many practical matters still need to be solved with respect to the usufruct model. Should a temporary protected usufruct be granted automatically or should we implement a licensing system? It seems logical to grant automatically some types of artistic product that require a substantial upfront investment (for example films and books) usufruct. But what are the drawbacks of this approach and should the duration of protection for all fields of the arts be the same? Other questions that come to mind are: Is there still a role to play for the collecting societies, and What is the effect of the one-year usufruct on the product life cycle of artistic products?

Most importantly, when will this new era of cultural production and creativity unhindered by copyright begin? How can we make it happen? Hans Christian Andersen has declared his entire oeuvre his gift to the world and we cite his inviting tale about the muse of the new century without hesitation.

> 'When will this new era begin? When shall we see and hear the muse of the next century?' [Who is she and what made her into who she is?] The muse of the next century is still a child, although she no longer sleeps in a cradle. She is still playing in the great kindergarten that is filled with treasures from the rococo and the distant past. [What are her intentions and ambitions?] What [we] ought to ask is, what she does not intend to do. She will not perform as a ghost of the past. She does not want to try to create new dramas out of leftovers. She will outdistance us, as the marble amphitheatre surpassed the mimer's cart . . . And when will she appear? For those of us who have gone before us and are familiar with eternity, it will be a short while; but for us who are alive now, it will be a long time to come. [Maybe] we shall never know her, but our children may and our grandchildren certainly will. (Hans Christian Andersen [1805–75] 1974, 729–34)

With digitization in mind, our guess is that we will not have to wait much longer before the copyright system will crumble.

NOTE

The authors wish to thank the following friends and colleagues for their kind and constructive comments on earlier drafts of this chapter: Maarten Asscher, Lee Davis, Christophe Germann, Willem Grosheide, Giep Hagoort, Eva Hemmings Wirtén, Pursey Heugens, Raj Isar, Lina Khamis, Jaap Klazema, Gerd Leonhard, Helle Porsdam, Alan Story, Ruth Towse, David Vaver, Catarina Vaz Pinto, Roger Wallis, Lior Zemer, as well as the Research Group Arts and Economics at the Utrecht School of the Arts (the Netherlands), the Copy/South Research Network and the AHRB Network on New Directions in Copyright Law (London).

REFERENCES

Alderman, John (2001), *Sonic Boom. Napster, P2P and the Battle for the Future of Music*, London: Fourth Estate.

Andersen, Hans Christian [1805–75] (1974), *The Complete Fairy Tales and Stories*, London: Victor Gollancz.

Barthes, Roland (1968), 'La mort de l'auteur', *Manteia*, 5, (4e trimestre 1968). Published as well in: Roland Barthes (1994), *Oeuvres complètes*, Tome II, 1966–1973, Paris: Editions du Seuil.

Bettig, Roland V. (1996), *Copyrighting Culture. The Political Economy of Intellectual Property*, Boulder, CO: Westview Press.

Bollier, David (2003), *Silent Theft. The Private Plunder of Our Common Wealth*, New York and London: Routledge.

Boyle, James (1996), *Shamans, Software, and Spleens. Law and the Construction of the Information Society*, Cambridge, MA and London: Harvard University Press.

Coombe, Rosemary J. (1998), *The Cultural Life of Intellectual Properties. Authorship, Appropriation, and the Law*, Durham, NC and London: Duke University Press.

Correa, Carlos M. (2000), *Intellectual Property Rights, the WTO and Developing Countries. The TRIPS Agreement and Policy Options*, London/Penang: Zed Books/Third World Network.

Daoudi, Bouziane and Hadj Miliani (1996), *L'aventure du raï. Musique et société*, Paris: Editions du Seuil.

Drahos, Peter and John Braithwaite (2002), *Information Feudalism. Who Owns the Knowledge Economy?* London: Earthscan.

Drahos, Peter and Ruth Mayne (2002), *Global Intellectual Property Rights. Knowledge, Access and Development*, Basingstoke and New York: Palgrave Macmillan and Oxfam.

Edelman, Bernard (2004), *Le sacre de l'auteur*, Paris: Seuil.

Fombrun, C.J. (1996), *Corporate reputation: How Companies Realise Value from the Corporate Brand*, Boston, MA: Harvard Business School Press.

Frith, Simon (ed.) (1993), *Music and Copyright*, Edinburgh: Edinburgh University Press.

Frith, Simon and Lee Marshall (eds) (2004), *Music and Copyright*, 2nd edn, Edinburgh: Edinburgh University Press.

Grandstrand, Ove (ed.) (2003), *Economics, Law and Intellectual Property*, Amsterdam: Kluwer Academic Publishers.

Grosheide, Willem and Jan Brinkhof (eds) (2002), *Articles on the Legal Protection of Cultural Expressions and Indigenous Knowledge*, Antwerp: Intersentia.

Hauser, Arnold (1972), *Sozialgeschichte der Kunst und Literatur*, München: C.H. Beck.

Hemmungs Wirtén, Eva (2004), *No Trespassing. Authorship, Intellectual Property Rights, and the Boundaries of Globalization*, Toronto: University of Toronto Press.

Kretschmer, Martin (1999), 'Intellectual Property in Music: A Historical Analysis of Rhetoric and Institutional Practices', in P. Jeffcutt (ed.), *Studies in Cultures, Organizations and Societies*, **6**, 197–223.

Kretschmer, Martin and Friedemann Kawohl (2004), 'The History and Philosophy of Copyright', in Simon Frith and Lee Marshall (eds) *Music and Copyright*, 2nd edn, Edinburgh: Edinburgh University Press, pp. 21–53.

Lessig, Lawrence (2002), *The Future of Ideas. The Fate of the Commons in a Connected World*, New York: Vintage.

Lessig, Lawrence (2004), *Free Culture. How Big Media Uses Technology and the Law to Lock Down Culture and Control Creativity*, New York: Penguin Press.

Lewinski, Silke von (2002), *Indigenous Heritage and Intellectual Property. Genetic Resources, Traditional Knowledge and Folklore*, The Hague: Kluwer Law International.

Litman, Jessica (2001), *Digital Copyright*, Amhers and New York: Prometheus Books.

Macmillan, Fiona (2002), 'Copyright and Corporate Power', in Ruth Towse (ed.) *Copyright in the Cultural Industries*, Cheltenham, UK and Northampton, MA: Edward Elgar, pp. 99–118.

McChesney, Robert W. (1999), *Rich Media, Poor Democracy. Communication Politics in Dubious Times*, Urbana and Chicago, IL: University of Illinois Press.

Mitsui, Tôru (1993), 'Copyright and Music in Japan. A Forced Grafting and its Consequences', in Simon Frith (ed.) *Music and Copyright*, Edinburgh: Edinburgh University Press, pp. 125–145.

Motavalli, John (2002), *Bamboozled at the Revolution. How Big Media Lost Billions in the Battle for the Internet*, New York: Viking.

Perelman, Michael (2002), *Steal This Idea. Intellectual Property Rights and the Corporate Confiscation of Creativity*, New York: Palgrave.

Picciotto, Sol (2002), 'Defending the Public Interest in TRIPS and the WTO', in Peter Drahos and Ruth Mayne (eds), *Global Intellectual Property Rights. Knowledge, Access and Development*, Basingstoke and New York: Palgrave Macmillan and Oxfam, pp. 224–43.

Rifkin, Jeremy (1998), *The Biotech Century. Harnessing the Gene and Remaking the World*, New York: Jeremy P. Tarcher/Putnam.

Rifkin, Jeremy (2000), *The Age of Access. The New Culture of Hypercapitalism, Where All of Life is a Paid-for Experience*, New York: Jeremy P. Tarcher/Putnam.

Schiller, Dan (2000), *Digital Capitalism. Networking the Global Market System*, Cambridge, MA and London: MIT Press.

Shiva, Vandana (1997), *Biopiracy. The Plunder of Nature and Knowledge*, Boston, MA: South End Press.

Shiva, Vandana (2001), *Protect or Plunder? Understanding Intellectual Property Rights*, London: Zed Books.

Shulman, Seth (1999), *Owning the Future*, New York: Houghton Mifflin Company.

Smiers, Joost (2001), 'La propriété intellectuelle, c'est le vol! Pladoyer pour l'abolition des droits d'auteur', *Le Monde Diplomatique*, September, 3*i*.

Smiers, Joost (2002), 'The Abolition of Copyrights: Better for Artists, Third World Countries and the Public Domain', in Ruth Towse (ed.), *Copyright in the Cultural Industries*, Cheltenham, UK and Northampton, MA: Edward Elgar, pp. 19–139.

Smiers, Joost (2003), *Arts Under Pressure. Promoting Cultural Diversity in the Age of Globalisation*, London: Zed Books.

Smiers, Joost (2004), *Artistic Expression in a Corporate World. Do We Need Monopolistic Control?* Utrecht: HKU/Utrecht School of the Arts.

Towse, Ruth (ed.) (2002), *Copyright in the Cultural Industries*, Cheltenham, UK and Northampton, MA: Edward Elgar.

Towse, Ruth (2003), 'Copyright and Cultural Policy for the Creative Industries', in Ove Grandstrand (ed.), *Economics, Law and Intellectual Property*, Amsterdam: Kluwer Academic Publishers, pp. 419–38.

Towse, Ruth (2004), 'Copyright and Economics', in Simon Frith and Lee Marshall (eds), *Music and Copyright*, 2nd edn, Edinburgh: Edinburgh University Press, pp. 54–69.

Vaidhyanathan, Siva (2003), *Copyrights and Copywrongs. The Rise of Intellectual Property and How It Threatens Creativity*, New York and London: New York University Press.

Index